studysync®

Teacher's Edition

Grade 8 | Volume 1

studysync.com

Send all inquiries to:
BookheadEd Learning, LLC
610 Daniel Young Drive
Sonoma, CA 95476

ISBN 978-1-94-973925-1

1 2 3 4 5 6 MER 24 23 22 21 20

A

Grade 8

Volume 1 Contents

Authors and Advisors

DR. DOUGLAS FISHER

Dr. Douglas Fisher is Professor of Educational Leadership at San Diego State University and a teacher leader at Health Sciences High & Middle College having been an early intervention teacher and elementary school educator. He is the recipient of a Christa McAuliffe award for excellence in teacher education and is a member of the California Reading Hall of Fame. He is a renowned speaker and author of numerous articles and books and is President of the International Literacy Association (ILA) Board.

DR. TIMOTHY SHANAHAN

Dr. Timothy Shanahan is Distinguished Professor Emeritus at the University of Illinois at Chicago where he is Founding Director of the UIC Center for Literacy. He was Director of Reading for Chicago Public Schools, and, among other awards, received the William S. Gray Citation for Lifetime Achievement and the Albert J. Harris Award for outstanding research on reading disability from the International Literacy Association (ILA). He is the author/editor of more than 200 publications and books, and his research emphasizes the connections between learning to read and learning to write, literacy in the disciplines, and improvement of reading achievement.

DR. MICHELLE H. MARTIN

Dr. Michelle H. Martin is the Beverly Cleary Endowed Professor for Children and Youth Services in the Information School at the University of Washington and from 2011-2016 was the inaugural Augusta Baker Endowed Chair in Childhood Literacy at the University of South Carolina. She published Brown Gold: Milestones of African-American Children's Picture Books, 1845-2002 (Routledge, 2004), and is the founder of Read-a-Rama, a non-profit that uses children's books as the springboard for year-round and summer camp programming.

CATLIN TUCKER

Catlin Tucker is a Google Certified Innovator, bestselling author, international trainer, and frequent Edtech speaker, who teaches in Sonoma County where she was named Teacher of the Year in 2010. Her books Blended Learning in Grades 4-12 and Blended Learning In Action are both bestsellers. She is currently in the doctoral program at Pepperdine University, and writes the Techy Teacher column for ASCD's Educational Leadership.

JEFF ANDERSON

Jeff has inspired writers and teachers with the power and joy of the writing process. His particular area of interest is in making editing and grammar in context a meaning-making experience for students and teachers. He has written five books on writing and teaching writing. More recently, he has taken up writing middle grade novels, including Zack Delacruz: Me and My Big Mouth, which was selected for the Keystone State Reading List in Pennsylvania.

DR. PATRICIA MORALES

Dr. Patricia Morales is founder of ellservices©, consultant, and a professional development provider in English as a Second Language (ESL), Bilingual Education, and Dual Language Education. She is also an independent educational consultant at the Teaching and Learning Division of the Harris County Department of Education in Houston, Texas. She has taught university courses focusing on language acquisition and pedagogy, and continues to prepare thousands of teachers pursuing certifications in bilingual education and English as a Second Language in Texas.

JESSICA ROGERS

Jessica Rogers is a Lecturer at Baylor University and founder of Rogers Education Consulting, which specializes in Balanced Literacy professional development. She has over fifteen years experience in education, including teaching ESL, inclusion, gifted and talented, self-contained classrooms, mentoring teachers, and designing and implementing professional development. Her passion is making abstract educational theory and cutting-edge techniques practical for the classroom teacher.

GERRIT JONES-ROOY

Gerrit Jones-Rooy is Director of Literacy at Collegiate Academies in New Orleans as well as a 9th grade teacher. Previously he worked as a Staff Developer for the Reading and Writing Project, leading work across the country as well as in Saudi Arabia, Colombia, Poland and Thailand. He is the author or co-author of several Teachers College units including "Turning Every Kid into a Reader, Really" and "All About Books: Writing in Non-fiction."

DR. MARCELA FUENTES

Dr. Marcela Fuentes is an Assistant Professor of Creative Writing and Latinx Literature at Texas A&M University. She is a graduate of the Iowa Writers' Workshop, and was the 2016-2017 James C. McCreight Fellow in Fiction at the Wisconsin Institute for Creative Writing. She co-founded The Iowa Youth Writing Project, a nonprofit dedicated to promoting writing programs and events for K-12 students in the Iowa City area.

J. SCOTT BROWNLEE

J. Scott Brownlee is a Career & Talent Development Consultant at UT-Austin's McCombs School of Business, and a core faculty member for Brooklyn Poets, a NYC-based literary nonprofit. The author of four books of poetry, he received the Texas Institute of Letters 2015 Bob Bush Award for Best First Book of Poetry, as well as the 2014 Robert Phillips Prize from Texas Review Press.

DR. LYNNE KNOWLES

Dr. Lynn Knowles spent the majority of her 28-year teaching career at Flower Mound High School in Texas, where she served as English department chair and taught English II pre-AP and Humanities, as well as AP Capstone. She holds a bachelor's degree in Journalism from The University of Texas, a master's in Humanities from the University of Texas at Dallas, and a Ph.D. in Rhetoric from Texas Woman's University.

RICHARD ORLOPP

Richard Orlopp moved to Texas after graduating from Rutgers University with degrees in English and Journalism. He never left. He has taught English for the past 17 years and currently teaches AP Literature and Composition and International Baccalaureate seniors at Coppell High School.

WENDY MASSEY

Wendy Massey has taught high school for 20 years now. She has experience teaching grades 9-12 but primarily has taught English II Pre-AP and PSAT/SAT Prep. She has served several years now as the English department co-chair; in addition, she has served on the curriculum writing team for her district and has been the Academic Decathlon language coach.

MUHAMMAD SHIMAL

Mr. Shimal has been teaching for eleven years now. His teaching experience spans high school to college classes domestically and internationally. He current ly teaches English Language AP/Dual Credit for Juniors and College Prep classes for Seniors. He holds a Bachelor's degree in English Language and Literature, a Masters degree in Linguistics, and is currently finishing his PhD in English at the University of Texas at San Antonio.

VALENTINA GONZALES

Valentina Gonzalez is a Professional Development Specialist for English Language Learners in Texas, coaching teachers in ELL strategies and leading professional development at the state and national level. She has a natural love of language stemming from her experience as an immigrant from Serbia, Yugoslavia. Her years in education include roles as a classroom teacher, ESL Specialty Support Teacher, and ESL Facilitator. She holds a bachelor's degree in Interdisciplinary Studies from The University of Houston, and a master's in Educational Administration from Lamar University.

Everyone Loves a Mystery

What attracts us to the mysterious?

Integrated Reading and Writing

Genre Focus: FICTION

242   Extended Writing Project and Grammar

English Language Learner Resources offer instruction using texts written at four distinct levels that serve as structural and thematic models of authentic texts in the unit.

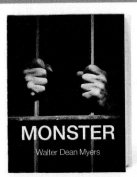
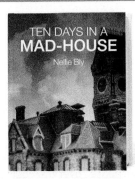
End-of Unit Assessments gauge students' understanding of key instuctional content and mastery of standards covered in the unit.

Author Biographies

NELLIE BLY

Reporter Nellie Bly (1864–1922) feigned insanity to gain admittance to the Blackwell's Island Insane Asylum in New York City, the subject of her 1886 exposé, which began as a series of newspaper articles and was eventually published as a book, *Ten Days in a Mad-House* (1887). Her report on the inhuman conditions she encountered there—from mandatory ice baths to confinement in small, damp, vermin-infested rooms—resulted in increased government oversight and improved overall conditions. Bly's pioneering tactic developed into modern investigative journalism.

PAUL LAURENCE DUNBAR

In his lifetime, Paul Laurence Dunbar (1872–1906) achieved national recognition for his writing reflecting black life in turn-of-the-century America. Known for his innovative use of dialect in his poems, his first collection of poems, *Oak and Ivy* (1893), was written in dialect and in standard English. It includes "Sympathy," one of his most popular poems addressing the plight of black people in American society, which contains the famous line "I know why the caged bird sings," the inspiration for the title of Maya Angelou's autobiography.

RUDOLPH FISHER

Considered one of the central literary figures of the Harlem Renaissance, Rudolph Fisher (1897–1934) was also a practicing physician and esteemed orator. Much of his work dealt with the adjustment of Southern black migrants to the urban enclave of Harlem. His second novel, *The Conjure-Man Dies* (1932), is regarded as the first detective novel by an African American author. Fisher published at least two novels and two short stories before his untimely death at the age of thirty-seven.

NEIL GAIMAN

A self-described "feral child who was raised in libraries," Neil Gaiman (b. 1960) devoured fantasy and science-fiction books from a young age. Best known for his novella *Coraline* (2002), he is credited with being one of the first creators of modern comics and an author of genre works that refuse to stay true to their genres. Gaiman's *The Graveyard Book* (2008), conceived of as a take on Kipling's Mowgli stories, involves an orphaned toddler finding a safe haven in the local graveyard.

ALFRED HITCHCOCK

British film director Alfred Hitchcock (1899–1980) earned the nickname "The Master of Suspense" over the course of his long and prolific career. His distinct directorial style in films like *Rear Window* (1954), *Psycho* (1960), and *The Birds* (1963) had a lasting impact on cinema. Film critic Peter Conrad wrote that in his work, "Hitchcock diagnosed the discontents that chafe and rankle beneath the decorum of civilization."

W.W. JACOBS

English short-story writer and novelist W. W. Jacobs (1863–1943) grew up in a house on a River Thames wharf. His is best known for his horror story, "The Monkey's Paw," published in his 1902 collection, *The Lady of the Barge*. In the story, a couple is presented with a magical monkey's paw from India. Set in Victorian England, the ensuing tale of superstition and terror unfolds in a domestic setting. Jacobs's first collection had immediate success and he published more than a dozen volumes in his lifetime.

SHIRLEY JACKSON

Called the master of the creepy story, Shirley Jackson (1916–1965) was interested in witchcraft, she writes, as "a way of embracing and channeling female power at a time when women in America often had little control over their lives." Her stories and novels of the supernatural included the well-known short story "The Lottery" and the best-selling novel *The Haunting of Hill House* (1959). When the former was first published in The New Yorker in 1948, it generated the largest volume of mail ever received by the magazine, most of it hateful.

WALTER DEAN MYERS

American children's book author Walter Dean Myers (1937–2014) wrote books that reflected the lives of young people he met visiting schools and prisons around the country, whose life experiences often resonated with his own. Although he wrote over a hundred books in his lifetime, he is best known for *Monster*, his 1999 drama about a teenager who writes a movie script while incarcerated. This stylistically innovative work alternates between suspenseful courtroom scenes and introspective journal entries.

EDGAR ALLEN POE

Widely regarded as one of the foremost progenitors of modern Gothic literature, Edgar Allan Poe (1809–1849) was born the son of two actors in Boston, but grew up in foster care in Richmond, Virginia. Much of his work, especially his best-known horror tales, achieve a psychological intensity through the use of a first-person narrator. Poe had written numerous short stories, poems, and works of criticism by the time he died at the age of forty from suspected alcohol poisoning.

JOHN FLEISCHMAN

John Fleischman (b. 1948) began writing non-fiction for young adults when he noticed how engrossed a group of adolescents was looking at a scientific display of the skull of Phineas Gage. The subject of Fleischman's first book, Gage was a construction foreman who became an important case study in the field of neurology when he miraculously survived a freak accident. Fleischman has also published three non-fiction books about the history of his adopted city, Cincinnati, Ohio, and has written articles for numerous science magazines.

Past and Present

What makes you, you?

Integrated Reading and Writing

Genre Focus: POETRY

Every lesson in the unit features integrated scaffolding and differentiation for all levels of English Language Learners. Approaching grade-level readers, and Beyond grade-level readers.

532 | Extended Writing Project and Grammar

Grammar instruction is embedded in the Extended Writing Project. Additional grammar lessons are available in the Skills library.

Each Core ELA Unit contains two options for Novel Study with lessons supporting the close reading of the complete text.

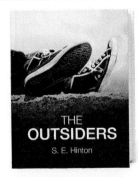

Author Biographies

SWIN CASH

Swin Cash (b. 1979) played fourteen seasons in the WNBA, winning three championships, appearing on four all-star teams, and winning two Olympic gold medals. In addition to her stellar playing record, she has worked to establish the WNBA players' union and to increase community involvement where she's lived. In a 2016 essay announcing her retirement, she paid tribute to the women who paved the way for her and made clear her commitment to ensuring that subsequent generations of women could play basketball professionally.

SANDRA CISNEROS

Regarded as a prominent figure in the Chicana literary movement, Sandra Cisneros (b. 1954) is a dual citizen of the United States and Mexico. In works like her classic coming-of-age novel, *The House on Mango Street* (2009), about a Latina girl growing up in a Chicago barrio, Cisneros explores themes related to Latina identity and working-class culture. In an *Electric Literature* interview, she said "the more you reach into the different things that make you who you are, the more you hold up a mirror to what makes you different from others."

JUDITH ORTIZ COFER

Born in Hormigueros, a small town in Puerto Rico, Judith Ortiz Cofer (1952–2016) moved with her family to Augusta, Georgia, at the age of fifteen. With characteristic vitality, Cofer's writing addresses the experience of living in the breach between these disparate cultures. Best known for her works of creative nonfiction, Cofer also published at least four collections of poetry, several novels, and a memoir.

EMILY DICKINSON

As early as 1850, just a few years after dropping out of Mount Holyoke and moving back into her family's estate in Amherst, Massachusetts, Emily Dickinson (1830–1886) started thinking of writing her life's work. She recognized that her aims in life were different from those of her peers and began to retreat from polite society. As a result, the speakers in Dickinson's poetry are often sharply critical of society and express a desire to be liberated from its constraints.

ROBERT FROST

Though he was born in San Francisco, Robert Frost (1874–1963) wrote mostly about New England, where he moved in 1884 following his father's death. He became known for his innovative use of New England vernacular in his writing. Objects, people, or events sparked meditations on large concepts in his poems. In "The Road Not Taken," one of Frost's most iconic poems, a fork in a woodland path becomes a metaphor.

S.E. HINTON

With her influential coming-of-age novel *The Outsiders* (1967) S. E. Hinton (b. 1948), who was seventeen at the time of writing, in large part inaugurated the young adult fiction genre. Set in Tulsa, Oklahoma, where she was born and has lived for the majority of her life, Hinton's novel about violence, prejudice, and class conflict in 1960s America stood out for its nuanced portrayals of teenage life. Four of Hinton's novels have been adapted into film, including *The Outsiders*, which has also been translated into thirty languages.

YUSEF KOMUNYAKAA

Born in Bogalusa, Louisiana, Yusef Komunyakaa (b. 1947) considers his first exposure to poetry to be the Old Testament–inflected cadence of his grandparents' voices. Komunyakaa would assert his distinctive style combining personal narrative, jazz rhythms, and vernacular language in two poetry collections in particular: *Magic Bus* (1992), about growing up in the South in the 1950s, and *Neon Vernacular: New and Selected Poems* (1994), which also dealt with the culture of the South as well as war in Southeast Asia, urban life, and music.

MICHELLE OBAMA

Lawyer, writer, public servant, and former First Lady, Michelle Obama (b. 1964) grew up on the South Side of Chicago, studied sociology and African American studies at Princeton University, and graduated from Harvard Law School. She has led initiatives to empower youth through higher education and to aid underserved communities throughout the United States, among many others. In her 2016 commencement address delivered at the Santa Fe Indian School, she reflects on how her family background shaped her character and contributed to her lifetime achievements.

NATASHA TRETHEWEY

Being born black and biracial in Gulfport, Mississippi, is one of the two "existential wounds" poet Natasha Trethewey (b. 1966) says she's been writing with her whole adult life. The other was losing her mother at the age of nineteen. In poetry collections like *Native Guard* (2006), *Bellocq's Ophelia* (2002), and *Domestic Work* (2000), she explores how her personal history is tied to larger historical narratives and the way private recollection often diverges from collective memory.

NAOMI SEPISO

Naomi Sepiso (b. 1998) is a writer of Kenyan and Zambian descent living in Australia. Her work often deals with the immigrant experience and the experience of being a young person of color. Her 2016 essay "So where are you from?" considers the sometimes damaging implications of this seemingly innocuous question.

THANHHÀ LAI

Children's book author Thanhhà Lai (b. 1965) was born in Saigon, Vietnam, and immigrated to Montgomery, Alabama, in 1975. Like the main character, Hà, of her first novel, Inside Out and Back Again (2011), Lai witnessed the harsh realities of the Vietnam War, had a father who was missing in action, and fled with her family to the United States. The emotions Lai conveys through her character Hà powerfully resonate with immigrant experiences everywhere. Lai's second novel, Listen, Slowly (2015) also explores themes related to heritage and identity.

No Risk, No Reward

Why do we take chances?

Integrated Reading and Writing

Genre Focus: INFORMATIONAL TEXT

Independent Reads provide opportunities to focus on reading comprehension and skills application.

Students self-select a text that corresponds to the unit's theme and essential question and then write a response.

814 | Extended Writing Project and Grammar

In the Extended Oral Project, students apply the structure and approach of the Extended Writing Project to an oral presentation.

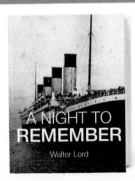

Author Biographies

FREDERICK DOUGLASS

Born into slavery in Baltimore, Maryland, Frederick Douglass (1818–1895) was twenty years old when he escaped to freedom and became an active abolitionist. He taught himself to read despite laws prohibiting enslaved people from doing so, and only seven years after attaining his freedom, published the first of his three memoirs, *Narrative of the Life of Frederick Douglass, An American Slave* (1845). An account of his journey from slavery to freedom, it played a key role in fueling the abolitionist movement prior to the Civil War.

ANYA GRONER

A resident of New Orleans, Louisiana, Anya Groner has written essays, stories, and poems covering a wide range of subjects, from her childhood growing up in Virginia to the politics of drinking water. In "The Vanishing Island" (2017), Groner discusses the plight of the Native American inhabitants of the Isle de Jean Charles off the coast of Louisiana, as rising water levels threaten their ancestral homeland.

FRANCES ELLEN WATKINS HARPER

Writer, abolitionist, and civil rights activist Frances Ellen Watkins Harper (1825–1911) is credited with establishing the tradition of African American protest poetry. Born a free woman in Baltimore, Maryland, Harper traveled extensively throughout the eastern United States, often under hazardous circumstances, to voice her opposition to slavery and to advocate for the burgeoning feminist movement. As a result of her constant effort to raise awareness around these issues, she was elected vice president of the National Association of Colored Women in 1897.

LANGSTON HUGHES

Now regarded as a leading figure of the 1920's cultural and intellectual movement known as the Harlem Renaissance, Langston Hughes (1902–1967) initially faced widespread criticism from African American intellectuals for his unvarnished portrayals of African American life in his poetry. Despite the criticism he received, he maintained his commitment to writing for and about regular people throughout his life, earning him the moniker "poet of the people."

JACK LONDON

Turn-of-the-century American novelist and short-story writer Jack London (1876–1916) is best known for his novels *The Call of the Wild* (1903) and *White Fang* (1906) about wild wolf dogs in the Yukon Territory and the Northwest Territories of Canada during the Klondike Gold Rush of the 1890s. Writing between the Civil War and World War I, London's work reflected the nation's transformation into a modern, industrial society, and appealed to readers desiring a sense of adventure and vitality.

THOMAS PONCE

An animal rights activist and citizen lobbyist from Casselberry, Florida, Thomas Ponce (b. 2000) became a vegetarian at age four, attended his first protest at age five, and founded the animal rights organization Lobby For Animals at age twelve. He now works as a coordinator for Fin Free Florida, working to limit the sale, distribution, and trade of shark fins and shark fin products in the state of Florida. For his dedication to animal rights, he has received awards from major organizations like PETA and the Farm Animal Rights Movement.

RONALD REAGAN

Though he had an average, midwestern upbringing, Ronald Reagan (1911–2004) became the fortieth president of the United States and is the only Hollywood actor ever to become president. He is remembered for his conservative political beliefs and his policies toward the dissolution of Soviet communism. A major event of his presidency was the explosion of the Space Shuttle *Challenger* resulting in the deaths of its seven passengers. His address to the nation on January 28, 1986, lauded the bravery of the fallen crew.

NINA GREGORY

Throughout her career, news editor and journalist Nina Gregory has covered topics ranging from the financial crisis to elections, and has interviewed many influential figures including director Ava DuVernay and Facebook COO Sheryl Sandberg. One of her most intriguing stories profiles Richard Turere, a young boy living among the Maasai people near Nairobi National Park, a refuge for endangered lions in Kenya. As a thirteen-year-old, Turere came up with an inventive solution for protecting both the locals' livestock and the encroaching lions.

WALTER LORD

Walter Lord (1917–2002) had been obsessed with the story of the RMS Titanic since he came across a small book written by a survivor of the shipwreck in his aunt's home in 1927. Lord studied American and modern European history at Princeton University, but it wasn't until an editor friend suggested he turn his obsession with the Titanic into a book that he undertook the endeavor. With A Night to Remember (1955), Lord popularized the story and developed an innovative technique of telling history through the eyes of those who lived it.

MAHVASH SABET

Teacher, principal, and Bahá'í community leader Mahvash Sabet (b. 1953) was fired from her job and blocked from working in public education following the Islamic Revolution of 1979. She and the rest of the seven leaders that comprised an informal council working to support Iran's 300,000-member Bahá'í community were arrested in 2008. While serving her twenty-year prison sentence, she began writing poetry, and in 2013 published her first collection in English translation.

Bring Literature to Life

- Instructional choice from thematic units, novel studies, and teacher-created units.

- Interchangeable print and digital use.

- A continuously growing library of over 1,600 classic & contemporary texts.

Student Print Edition

Novel Options

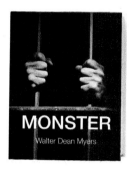

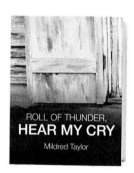

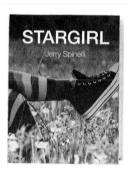

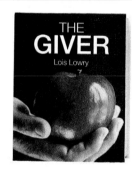

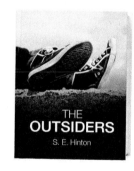

- Extensive writing and research practice.

- Automatically embedded scaffolds so ALL students reach their potential.

- Data-driven assessment to track progress and inform instruction.

Teacher Print Edition

Data Driven Assesment

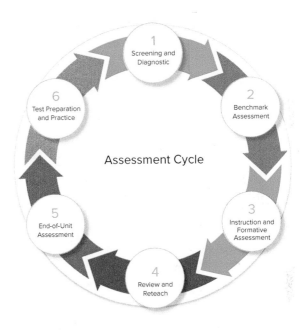

Comprehensive Student and Teacher Digital Experience

Lead to Achievement

StudySync's integrated reading and writing routines hone foundational language, reading comprehension, and analytical reading and writing skills as students respond to multiple genres of increasingly complex texts.

- StudySync's close reading routines ensure progress toward standards mastery.

- Novel Studies provide teachers with key vocabulary, reading quizzes, comparative texts, and other curriculum supports to teach from any of the 12 complete works suggested in each grade.

- Independent and self-selected reading lessons provide students opportunities to practice and apply skills while exercising more choice over their readings and responsesTwo comparative text sets in every unit challenge students to make connections and compare texts within and across genres.

- Extended Writing Projects teach writing with embedded grammar instruction.

Support Every Student

With StudySync, every student has the same opportunity and access regardless of native language, learning level, or physical, social and emotional ability.

Supports for English Language Learners

- Targeted scaffolds for 4 different levels of English Language Learners automatically appear with every digital assignment.

- Two leveled texts per unit introduce English Language Learners to the text types they'll encounter in the core curriculum.

- Additional ELL skills lessons emphasize/vocabulary development, language acquisition, spelling and grammar, and reading comprehension.

- Extended Oral Projects build language proficiency and offer students opportunities to collaborate and build academic language skills.

Supports for Approaching and Beyond Grade-level Learners

- Intentional scaffolds such as annotation guides, and sentence frames help Approaching-level students interact meaningfully with on grade-level curriculum.

- A digital Library of 1000s of additional skill mini-lessons and texts is searchable by standard and Lexile, allowing teachers to quickly and easily differentiate, remediate, or extend lessons.

- Lesson-specific suggestions such as Beyond the Book and Prepare for Advanced Courses drive Beyond grade-level learners to further engage with texts and extend their learning.

Amplify Student Voices

StudySync helps students think critically and thoughtfully. All StudySync students see themselves in their curriculum. StudySync encourages students to develop their own unique voices while they grow as readers, writers, and future leaders in college and career settings.

- StudySync's curriculum is centered around students. Lesson activities and the digital platform enable teachers to easily facilitate peer review and other on and offline collaborative approaches that transform classrooms into workshops of great reading and writing.

- The Table of Contents for every grade features at least 50% of texts written by female authors and at least 50% of texts written by authors from diverse backgrounds.

- Each grade's Table of Contents includes stories about extraordinary young people. Whether it's Olympic gold medalist Simone Biles or animal rights advocate Thomas Ponce, students will learn how other young people like them are changing the world today.

- Integrated media such as StudySyncTV and SkillsTV models collaborative and academic conversations, providing students the roadmap they need to develop their own voices.

- Unique media like the "School of Thought" podcast series helps teachers meet multimedia and digital literacy standards with high-quality resources that are relevant to the lives of today's students.

- Blast lessons help students understand the most important issues in today's world. Teachers have access to a brand new Blast article - leveled for 3 different Lexiles - every single school day, helping them deliver a fresh, relevant learning experience every year.

No Risk, No Reward

Why do we take chances?

UNIT 3

No Risk, No Reward

Why do we take chances?

Why do we take chances? Every time a person takes a chance, he or she risks losing something for the possibility of a reward. Sometimes these chances pay off, and sometimes they don't. Yet, people still take risks every day. With a genre focus on informational texts, this Grade 8 unit prepares students to explore questions about why we take chances.

Nonfiction authors explore risk-taking from a variety of viewpoints. Walter Lord takes a historical approach to the topic, sharing an account of a real event with a surprising outcome that still affects people today. Anya Groner and Nina Gregory look at contemporary risk-takers who search for solutions in the face of environmental challenges, while essayist Thomas Ponce is a current risk-taker seeking environmental justice. President Ronald Reagan shares his perspective after a shocking national tragedy. Frederick Douglass explains risks he had to take in order to improve his own life as an enslaved person in the time before the Civil War; poets Langston Hughes and Frances Ellen Watkins Harper reveal how taking risks was historically necessary for African Americans. Classic American novelist Jack London depicts a risk-taking fictional character—a dog.

After reading about these ideas within and across genres, your students will write an informative essay, applying what they have learned from the unit's literature, speeches, and informational texts to an informative writing project.

Integrated Reading and Writing

Extended Writing Project and Grammar

English Language Learner Resources

906 | Novel Study Choices

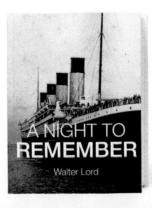

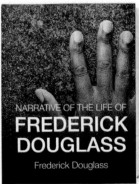

909 | End-of-Unit Assessment

No Risk, No Reward

tv StudySyncTV or SkillsTV Episode

Pacing Guide

Days	Readings	Skill and Standard Instruction	Skill Practice and Spiraling
1–2	**Essential Question** **The Big Idea: Why do we take chances?** p. 630	• Recognizing Genre: Informational Text • Academic Vocabulary	• Write: Analyzing Genre
3–5	**The Vanishing Island** p. 634	• Evaluating Details • Greek and Latin Affixes and Roots • Media	• Textual Evidence • Informative Writing
6–9	**PAIRED READINGS** **A Night to Remember** tv p. 670 **Address to the Nation on the Explosion of the Space Shuttle** *Challenger* p. 680	• Summarizing • Informational Text Structure tv	• Textual Evidence • Comparative Writing • Collaborative Conversations
10–12	**A Kenyan Teen's Discovery: Let There Be Lights to Save Lions** p. 698	• Synthesizing • Media • Word Patterns and Relationships	• Textual Evidence • Summarizing • Informative Writing
13–17	**PAIRED READINGS** **Mother to Son** p. 716 **Learning to Read** p. 726 **Narrative of the Life of Frederick Douglass, An American Slave** tv p. 736	• Adjusting Fluency • Informational Text Elements • Figurative Language tv	• Textual Evidence • Central or Main Idea • Author's Purpose and Point of View • Comparative Writing • Collaborative Conversations

THEMATIC PACING AT A GLANCE — 30 DAYS

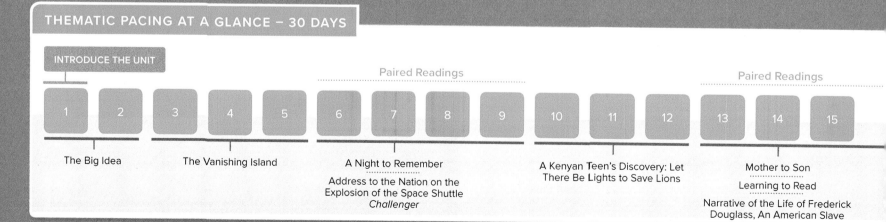

INTRODUCE THE UNIT

Paired Readings   Paired Readings

1 2   3 4 5   6 7 8 9   10 11 12   13 14 15

The Big Idea   The Vanishing Island   A Night to Remember   A Kenyan Teen's Discovery: Let   Mother to Son
                                          Address to the Nation on the   There Be Lights to Save Lions   Learning to Read
                                          Explosion of the Space Shuttle   Narrative of the Life of Frederick
                                          Challenger   Douglass, An American Slave

Days	Readings	Skill and Standard Instruction	Skill Practice and Spiraling
18–21	**The Day I Saved a Life** p. 758	• Context Clues • Technical Language • Write: Analyzing Genre	• Textual Evidence • Argumentative Writing
22–24	**The Call of the Wild** 📺 p. 778	• Language, Style, and Audience • Media	• Textual Evidence • Theme • Literary Analysis Writing • Collaborative Conversations
25–27	**Cocoon** p. 796	• Connotation and Denotation	• Textual Evidence • Literary Analysis Writing
28	**Self-Selected Reading and Response** p. 812	• Independent Reading	• Personal Response Writing

Review and Assessment   See page 908.

Days	Review and Assessment	Skill Practice and Assessment
29	**Skills Review** p. 908	Students will have the opportunity to complete one or more Spotlight skill lessons in order to improve understanding and further practice skills from the unit that they found most challenging.
30	**End-of-Unit Assessment** p. 909	For more detail, please see the End-of-Unit Assessment information for Grade 8 Unit 3 on page 909.

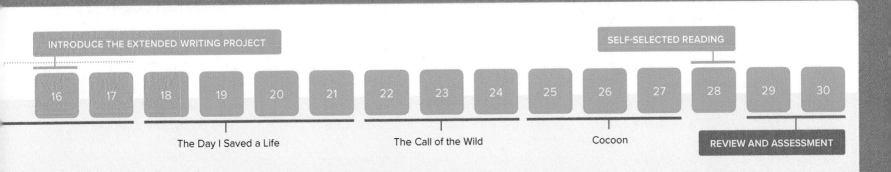

Extended Writing Project and Grammar

Pacing Guide

In the second half of the unit, students continue exploring texts that address the unit's Essential Question and begin crafting a longer composition to share their own ideas about the Essential Question in the Extended Writing Project. The writing project will take your students through the writing process to produce an informative essay.

Extended Writing Project Prompt

What happens when we take risks?

Choose three informational texts from this unit, including research links in the Blasts, and explain how the authors inform readers about their risk-taking subjects. Identify the risks individuals take and the outcomes of those risks. Include a clear main idea or thesis statement, and cite evidence from each text to explain your conclusions.

Days	Extended Writing Project and Grammar	Skill and Standard Instruction	Connect to Mentor Texts
16	**Informative Writing Process: Plan** p. 822		
17-20	**Informative Writing Process: Draft** p. 838	• Thesis Statement • Organizing Informative Writing • Supporting Details	• Address to the Nation on the Explosion of the Space Shuttle *Challenger* • Narrative of the Life of Frederick Douglass, An American Slave • The Day I Saved a Life
21-25	**Informative Writing Process: Revise** p. 858	• Introductions • Transitions • Precise Language • Style • Conclusions	• The Vanishing Island • A Night to Remember • The Day I Saved a Life
26-28	**Informative Writing Process: Edit and Publish** p. 867	• Participles • Gerunds • Infinitives	Additional grammar lessons can be found in the StudySync Skills Library.

Research

The following lessons include opportunities for research:

Blast **No Risk, No Reward** Research Links*

Close Read **The Vanishing Island** Beyond the Book

Blast **Risky Business** Research Links*

Close Read **Address to the Nation on the Explosion of the Space Shuttle** *Challenger* Beyond the Book

Close Read **A Kenyan Teen's Discovery: Let There Be Lights to Save Lions** Beyond the Book

Blast **Now, That's an Idea** Research Links*

Close Read **Narrative of the Life of Frederick Douglass, An American Slave** Beyond the Book

First Read **The Day I Saved a Life** Independent Research (Beyond)

First Read **The Day I Saved a Life** Beyond the Book

*See the teacher lesson plan online

Self-Selected Reading Prompt

After reading a self-selected text, students will respond to the following narrative prompt:

Have you ever heard the expression "walk a mile in someone else's shoes"? It means you can't really understand someone until you've spent some time imagining the world from his or her perspective.

Why do we take chances?

Assume the role of a character, individual, or narrator/speaker from your self-selected text. Imagine that a journalist has asked your chosen character to respond to the question "Why do we take chances?" Think about how your chosen character, individual, or narrator/speaker would respond, and write a personal response as this character, individual, or narrator/speaker.

Integrated Scaffolding

ELL and Approaching grade-level students receive scaffolds for every lesson, whether in the Thematic, Novel Study or ELL Resources sections of the unit. Specific scaffolds are intentionally designed to support the needs of English Language Learners and Approaching grade-level students in the ELA classroom. Other scaffolds exist as part of the many standard features in the StudySync digital platform and can be strategically utilized to support students' comprehension and engagement.

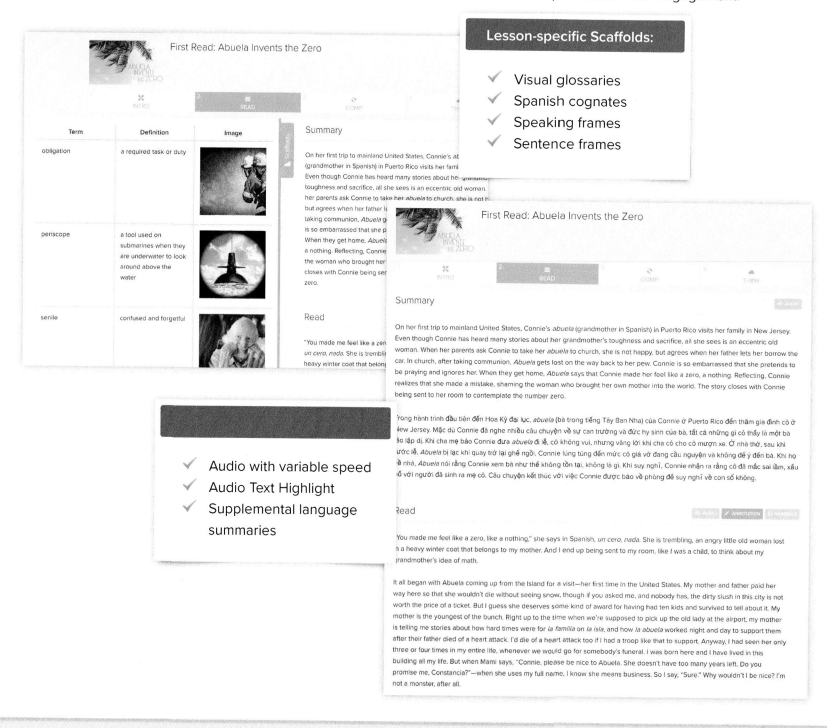

Lesson-specific Scaffolds:

- ✓ Visual glossaries
- ✓ Spanish cognates
- ✓ Speaking frames
- ✓ Sentence frames

- ✓ Audio with variable speed
- ✓ Audio Text Highlight
- ✓ Supplemental language summaries

English Language Learner Resources

Both Thematic and Novel Study units include English Language Learner resources designed to match the thematic focus, text structures, and writing form of the unit. ELL resources include two leveled texts and an extended oral project.

ELL Texts	Differentiated Text Levels	Skill and Standard Instruction
	**BEGINNING** 540L I 377 words **INTERMEDIATE** 620L I 416 words **ADVANCED** 770L I 467 words **ADVANCED HIGH** 810L I 545 words Use this text in place of or as an extension to "Address to the Nation on the Explosion of the Space Shuttle *Challenger*."	• Sight Vocabulary and High-Frequency Words • Using Prereading Supports • Analyzing Expressions • Main Ideas and Details • Spelling Patterns and Rules
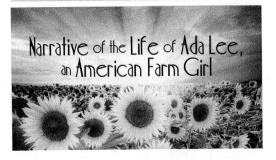	**BEGINNING** 390L I 257 words **INTERMEDIATE** 700L I 416 words **ADVANCED** 830L I 456 words **ADVANCED HIGH** 900L I 567 words Use this text in place of or as an extension to *Narrative of the Life of Frederick Douglass, An American Slave*.	• Classroom Vocabulary • Making Connections • Language Structures • Comparing and Contrasting • Main and Helping Verbs
	In this Extended Oral Project, students will write and perform an informative presentation. This may be assigned in place of this unit's EWP.	• Acquiring Vocabulary • Sentence Types

Focus on English Language Proficiency Levels

ADVANCED HIGH
ADVANCED
INTERMEDIATE
BEGINNING

ELL Resources provide targeted support for four levels of proficiency: Beginning, Intermediate, Advanced, and Advanced High. Instruction and scaffolds, as well as the texts themselves, are differentiated based on these levels.

Additional differentiated scaffolds include visual glossaries, speaking and writing frames, and suggested grouping for peer and teacher support. Lessons also include suggested extension activities to challenge Advanced and Advanced High students as they progress through the year.

Assessment

Assessment in StudySync is built upon a recursive cycle that includes assessment, instruction, and review. Screening, placement, and benchmark assessments help teachers establish baselines and determine scaffold needs. Throughout the course of instruction, teachers regularly assess student progress using formative and summative measures, and use the individualized data from those assessments to guide choices about instruction, review, remediation, and enrichment to bring all students to standards mastery and College and Career Readiness.

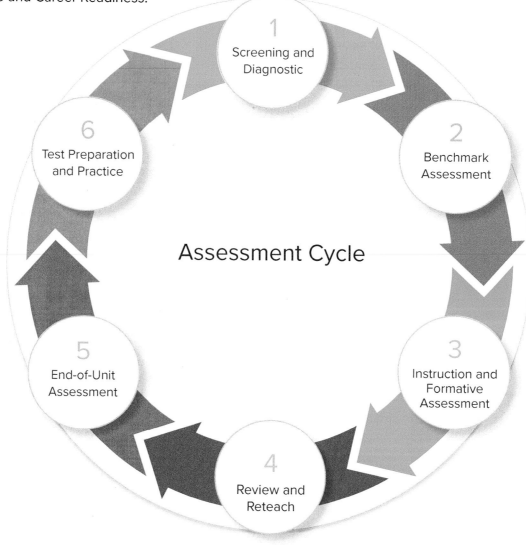

Assessment Cycle

1 Screening and Diagnostic

2 Benchmark Assessment

3 Instruction and Formative Assessment

4 Review and Reteach

5 End-of-Unit Assessment

6 Test Preparation and Practice

What's Next?

Assessment results can be viewed by item, standard, and skill to monitor mastery and make decisions for upcoming instruction.

✓ Reteach skills that students have not yet mastered, using Spotlight Skills or the Test Preparation and Practice book.

✓ Revise your teaching plan to provide more or less explicit instruction into a skill or text, using Beyond the Book activities for enrichment.

✓ Regroup students and levels of scaffolding based on standards progress.

Review

Spotlight Skills Review

A review day before the end-of-unit assessment gives you an opportunity to review difficult concepts with students using Spotlight Skills lessons. Spotlight Skills are targeted lessons that provide you resources to reteach or remediate without assigning additional readings. Every Core ELA Skill lesson has a corresponding Spotlight Skill lesson. Spotlight Skills can be assigned at any point in the year, but the end of each unit provides a natural moment to pause, review data collected throughout the unit, and reteach skills students have not yet mastered.

Progress Monitoring

The Progress Monitoring charts that appear before every text in this unit identify standards and associated Spotlight Skills. On review day, you may want to give preference to reteaching skills that are not revisited in later units. You can see where Skills are covered again in the Opportunities to Reteach column.

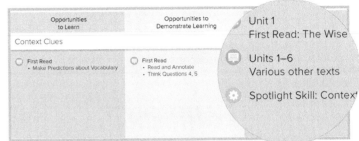

StudySync Gradebook

As students submit assignments on StudySync, their mastery of skills and standards is tracked via the gradebook. The gradebook can be sorted and viewed in a variety of ways. Sorting by assignment shows overall student performance, while sorting by standards or by Skill lessons displays student progress toward mastery goals.

	First Read	Skill: Text	Close Re...	
MAX SCORE	10	2	12	
STUDENT				
Tate O'Brien	10	2	9	
Olivia Adams	8	1	11	

Skills Library

Spotlight Skills are located in the Skills section of the StudySync Library. You can assign Spotlight Skills to individual students or groups of students. Search tools allow you to search by Skill type or name.

End-of-Unit Assessment

Assessed Reading Skills

- ✓ Connotation and Denotation
- ✓ Context Clues
- ✓ Figurative Language
- ✓ Greek and Latin Affixes and Roots
- ✓ Informational Text Elements
- ✓ Informational Text Structure
- ✓ Language, Style, and Audience
- ✓ Point of View
- ✓ Summarizing
- ✓ Technical Language
- ✓ Textual Evidence
- ✓ Word Patterns and Relationships

Assessed Revising, Editing, and Writing Skills

- ✓ Conclusions
- ✓ Gerunds
- ✓ Infinitives
- ✓ Introductions
- ✓ Organizing Informative Writing
- ✓ Participles
- ✓ Precise Language
- ✓ Style
- ✓ Supporting Details
- ✓ Thesis Statement
- ✓ Transitions

Unit Preview

Introduce the Unit

As a class, watch the unit preview ▶ and discuss the questions below.

- What two words would you use to describe this video?
- What key words or images from the video do you think will be most important to this unit?

Instructional Path

Big Idea Blast

Objectives: After exploring background information and research links about a topic, students will respond to a question with a 140-character response.

Skill: Recognize Genre

Objectives: After learning about the genre of informational text, students will be able to identify and describe characteristics of memoir, articles, speeches, biography, and essays.

Skill: Academic Vocabulary

Objectives: After learning the meanings of ten academic vocabulary words, students will be able to recognize and use them in a variety of contexts.

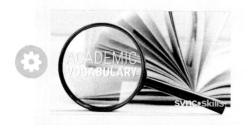

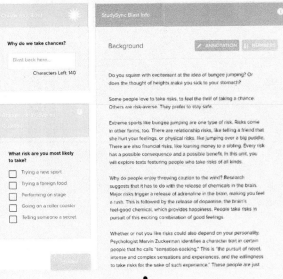

 ## Blast: No Risk, No Reward

Why do we take chances?

Ask students:

- What do you think this Blast will be about? Make a prediction.

 ## TEXT TALK

What are the possible results of taking a risk?

Risks have possible consequences and benefits.

Why do some people like taking risks more than others?

According to Marvin Zuckerman, some people have a "sensation-seeking" character trait.

Why do people sometimes take "senseless" risks?

They make emotional choices and base their choices on personal experience rather than logic.

Create Your Own Blast

 SCAFFOLDS

Ask students to write a 140-character Blast after they complete the QuikPoll.

Use the scaffolds below to differentiate instruction for your **ELL** English Language Learners.

ELL **BEGINNING** Write a response using the word bank to complete the sentence frame.

INTERMEDIATE Write a response using the sentence frame.

ADVANCED, ADVANCED HIGH Write a response using the sentence starter.

BEGINNING	INTERMEDIATE	ADVANCED, ADVANCED HIGH
Word Bank	Sentence Frame	Sentence Starter
fun improvement a bad outcome high reward low	A chance is worth taking when you think the likelihood of ____ is ____.	• A chance is worth taking when . . .

Skill: Recognize Genre

Introduce the Genre: Informational Text

Watch the Concept Definition video 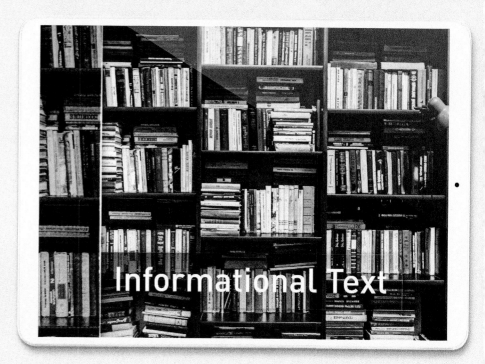 and read the following definition with your students.

Informational text presents readers information or ideas about real people, places, things, and events. In order to express information clearly, writers use a set of informational text elements, including a **thesis**, or main idea, and supporting **evidence** in the form of details, facts, examples, statistics, and expert opinions.

A typical informational text includes an introduction that builds to a thesis, body paragraphs that include key ideas and supporting evidence, and a conclusion that restates the most important ideas to remember.

Within body paragraphs, writers might use specific **text structures**, or organizational patterns. For instance, a writer may discuss ideas in order of importance, tell about events in chronological order, or present causes and then describe their effects.

Informational writing can take many forms, including essays, pamphlets, news and magazine articles, textbook articles, and nonfiction books.

 TURN AND TALK

Use the questions to discuss informational texts.

- What features in an informational text convey information?

- What feature do you find the most useful and why?

 SPEAKING FRAMES

- The text features that make up an informational text are ____, ____, ____, ____, and ____.

Your Turn

Ask students to complete the Your Turn activity.

Description	Text Feature
A chart shows the number of cases of the flu over the course of 12 months.	graphic feature
Ninety-eight percent of adults have drivers licenses.	statistics
The flu is a contagious viral infection of the respiratory passages and causes fever, severe aching, and catarrh, and often occurs in epidemics.	specialized vocabulary
The flu is a virus.	facts
The author interviewed several experts on the different techniques for treating the flu.	research

Skill: Academic Vocabulary

Introduce the Terms

asterisk / el asterisco *noun* a star-shaped character (*) used in printing COGNATE

asteroid / el asteroide *noun* a small space object made up of rock and metal that moves around the sun COGNATE

astronaut / el/la astronauta *noun* a person trained to travel in a spacecraft COGNATE

deduce / deducir *verb* to conclude by reasoning COGNATE

induce / inducir *verb* to bring about; to cause something to happen COGNATE

introduce / introducir *verb* to bring into notice, practice, or use, as in to introduce a new fashion COGNATE

apathetic / apático/a *adjective* showing little or no emotion

empathy / la empatía *noun* the feeling that you understand and share another person's experiences and emotions COGNATE

pathologist / el/la patólogo/a *noun* a doctor who specializes in medical diagnosis COGNATE

sympathy / la compasión *noun* sharing the feelings of others, especially feelings of sorrow or anguish

Your Turn

Ask students to complete the Your Turn activities.

Your Turn 1

Word	Root	How can the word part help you remember the meaning of the word?
introduce	duc (Latin) "lead"	If you introduce a topic, you are leading the discussion toward that topic.
deduce	duc (Latin) "lead"	When you deduce a solution, you follow where the evidence leads to draw a conclusion.
induce	duc (Latin) "lead"	When you try to induce someone to accept your opinion, you are trying to lead them toward your way of thinking.
apathetic	path (Greek) "feeling, disease"	If you are bored and don't care or have any feelings about a situation, you are apathetic.
asterisk	ast(er) (Greek) "star"	The star-shaped symbol you put next to an important item on a list is called an asterisk.

Your Turn 2

QUESTION 1: B **QUESTION 2:** D **QUESTION 3:** A **QUESTION 4:** C **QUESTION 5:** C

Your Turn 3

See digital teacher's edition for complete sample activity."

Practice Using Vocabulary

Divide the vocabulary words into two lists. Pair students and give each student one half of the list. Challenge students to have a casual conversation with each other that uses every word on their list. Students should aim to insert their vocabulary words in a way that sounds natural. You may wish to turn this activity into a game, allowing partners to award each other points if they effectively use each word on their list.

The Vanishing Island

INFORMATIONAL TEXT
Anya Groner
2017

Introduction

Author Anya Groner offers an intimate perspective of the Biloxi-Chitimacha-Choctaw Native American tribe and the trials they face as their ancestral homeland disappears before their eyes. As creeping water threatens the tribe and much of the Louisiana coast, the tribe must take on the challenge of seeking a new and safe place to live. In a race against the clock, the tribe seeks ways to preserve community and protect their culture from eroding along with

The ancestral homeland of the Biloxi-Chitimacha-Choctaw Native American tribe, Isle de Jean Charles, is being threatened by rising sea levels. In the past, the small Louisiana island was eleven-by-five miles, but over time it has shrunk to only two miles long by a quarter mile wide. The tribe originally settled on the island in the early 1800s and was self-sufficient for years. However, the loss of land has meant that the tribe can no longer grow food to sustain themselves. In 2002, the tribe had an opportunity to relocate, but the residents voted against it. In 2009, after Hurricanes Katrina and Rita, the residents agreed to leave, but potential future neighbors did not want the tribe in their backyard. In 2016, the government gave the tribe a $48 million grant, which will allow the tribe to stay together and maintain their community when they find a new home.

 Proficiency-leveled summaries and summaries in multiple languages are available digitally.

 Audio and audio text highlighting are available with this text.

CONNECT TO ESSENTIAL QUESTION

Why do we take chances?

Why would a group of people stay in a dangerous location? In this informational text, author Anya Groner describes the struggle faced by the Biloxi-Chitimacha-Choctaw Native American tribe as their homeland vanishes into the surrounding water.

Access Complex Text

LEXILE: 1000L   **WORD COUNT:** 5,780

The following areas may be challenging for students, particularly **ELL** English Language Learners and **A** Approaching grade-level learners.

Prior Knowledge	Connection of Ideas	Specific Vocabulary
• Students may be unfamiliar with environmental and geological changes that cause massive land erosion. • References to historical events, such as the Indian Removal Act and the Trail of Tears, as well as references to French influence on Louisiana culture, may need explaining.	• This article interweaves information involving Louisiana geology, political and social history, the culture and lives of Native Americans, and historical events in a long and complex narrative, and the narration moves back and forth in time. Students may need support as the topics and time periods shift.	• Students may be unfamiliar with domain-specific vocabulary, such as *anhingas*, *arsenic*, and *palmetto(s)*, as well as French words, such as *bousillage*. • Using Greek and Latin roots, as well as a dictionary, can help students with words such as *biannual*.

◢ SCAFFOLDS   **ENGLISH LANGUAGE LEARNERS**   **APPROACHING GRADE LEVEL**   **BEYOND GRADE LEVEL**

These icons identify differentiation strategies and scaffolded support for a variety of students. See the digital lesson plan for additional differentiation strategies and scaffolds.

Instructional Path

Skill: Evaluating Details

Objectives: After reading and discussing a model, students will be able to evaluate details in order to determine key ideas.

First Read: The Vanishing Island

Objectives: After an initial reading and discussion of an informational text, students will be able to identify and restate the text's key ideas and details.

Skill: Greek and Latin Affixes and Roots

Objectives: After rereading and discussing a model of close reading, students will be able to determine the meaning and usage of grade-level academic English words derived from Greek and Latin roots.

Skill: Media

Objectives: After rereading and discussing a model of close reading, students will be able to analyze and evaluate the author's use of media to achieve specific purposes.

Close Read: The Vanishing Island

Objectives: After engaging in a close reading and discussion of the text, students will be able to explain why people fight hard for their cultural survival, citing different media in a short, written response.

Blast: Risky Business

Objectives: After exploring background information and research links about a topic, students will respond to a question with a 140-character response.

Progress Monitoring

Opportunities to Learn	Opportunities to Demonstrate Learning	Opportunities to Reteach
Evaluating Details		
⚙ Skill: Evaluating Details	🖥 **First Read** • Read and Annotate	⚙ Spotlight Skill: Evaluating Details
Greek and Latin Affixes and Roots		
⚙ Skill: Greek and Latin Affixes and Roots	⚙ Skill: Greek and Latin Affixes and Roots • Your Turn 🖥 **Close Read** • Skills Focus	⚙ Spotlight Skill: Greek and Latin Affixes and Roots
Media		
⚙ Skill: Media	⚙ Skill: Media • Your Turn 🖥 **Close Read** • Skills Focus • Write	⚙ Unit 3 Skill: Media - A Kenyan Teen's Discovery: Let There Be Lights to Save Lions ⚙ Unit 3 Skill: Media - The Call of the Wild ⚙ Spotlight Skill: Media

First Read

Anya Groner

The Vanishing Island

 ## Introduce the Text

As a class, watch the video preview and have students read the introduction in pairs to make connections to the video preview.

To activate prior knowledge and experiences, ask students:

- What key words or images from the video do you think will be most important to the text you are about to read?

- Why do you think it's important to learn about this topic?

ELL **SPEAKING FRAMES**

- The ____ in the video makes me think ____.
- The video shows ____. This makes me wonder ____.
- I think the text will ____. I think this because ____.
- I predict that there will be ____. I believe this because ____.

Entry Point

As students prepare to read "The Vanishing Island," share the following information with them to provide context.

✓ A coastal area can be protected from hurricane damage by barrier islands and wetlands. A barrier island lies just off the coast and takes the brunt of a storm as it approaches the coast from the ocean. During a hurricane, a wetland absorbs much of the water from the initial storm surge, as well as water from the pounding rains, reducing flooding in populated areas. When these natural protective features disappear through erosion or destruction, an area like Isle de Jean Charles is much more at the mercy of hurricanes.

✓ Louisiana was part of France's colonial empire in North America until the late 1700s. French culture remains strong in the area, influencing cuisine, place-names, religious practices, and other cultural characteristics.

✓ French-speaking Acadians (descendants from French settlers in North America) migrated from Canada to what is now Louisiana in the late 1700s and developed a distinct local culture, including a popular cuisine and the Cajun French dialect.

"We know we are going to lose it. We just don't know when."

The Lay of the Land

At first glance, the Isle de Jean Charles, a skinny, two-mile long Louisiana island 75 miles south of New Orleans, looks like a tropical paradise. Beards of Spanish moss sway from the branches of oak trees. Orange and white wildflowers brighten both sides of the only street. Snow-white egrets, blue and green herons, and ebony anhingas stretch their necks, balancing on fallen trees. A flock of red-winged blackbirds takes flight, swooping before landing on the power lines. Even the houses have a bird-like quality. Teal, maroon, and gray, the buildings perch on stilts, fourteen feet off the ground. Wide porches and open front doors welcome visitors. A group has gathered for a fresh crawfish and crab boil. Everyone knows each other here: they grew up together, fishing and crabbing and catching game. Of the two dozen families that still live here, most are relatives and members of the Biloxi-Chitimacha-Choctaw Native American tribe. But the island is not what it used to be. In fact, the island is vanishing. By 2050, Isle de Jean Charles may be completely gone.

Isle de Jean Charles

NOTES

Skill: Media

The boldface text sitting on its own line shows that this is a heading. The heading gives clues about the information in this section. The word land *indicates it will be about the geography of the island.*

Reading & Writing Companion 1

Analyze Vocabulary Using Context Clues

In paragraph 7, focus on the sentence that uses the word *subsistence*. Point out these context clues:

1. First, I notice there is a phrase that follows the word *subsistence*.

2. The phrase seems to be the definition of the word.

3. I read the paragraph again. The meaning fits the context because the forests and fish nurseries are gone. That means people can no longer live off their natural surroundings.

Media

How did the reader use a feature of the print medium to better understand the text?

The reader used a boldface section heading and a key word to identify what information the author will give in that section.

TEXT TALK

How many people live on Isle de Jean Charles, and how are they related?

See paragraph 1: Two dozen people still live there. Most of them are relatives and members of the Biloxi-Chitimacha-Choctaw tribe.

The Vanishing Island

NOTES

2   "Way back in the old days," lifetime resident Wenceslaus Billiot Sr. says in the film *Can't Stop the Waters,* "you had trees. There was no bay. All this water used to be marsh." Billiot Sr. is an 89-year-old boat builder and lifelong resident who has watched the landscape transform. "I built this house in the 1960s. I have another I built in '49. I built it all." Since 1955, the tribe has lost 98 percent of their land to encroaching waters. What was once an eleven-by-five mile island that contained forests and cattle farms is now just two miles long and a quarter of a mile wide. The land, composed of soft, silty dirt, has dissolved, much of it giving way to the waters of the Gulf of Mexico—and the population has shrunk along with the island.

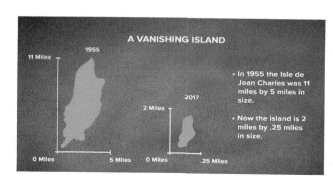

3   "Just in my lifetime, the amount of land loss is astonishing," says tribal secretary Chantel Comardelle. She spent her early years on the island, but her family left when she was four because life on the mainland is more stable than an uncertain future on Isle de Jean Charles. Nonetheless, like many tribal members who've moved away, the island remains her cultural home. She visits nearly every weekend, usually bringing her children with her. "Every time I go back, I see a little bit less."

4   "I grew up here," echoes Emray Naquin. "The land is going like you wouldn't believe."

5   When he was a child, the tribe's leader, Chief Albert Naquin, set traps in the woods with his father. Now, though, that forest is part of the bay, a place where fishermen search for crabs. Farms have vanished, too. There's no place for livestock. Even small vegetable gardens are hard to keep. Over time, the earth has absorbed salt and arsenic from the polluted waters that sweep across the land with increasing frequency.

2   Reading & Writing Companion

Please note that excerpts and passages in the StudySync® library and this workbook are intended as touchstones to generate interest in an author's work. The excerpts and passages do not substitute for the reading of entire texts, and StudySync® strongly recommends that students seek out and purchase the whole literary or informational work in order to experience it as the author intended. Links to online resellers are available in our digital library. In addition, complete works may be ordered through an authorized reseller by filling out and returning to StudySync® the order form enclosed in this workbook.

TEXT TALK

Where has the lost land gone?

See paragraph 2: The land has disappeared under the waters of the Gulf of Mexico.

NOTES

6 "We were so self-sufficient as a tribe, that [in the past] we were unaware of the outside world," explains Damian Naquin. He's eighteen years old. He grew up in nearby Pointe-aux-Chenes. "When the Great Depression happened, the tribe didn't know it." He says that during the nation's greatest economic collapse, tribe members suffered no shortage of food. "It didn't affect us."

7 Self-sufficiency used to be a point of pride for islanders who found freedom in working for themselves. **Subsistence**, the ability to live off one's natural surroundings, is no longer possible because of land loss. The forests are gone, and without the marshes to sustain fish nurseries and provide habitats, the once abundant sea life has diminished.

8 "At one time, water was our life. Now it's almost our enemy because it is driving us out," says Comardelle. "It's a double-edged sword. Our life and our death."

9 Between August and October, the peak months of hurricane season, day-to-day erosion is worsened by storms. Since 1998, Terrebonne Parish, the region that encompasses the Isle de Jean Charles, has suffered a federally-declared disaster every two years. The big ones arrive with more strength and more frequency than in the past. The natural features that used to protect land—wetlands and barrier island—are gone. During hurricanes, waist-deep water rises over the only exit road, cutting off the island from rescue crews. Trees fall and wind rips walls and roofs from buildings. Before residents began elevating their homes atop stilts, biannual flood waters swept furniture and belongings into the bay. "Every time there's a flood, we lose everything," explains Damian. "We don't have any valuables. We know, if we get something, the next storm that comes through, it's going to ruin it. It's going to carry it away."

10 When storms subside, weary residents paddle through town checking up on one another and assessing the damage. After the waters recede, mold and mildew linger, which causes respiratory problems and makes residents ill. The cycle of devastation and rebuilding is exhausting. But it wasn't always like this.

11 "Now [folks] evacuate for hurricanes. Back then they didn't," recalls Comardelles's father, Deputy Chief Wenceslaus Billiot Jr. As a child in 1965, he spent Hurricane Betsy in his father's boat, in the canal in front of their house. "We would get hit by storms but it wouldn't be as bad because we had protection. When Camille hit we didn't have any damage at all. Now, a hurricane like Betsy hits? Shooo." His voice drops to a whisper and he shakes his head.

12 With such severe conditions, outsiders are often baffled to learn that many of the remaining residents of Isle de Jean Charles refuse to leave. The island, which some affectionately refer to as "the bathtub," isn't simply a place to

Reading & Writing Companion   3

Prepare for Advanced Courses

Use the activity below to differentiate instruction for your **B** Beyond grade-level learners.

Look at paragraph 6. Have students discuss what they already know about how Native Americans lived off the land and their treatment of the environment. Ask students to conduct informal research to answer the following questions: How do Native Americans rely on self-sufficiency? How have Native American survival practices changed over time?

V **SELECTION VOCABULARY**

subsistence / la subsistencia *noun* the tools and ability needed to survive **COGNATE**

The Vanishing Island

live—it is the center of tribal life and a cultural homeland. Eight generations have grown up on Isle de Jean Charles, surviving off the bounty of the water and land around them: hunting, fishing, trapping, and gardening. As the land **erodes**, the Biloxi-Chitimacha-Choctaw tribal culture erodes with it. "Once our island goes, the core of our tribe is lost," says Comardelle. "We've lost our whole culture—that is what is on the line."

13 Many elder tribe members don't want another way of life. They grew up here. Though the island has changed, giving up on their homeland is simply too hard. For them, staying put is a way of maintaining traditional life. Others lack the financial resources to live elsewhere. They have come to terms with cleaning up flood damage every two to three years.

14 Island life has changed dramatically over the past few decades. "The old chief, a great-great-great-grandpa of mine, he owned the [island] store," remembers Comardelle. "The store was also the dance hall, it was the church, it was the wedding hall, it was everything." When the population began shrinking, the store shut down. Today the closest grocery store is fifteen miles away. Other community spaces have disappeared as well. There are no longer event grounds on the island. Grand Bois Park, a public event space on the mainland once used for pow wows, has been destroyed by flooding, too. The tribe hasn't held a pow wow—a traditional Native American festival—since before Hurricane Katrina hit Louisiana in 2005. "We have no place," says Comardelle. "I used to dance in pow wow dress. My kids have never experienced that."

15 What remains are the Isle de Jean Charles firehouse and the local marina. Above the tin roof, an orange flag flaps in the wind. It is the flag of Houma Nation, the name of another local Native American tribe. On weekends, visitors come to the island to eat fresh crawfish, shrimp, and crabs; the rest of the week the marina is quiet, as though already abandoned.

16 For more than fifteen years, Chief Naquin has been trying to relocate his people. "The longer we wait," Naquin says in the documentary *Can't Stop the Water*, "the more hurricane seasons we have to go through. We hate to let the island go, but we have to. It's like losing a family member. We know we are going to lose it. We just don't know when."

17 As chief, Naquin believes he must have a good heart in order to know right from wrong and determine what's good for his people. "We're washing away, one day at a time," he says. It is painful for him to admit, but Naquin believes the tribe's future lies elsewhere.

18 In January of 2016, Chief Naquin received good news. Through a Housing and Urban Development grant, his tribe received $48 million, about half the

Skills Focus

QUESTION 1: Greek and Latin Affixes and Roots

The word *education* has the Latin root *duc*. The root helps me understand the meaning of the word because education leads people to knowledge.

SELECTION VOCABULARY

erode / erosionar **verb** to become worn down or to deteriorate, usually caused by natural forces

- What is happening to the island?
- How do clues such as "once our island goes" show the meaning of *erode*?

NOTES

estimated cost of resettling the tribe. The money would help build a community center, medical facilities, and housing for tribe members. That includes the 600 or so people who left Isle de Jean Charles and scattered throughout Louisiana. The grant would also help fund an education program so visitors can learn about the island's history and the difficult process of relocation.

19 "I'm flying high as a kite," Naquin told the newspaper *Houma Today* after receiving the news. It's easy to understand why the grant would make him so happy. Though the island is vanishing, with this money the Biloxi-Chitimacha-Choctaw tribe just may have a future.

Eight Generations of History

- Early 1800s — Jean Marie Naquin and Pauline Verdin are married
- 1830 — Indian Removal Act
- 1876 — Decendants of tribe purchase Isle de Jean Charles legally
- 1910 — Sixteen families living on Isle de Jean Charles
- 1930 — Children begin traveling to Point-aux-Chenes to go to school
- 1940 — The Mission School built for young islanders
- 1952 — Island builds first "Indian High School"
- Local high schools begin admitting Native American Students — 1967
- Hurricanes Katrina and Rita hit; 200 square miles of wetlands lost — 2005
- Hurricane Gustav damages only road to Isle de Jean Charles — 2008
- Tribe receives $4.8 million grant to move — 2016
- Island will be gone due to erosion — 2050

20 Jean Marie Naquin and Pauline Verdin married in the early 1800s. After their wedding, though, they needed to hide: Jean Marie was French and Pauline was Native American. At the time in Louisiana, interracial couples faced discrimination and even violence. Jean Marie's family disowned him because of the marriage. To escape persecution, Jean Marie and Pauline built their home on an "uninhabited" island. The landscape was rich with palmettos, alligators, crawfish, and sea birds.

21 Ironically, it was Jean Marie's disapproving father, Jean Charles, for whom the Isle de Jean Charles was likely named. He was the one who first showed his son the island, hidden in the coastal wetlands. Jean Charles had first come to the island while he was employed by the notorious privateer and outlaw, Jean Lafitte. At the time, Louisiana's wetlands were considered "uninhabitable" by the government. They weren't even mapped by Europeans. For a man like Jean Lafitte, a privateer who transported stolen goods and slaves to illegal markets, the maze of marshes provided a hiding place for his misdeeds.

Skills Focus

QUESTION 3: Media

The timeline is a good way to show me the events that happened over eight generations of history, but the disadvantage of a timeline is that it doesn't give any details about these events. When I go on to read the text, I see that it does explain the events with rich and interesting details.

TEXT TALK

What does Chief Naquin think about the tribe's future?

See paragraphs 16–19: He thinks the tribe can survive by resettling together in a new place.

Skills Focus

QUESTION 5: Connect to Essential Question

Jean Marie and Pauline took a risk when they built their home on an uninhabitable island. They took this chance because they were not safe on the mainland.

22 The coastal swamps provided safety for the newly married Jean Marie and Pauline. Not only was the island isolated, the land was also free. "Uninhabitable" land meant unwanted land, so Jean Marie and Pauline simply claimed it as their own. They built their home from mud, moss, and palmetto leaves, a kind of construction known as bousillage. Soon they started a family.

23 By the 1830s, Jean Marie and Pauline's children were having children of their own. Later, they married Native Americans from off the island and brought them to Isle de Jean Charles to live and start families as well. Once again, the remote location provided safety from a hostile society. In 1830, the United States Congress passed the Indian Removal Act, a federal law authorizing the forced removal of southern Native Americans from their ancestral land. The purpose of the law was to enable white settlers to move in. A few tribes, including the Mississippi Choctaws, signed treaties exchanging their homeland for payment and land rights west of the Mississippi. Other tribes resisted and the situation escalated. White men formed local and state militias, which forced southern and southeastern Native Americans to abandon their homes and march west to Oklahoma and Texas. The Native Americans were exposed to the elements. They lacked supplies. Thousands died and the march west became known as the Trail of Tears, in memory of the lives and culture lost.

24 Unlike so many other Native Americans, the growing Naquin family escaped the Trail of Tears because of their hidden island deep in the marshes. For the second time, the swamp saved their lives.

TEXT TALK

How did living in a hidden swamp help the people on Isle de Jean Charles survive in the past?

See paragraphs 23 and 24: The people on the island could stay on their ancestral land. Other Native Americans were forced off their land after the Indian Removal Act and lost their lives during the Trail of Tears.

NOTES

25   By 1876, Louisiana settlers were looking to expand their communities and build in new places. The state revoked the coastal marshes' official designation as "uninhabitable." It put the wetlands and their hidden islands up for sale. Four families, residents of Isle de Jean Charles and descendants of Jean Marie and Pauline, purchased the land they lived on, which gave them a legal claim to the island their families had been occupying for seven decades.

26   By 1910, sixteen families lived on Isle de Jean Charles. Residents were fluent in Cajun French and English. They lived a subsistence-based lifestyle. Families fished, trapped, and hunted for food. They added to their diets with gardens. They had domesticated livestock such as chickens and cows.

27   French, Native American, and African food cultures influenced their cuisine. For instance, Gumbo Fricassee, a popular dish, contains the following ingredients:

- Okra - a vegetable imported from West Africa during the slave trade
- Roux - a mixture of fat and flour often used as a base in French cooking
- Filé - a Choctaw spice made from ground sassafras leaves
- The Holy Trinity - a Catholic nickname for the celery, bell peppers, and onions, essential ingredients in any gumbo recipe
- Whatever seafood, chicken, or sausage is fresh and available

Skills Focus

QUESTION 2: Media

The photograph of gumbo fricassee shows the finished product of the recipe the author includes. This helps me understand the kind of food that is associated with the tribe's cultural heritage.

The Vanishing Island

NOTES

28 Religious practices on the island similarly combine French Catholic and Native American customs. To this day, many Biloxi-Chitimacha-Choctaw people attend both church and pow wows.

29 Masculinity was important in both games and government. On Christian or Native American holidays, men and boys often gathered to play pick, a game still played today. Damiann Naquin first played pick when he was six. Pick, he explains, is "a simple game. You have a circle in the mud. Everyone has a sharpened wooden stick, which you find from a tree and sharpen. . . . The point [is] to see who could keep their stick in the mud the longest [and] to knock another person's stick down."

30 The tribe's chief was always a man. As the tribal leader, he would **maintain** the grocery store, distribute mail, help **settle** disputes, represent the people of the island to outsiders, and gather residents for community service. Upon retirement, he chose his successor, a practice that continues to this day.

31 Despite the growing size of the community, for decades Isle de Jean Charles lacked a school. In the 1930s, children began traveling by small wooden boats called pirogues to the nearby town of Pointe-aux-Chenes, where a missionary school funded by donations and run by the Live Oak Baptist Church served both white and Native American children. At that time, though, Louisiana was committed to Jim Crow laws, which legalized racial segregation. The missionary school didn't last long. The superintendent visited, saw a racially mixed classroom, and shut the school down. The island children had nowhere to go.

V SELECTION VOCABULARY

maintain / mantener **verb** to keep or continue without changing COGNATE

ELL
- What goals are described in this paragraph?
- How do those goals show the meaning of *maintain*?

settle / resolver **verb** to resolve a problem or reach an agreement

ELL
- What is being "settled"?
- What other events are described in the sentence? Are they positive or negative?

NOTES

32 In 1940, Baptists tried again to provide education for the younger islanders by building the Mission School. It was a one room building on the Isle de Jean Charles. The mission school filled a gap, but it only ran to eighth grade. Eventually, some frustrated families moved off the island. In 1952, Louisiana built its first "Indian High School" in Houma, Louisiana. It was a segregated school for Native American teenagers 25 miles from Isle de Jean Charles. It was not until 1967 that local public schools admitted Native American students.

Reading & Writing Companion   9

Use the activity below to differentiate instruction for your **B** Beyond grade-level learners.

Direct students to reread paragraphs 31–33.

Ask students: How does the author's inclusion of the information about schools add complexity to the island problems?

Answers will vary; sample answer: The author shows that the island had to abide by state laws, which included racial segregation. Island life meant "traveling by small wooden boats," so a mix of geography, culture, and politics made attending school at times impossible. This made raising families there more stressful.

Media

How did the reader use a visual in the print medium to better understand the text?

The reader noticed a photograph that helped her visualize key details in the text about how flooding can trap people on the island.

Greek and Latin Affixes and Roots

How did knowledge of Greek roots and affixes help the reader define a word?

The reader combined the root *geo* and the affix *-logy* to confirm that *geological* had to do with the study of the earth.

**Skill:
Media**

The author talks about the road being low and easily flooded and then includes a photograph of it. The photo really helps me see how close to the water the road is. No one could get to school or work when it floods.

**Skill:
Greek and
Latin Affixes
and Roots**

I see the word geological, and I think it has to do with a study of Earth. I know that it combines the Greek root geo, meaning "earth," and the Greek root logy, meaning "the study of."

33   Even today, there are no schools on the island. The closest schools are on the mainland. In 2008, Hurricane Gustav damaged the only road connecting the mainland to the island, turning it from a two-lane road into a one-lane road. After that, school buses stopped coming to Isle de Jean Charles. All but one family with school-age children have moved away. Though the road has been repaired, it still sits only inches above open water. High winds can cause flooding over the pavement. "If you live on the island and the road is flooded then you can't go to school or go to work," explains Sheila Billiot.

Stomping Out the Boot

34   If you open a United States atlas or search the Internet for "Louisiana map," you'll discover a state shaped roughly like a boot. Louisiana is bordered by the Mississippi River to the east, Arkansas to the north, and Texas to the west. The foot of the boot stretches south and east into the Gulf of Mexico.

35   A state's shape sounds unchangeable, but some Louisianans believe their map needs to be redrawn. "The boot is at best an inaccurate approximation," writes Brett Anderson, staff writer for the New Orleans newspaper *The Times-Picayune*. Anderson isn't disputing Louisiana's borders with surrounding states; his contention lies with the southernmost border, where the state's marshy edges are rapidly slipping into the gulf.

36   Because marshlands are largely impassable except by boat, it's difficult to understand the magnitude of Louisiana's land loss unless viewing it from a plane. The United States Geological Service (USGS) reports that between 1932 and 2000, roughly 1,900 square miles of Louisiana's land vanished into the Gulf of Mexico. That's an area about the size of Delaware. Today, an

TEXT TALK

Why is it difficult for residents to travel off the island?

See paragraph 33: There is only one road that connects the island to the mainland. If that road is flooded, people cannot go to school or work.

Why do Louisiana residents want their state to be redrawn on maps?

See paragraphs 35 and 36: Land is disappearing into the Gulf of Mexico.

NOTES

estimated football field of land is lost every 45 minutes. That rate of land loss is higher than almost anywhere else on the planet. If no measures are put in place to prevent more erosion, another 1,750 square miles—a landmass larger than Rhode Island—will give way by 2064. "Our coast is going away faster than pretty much any other coast in the world," explains Pat Forbes. He's the Executive Director of the Louisiana State Office of Community and Development. Currently, Louisiana's greatest land loss occurs during storms. In 2005, the year Hurricanes Katrina and Rita hit, Louisiana lost more than 200 square miles of coastal wetlands in a single summer.

Louisiana Shoreline Change
1932–2000

37 In addition to hurricane damage and global sea level rise, other factors also contribute to land loss. The engineering of the Mississippi River, the land's natural propensity to sink and erode, and the dredging of canals throughout the wetlands have also contributed to the loss of land in Louisiana.

38 From its source in Minnesota, the Mississippi River winds its way through nine more states before spilling into the Gulf of Mexico: Wisconsin, Iowa, Illinois, Missouri, Kentucky, Tennessee, Arkansas, Mississippi, and Louisiana. The river, nicknamed the Big Muddy, picks up dirt and carries it downstream. Eventually, this dirt is deposited along the Louisiana Gulf Coast, a process that has replenished and maintained coastline marshes and islands that would otherwise erode into the sea. "Essentially," explains Forbes, "most of Southern Louisiana has been built up by sediment carried down the Mississippi over thousands of years." Without this sediment to constantly build back the land, Louisiana's coastline would naturally diminish.

39 In 1927, unusually heavy rains overwhelmed the Mississippi River, flooding an area the size of Ireland and causing the current to run backwards. Levees broke. Floodwaters swept away farms and towns. In some places the swollen river stretched more than 60 miles wide. More than 700,000 people lost their homes. The damage cost about $1 billion at the time to fix.

Reading & Writing
Companion

11

Prepare for Advanced Courses

Use the activity below to differentiate instruction for your **B** Beyond grade-level learners.

Note the word *dredge* in paragraph 37. Explain to students the idiomatic use of *dredge*. Ask students to consider how the idiomatic usage plays into the text. Have students look up meanings of the word *dredge* and explore how those various meanings are connected.

The Vanishing Island

40   To prevent such a disaster from happening again, the US government constructed the world's largest river containment system around the Big Muddy. The Army Corps of Engineers built dirt barriers called levees on either side of the river to prevent the floodwaters from spilling over the banks. They also dug man-made canals, called floodways. That way, when the river swelled, the water could be released along predictable routes. Rather than carving a new riverbed every spring, as the Mississippi had done annually since the last Ice Age, the massive waterway was given a fixed path which ended in the Gulf of Mexico.

41   The levees and floodways prevented the Mississippi from overflowing its banks, but they also stopped the river from carrying out many of the natural processes that surrounding states relied on. The levee system cut the Louisiana coast off from the sediment that nourished and created the land. The dirt that gave the Big Muddy its nickname no longer reached Louisiana's marshes.

42 The problems caused by river engineering are worsened by subsidence, or the natural propensity for wetlands to sink and erode. Louisiana contains 40% of the nation's wetlands. These marshes make up more than a third of the state. They provide habitats for shrimp, fish, crawfish, and crabs. These animals are crucial to Louisiana's fisheries. Built from soft mud, these wetlands are constantly sinking and eroding, a natural process called subsidence. When the river dumps sediment into the marshes, the wetlands rebuild and the lost land replenishes. Without river sediment to continually build them back up, Louisiana's wetlands shrink, then vanish, a process that's been charted repeatedly along the coast.

43 In addition to subsidence, a system of canals crisscrosses the state's wetlands, further damaging the fragile ecosystem. In the swamp, these waterways function as roads, providing boats easy access to oil, gas, and fisheries; over time, however, they've created pathways for saltwater from the Gulf of Mexico to leach into the freshwater wetlands. Salt is poisonous to wetland plants such as Cypress and Tupelo Gum trees. As the flora dies off, the wetlands give way to open water.

44 The disappearance of the wetlands has had another unintended consequence. Marshes and swamps are like sponges; they can expand and soak up water, protecting the mainland and inland islands from storm surges and flooding—but without wetlands to provide natural barriers, hurricane damage can be even more **catastrophic.**

45 For Louisianans, restoring the coast is a race against time. The goal is not only to protect the land, but also to care for the humans, plants, and animals that live there. The US economy is deeply linked to Louisiana's wellbeing. The state's commercial fishing industry produces a quarter of US seafood, and nearly half of the nation's grain supply passes through the port of New Orleans. Since 2007, the state has built 250 miles of levees and constructed 45 miles of barrier islands and berms. But this massive effort has not been able to keep up with the rate of land loss.

Stay or Go?

46 The first opportunity for the Biloxi-Chitimacha-Choctaw tribe to relocate came in 2002. The Army Corps of Engineers redrew the path of the Morganza-to-the-Gulf Levee. This 98-mile earthen wall was designed to protect people and property from hurricanes and storm surges. Originally, Isle de Jean Charles was included in this plan. The levee would keep water off the island and the land would regenerate. However, in 2002, the Army Corps of Engineers decided to bypass Isle de Jean Charles. For islanders, the news was devastating.

Reading & Writing Companion 13

Why is hurricane damage worse since the disappearance of wetlands in the area?

See paragraph 44: Marshes and swamps soak up extra water, so hurricane-related flooding is worse without them.

V SELECTION VOCABULARY

catastrophic / catastrófico/a *adjective* causing ruin; disastrous COGNATE

ELL
- What effects are being described in these paragraphs?
- Are the effects positive or negative?

Greek and Latin Affixes and Roots

How did the reader determine the meaning of the word *relocate*?

The reader looked up the word in a dictionary. He learned the prefix *re-* means "again," the root *loc* means "place," and the verb suffix *-ate* means "to make."

Greek and Latin Affixes and Roots

How does the reader determine the meaning of the word *relocation*?

The reader used his knowledge of the root and affixes of *relocate* and the noun suffix *-tion* to make a guess before looking up the word in a dictionary.

TEXT TALK

How did the tribe's feelings about relocating change over time?

See paragraphs 47 and 48: People reconsidered the option of relocating after hurricanes badly damaged the land.

The Vanishing Island

NOTES

Skill:
Greek and
Latin Affixes
and Roots

I'm not sure what the word relocate means. I can tell it is a verb because the word to comes before it. I think it may have a Greek or Latin root, but I need to look it up to be sure.

Skill:
Greek and
Latin Affixes
and Roots

Relocation looks like relocate, so the words probably have a similar meaning. I know the suffix -ion forms nouns. Based on these clues, I think the word relocation might mean "the act of moving to a new place."

47   The Army Corps of Engineers offered to relocate the community. But it would only happen if the residents voted unanimously in favor of resettling. "The plan was dead in the water," Comardelle recalls. "At the time, we'd had a lot of land loss, but we hadn't had major structural issues [with buildings and infrastructure]." The majority of residents were in favor of the relocation. However, some residents, particularly tribal elders, were reluctant to leave. "It's home for them, you know," Dominick explains. "They were born, raised, grew up, lived their whole entire lives there. Even though their home is being stripped away, they still don't want to leave because of the sentimental value." Others worried the relocation was part of a dishonest effort to take over their island. In the end, the tribe couldn't get unanimous support. The relocation was voted down by the people.

48   Several years after the vote, storm damage caused tribe members to reconsider their stance. In 2005, Hurricanes Katrina and Rita flooded the island, badly damaging the land. Three years later, when Hurricane Gustav hit Isle de Jean Charles directly, houses lost roofs and walls, gas lines broke, and the utility company refused to replace the lines. Many residents left, and those who stayed behind reconsidered their options.

49   In 2009, the tribal council restarted the relocation process. This time, plans progressed much further. Most residents were ready to leave. The tribal

NOTES

council found land to purchase. This time the relocation was halted by their future neighbors. "We were going forward and some issues came up with the [adjacent] neighborhood," remembers Comardelle. "That community rose up and said they didn't want [us] in their backyard." With no place to move, tribe members wondered if their culture was fated to vanish along with the island.

50 Good news came in early 2016. That's when the Biloxi-Chitimacha-Choctaw tribe learned they would receive the $48 million relocation grant from the federal office of Housing and Urban Development. Beginning with the marriage of Jean Marie Naquin and Pauline Verdin, eight generations of tribal members made their home on the Isle de Jean Charles. The relocation grant meant the tribe could have a future, but it would have to be elsewhere. Though he was thrilled to receive the grant, in an article in *National Geographic* Chief Naquin compared "losing the island" with "losing a family member."

51 Federal grants have supported resettlement projects for storm victims for decades. They've enabled, for example, families who lost houses in Hurricane Katrina and Hurricane Sandy to live elsewhere. The Isle de Jean Charles relocation, however, is an entirely new endeavor. "Resettling a community is entirely different from relocating individuals," explains Pat Forbes. "In the past, when an area's been declared unsafe to live, the state or federal government has offered buyouts to affected landowners. In other words, they pay residents to leave. The problem with buyouts is that communities don't stay together."

52 In contrast, the primary goal of the Isle de Jean Charles relocation is to preserve the community and culture of the Biloxi-Chitimacha-Choctaw tribe. Rather than splitting up tribe members, the grant aims to bring people together. The grant proposal explains, "The tribe has physically and culturally been torn apart with the scattering of members. . . . A new settlement offers an opportunity for the tribe to rebuild their homes and secure their culture on safe ground." With this funding, island residents and tribal members who left their homeland due to land loss and flooding can also rejoin their community in a new location.

53 "The people of the Isle de Jean Charles Band of Biloxi-Chitimacha-Choctaw tribe are situated on the front line of Louisiana's coastal land loss disaster and their ancestral home is sinking into the marsh," explains Forbes. "This $48 million grant will allow the state to help them resettle their entire community to a safer place with minimum of disruption to livelihoods and lifestyles.

Skills Focus

QUESTION 4: Textual Evidence

Most groups have to split up when they relocate. However, the federal grant money will help the tribe rebuild their community in a new location.

TEXT TALK

How will the relocation grant help the community?

See paragraphs 50–52: The grant will help the community move together to a new location.

Together we'll be creating a model for resettlement of endangered coastal communities throughout the United States."

54   To accomplish this lofty goal, tribal members have been dreaming big. "We could have our own community center," says secretary Comardelle. "We could have room to grow. We could have our own crops, our own industry if we wanted. We want to be our own place again."

55   Community members are working hard to make the relocation happen. "It's about family," says Dominick Naquin. "No matter how many times we've been shot down, we came back stronger and kept fighting." Perhaps everything that the Isle de Jean Charles' residents and their ancestors have overcome has set them up for this moment. With ancestors who escaped the Trail of Tears and families who've survived numerous hurricanes, they're well equipped to triumph despite unfavorable odds.

A Vision of Community

56   "I want you to feel like you have just walked onto the original island, with the way the trees look, the way the vegetation looks," says Chantel Comardelle. She's leaning back in a brown armchair in her two-bedroom house in Houma, Louisiana, 45 minutes from the Isle de Jean Charles. To her right sits her daughter's three-story plastic dollhouse; to her left, giant containers filled with quilts and photo albums. Heirlooms inherited when her mother-in-law passed away. One room over, one of her young sons is crying. Comardelle's mother, Sheila Billiot, is talking to him softly, comforting him. The emphasis on family, a value nearly every member of her tribe seems to cherish, is abundant in this house.

57   Comardelle's eyes are closed as she talks. Physically, she's here, in her living room. Spiritually, she's in the future, imagining what her tribe's relocation will look like. What will it mean for her family and for the future of her people? Her voice is confident as if she's describing a place that already exists.

58   "When you pull up, when you approach the community, the center grounds are also pow wow grounds." In the front of the facility, she imagines a museum. It's a wooden building with a front porch. When visitors enter, they feel like they're walking into someone's house. "I want guests to walk through the history of the island with the original settlers. The ceiling, I want it to be the road to show how it progressed. With no road, just water and canoes, and then you have the road, and then you start to see the road on the floor. I want to have a big map on the wall and show the island. I want it to be digitized to show you how the island's progressed in digital pictures as far as land loss, how it's shrunk."

59   Comardelle's belief in the museum is so great that she's begun taking online graduate courses in museum studies, using her class assignments to start planning exhibits and features. "Even the sounds will be like you're on the island," she says. "I want French music playing in some sections. I want people talking in other sections. I want animal sounds in other sections. I want you to be fully immersed." Comardelle's vision is so detailed and her belief so firm that it's hard to imagine the future panning out any other way.

60   Besides the museum, Comardelle imagines the new site hosting other public facilities. There will be a store, a clinic, and a restaurant. "We hope to have a kitchen. The food's traditional Cajun food. Gumbo. Gumbo fricassee. We're going to have a healthcare facility. We want to have a 24-hour nurse, and we'll also service the outside, so it'll be like a both-ways kind of thing. We also want to have a childcare facility. An elderly senior center. Our kitchen will cook and serve food for the outside, but daily they'll make a plate lunch for our residents who are elderly."

61   Comardelle's idealism is intentional. In 2010, the tribe began working with a non-profit called the Lowlander Center, a community-run organization aimed at helping lowland residents build a future while adapting to an ever-changing coastline. After Hurricane Gustav, volunteers at the Lowlander Center heard about the tribe's resettlement plan. They encouraged the council of elders to come up with their best-case scenario. "All the bells and whistles," recalls Comardelle. "Everything you want. Everything you desire."

62   Beyond the pow wow grounds, the museum, and the restaurant, Comardelle envisions a less public part of the community where residents live. Designed to accommodate up to 400 members, the houses will be arranged, as they were on the the island, so that extended families share backyards. Aunts and uncles and grandparents will be able watch each other's children. They'll call across to each other from porch to porch. "I want to build that family unit back," says Comardelle.

63   Comardelle isn't the only one to prioritize shared responsibility and familial interactions. At eighteen, Damian and Dominick Naquin are the youngest members of the resettlement committee. They see blood relationships as the glue that holds their community together.

64   "As a future, I would love to see us stay as a family," explains Damian. "Some elders don't want to give up what they remember, what they hold onto, but their grandchildren, they would love to see another future for them. They want to save the family values and the culture so that the younger generation can experience what they experienced."

NOTES

TEXT TALK

What is being planned for the tribe's new community?

See paragraphs 56–62: The plans include a museum, pow wow grounds, a store, a clinic, a childcare facility, a senior center, and a restaurant.

Use the activity below to differentiate instruction for your **B** Beyond grade-level learners.

Look at the accomplishments and desires of Comardelle in paragraphs 60–65.

Initiatives like Comardelle's museum and public facilities are often driven by a variety of social and cultural values. Ask students: What is the driving force of Comardelle's museum and future plans? What controversies might emerge from Comardelle's idealism?

NOTES

65   "If we're successful with the relocation," adds Dominick, "then the elders will know the younger generation will experience what they experienced."

66   As for their own future, the twin brothers hope to return to their tribe equipped with skills to help their community thrive. Both are currently freshmen at Louisiana State University in Baton Rouge. "I'm trying to become a pediatrician, a child doctor," says Damian. "If I achieve that goal, I know I'm able to bring a very valuable resource back. I see my role in the future of the tribe, to support wherever the tribe goes."

67   Dominick, who's majoring in computer science, echoes his brother's wish to contribute to the well-being of his people. His ideal day in the new community includes multigenerational activities. "I'll wake up. I'll do my job, whatever that may be," he says. "Hopefully, when the time comes, I would have the privilege to sit down with a whole bunch of children and be able to sit down in a circle drum and teach them how to drum and sing. To pass down our culture, that would bring me great joy."

68   Damian and Dominick's plans are exactly what the tribe needs for the resettlement to work. Maintaining a cultural identity is the primary goal of the resettlement, but the only way that can happen is through interaction across age groups. Already, the culture is being lost. Comardelle's grandmother was a medicinal herbalist, who used teas and plants to cure others. Those skills weren't passed down and the tradition was lost.

69   Until the relocation is complete, Comardelle does her best to transfer culture by taking her children to Isle de Jean Charles, explaining, "If you can keep the younger generation connected with the oldest generation, you can keep that transition. I notice it with my kids, when we go visit my grandma. They're learning French in school and they're tickled to go over there and talk French with my grandma."

70   Perhaps, years from now, Comardelle's children will recall these trips to Isle de Jean Charles, an island homeland that no longer exists. Sitting on a back porch, they'll tell their children about how they caught crabs in the bayou. How they listened to their grandparents speak in Cajun French about weddings in general stores and waiting out hurricanes in their daddy's boats. Around them the egrets will take flight as Spanish moss sways in the breeze. Relatives might wave from nearby porches. After all, history isn't just what happened a long time ago. The creation of a new homeland, the tribe's relocation, and the council's efforts to maintain culture are all history in action. If the relocation works, Comardelle, the Naquins, and the other members of

18   Reading & Writing Companion

the Biloxi-Chitimacha-Choctaw tribe will achieve something amazing. Their people and their culture will have a safe home in coastal Louisiana for centuries to come.

Anya Groner's essays and stories can be read in journals including *The New York Times, Ecotone, The Oxford American,* and *The Atlantic.* A resident of New Orleans, Groner teaches creative writing at the New Orleans Center for Creative Arts and through the New Orleans Writers Workshop.

NOTES

TEXT TALK

How is preserving the Biloxi-Chitimacha-Choctaw Native American tribe's land like preserving their culture?

Answers will vary.

B   Ask each Beyond grade-level student to write one additional discussion question. Then have one or two students facilitate a discussion, using their questions to guide the conversation.

Think Questions

Circulate as students answer Think Questions independently. Scaffolds for these questions are shown on the opposite page.

QUESTION 1: Textual Evidence

Jean Marie Naquin and Pauline Verdin were the first people to move to Isle de Jean Charles. They were an interracial married couple who moved to the uninhabited island "to escape persecution." Later, their children married Native Americans from areas near the island and "brought them to Isle de Jean Charles to live and start families."

QUESTION 2: Textual Evidence

The tribe used to subsist on food they got for themselves on the island. They used to be able to trap animals, farm, and keep livestock. But "since 1955, the tribe lost 98% of their land to encroaching waters," so land loss prevents them from being able to support themselves.

QUESTION 3: Textual Evidence

Containment of the Mississippi River stopped natural processes that used to maintain the coastline: "The levee system cut the Louisiana coast off from the sediment that nourished and created the land." This has had long-term effects: "Without river sediment to continually build them back up, Louisiana's wetlands shrink, then vanish, a process that's been charted repeatedly along the coast."

QUESTION 4: Context Clues

I think *erodes* must mean "to disappear slowly over a long period of time." The word is used to tell what happens to the land, and the text is mostly about how the land is vanishing over time.

QUESTION 5: Word Meaning

Definition e most closely matches the meaning of the word *settle* in paragraph 30. In the text, the chief helps people end disputes, or arguments.

The Vanishing Island

First Read

Read "The Vanishing Island." After you read, complete the Think Questions below.

 THINK QUESTIONS

1. Why did people move to the Isle de Jean Charles? Provide two specific examples from the text to support your response.

2. Why is the Biloxi-Chitimacha-Choctaw tribe no longer able to subsist? Provide specific evidence from the text to support your response.

3. How does containment of the Mississippi River affect the Louisiana coastline? Provide specific evidence from the text to support your response.

4. Find the word **erodes** in paragraph 12 of "The Vanishing Island." Use context clues in the surrounding sentences, as well as the sentence in which the word appears, to determine the word's meaning. Write your definition here and identify clues that helped you figure out its meaning.

5. Read the following dictionary entry:

   settle
   set•tle \sedl\ *verb*

   a. to decide something
   b. to put things in order
   c. to move to a place to live
   d. to pay money that is owed
   e. to end an argument
   f. to get into a more comfortable position

   Which definition most closely matches the meaning of **settle** as it is used in paragraph 30? Write the correct definition of *settle* here and explain how you figured out the correct meaning.

Think Questions

Use the scaffolds below to differentiate instruction for your **ELL** English Language Learners and **A** Approaching grade-level learners.

ELL **BEGINNING** Write a response using the <u>word bank</u> and <u>sentence frames</u>.

INTERMEDIATE Write a response using the <u>sentence frames</u>.

ADVANCED, ADVANCED HIGH Write a response using the <u>Text-Dependent Question Guide</u>.

A **APPROACHING** Write a response using the <u>Text-Dependent Question Guide</u>.

BEGINNING	INTERMEDIATE	APPROACHING / ADVANCED, ADVANCED HIGH
Word Bank	**Sentence Frames**	**Text-Dependent Question Guide**
fish smaller accepted land loss disappear farm shrink married sediment Native Americans	The first people to move to the island were a _____ couple. They moved to the uninhabited island because interracial couples were not _____ at the time. Later, their children married _____ from nearby areas and brought them to the island to live.	1. • Why did they move to the island? • How did their children contribute to the island's population?
	The tribe used to _____ and _____ to live. Over time, _____ has made this impossible.	2. • How did people on the island subsist, or live off the land, in the past? • What changed on the island?
	The _____ from the Mississippi River used to naturally build up Louisiana's wetlands. Now that the river has been contained, these areas _____ and eventually vanish.	3. • What happened naturally before the containment of the Mississippi River? • What happened after the containment was complete? • How did the Louisiana coastline change?
	The island is getting _____. This gives me a clue that *erodes* means "to _____ over time."	4. • Read: "As the land **erodes**, the Biloxi-Chitimacha-Choctaw tribal culture **erodes** with it." • What is eroding? • What does that tell me about the meaning of the word *erodes*?
	Settle as used in the text matches definition _____.	5. • "As the tribal leader, he would maintain the grocery store, distribute mail, help **settle** disputes, represent the people of the island to outsiders, and gather residents for community service." • Does *settle* mean "make a decision" (a), "put things in order" (b), "move" (c), "pay back money" (d), "end an argument" (e), or "get more comfortable" (f)?

Reading Comprehension OPTIONAL

Have students complete the digital reading comprehension questions ✅ when they finish reading.

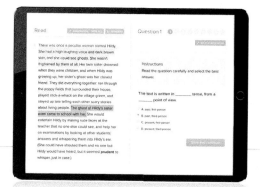

ANSWER KEY

QUESTION 1: D	QUESTION 5: A	QUESTION 9:
QUESTION 2: B	QUESTION 6: B	*See first chart.*
QUESTION 3: C	QUESTION 7: A	QUESTION 10:
QUESTION 4: D	QUESTION 8: C	*See second chart.*

Synonym	Word
continue	maintain
disastrous	catastrophic
upkeep	subsistence
crumble	erode
occupy	settle

Quote	Person
"I want to build that family unit back."	Chantel Comardelle
"To pass down our culture, that would bring me great joy."	Dominik Naquin
"We hate to let the island go, but we have to. It's like losing a family member."	Chief Albert Naquin
"I built this house in the 1960s. I have another I built in '49. I built it all."	Wenceslaus Billiot Sr.

Connect and Extend OPTIONAL

CONNECT TO EXTENDED WRITING PROJECT

Students can use "The Vanishing Island" as a resource when writing their informational essays. Have students analyze Anya Groner's use of details to help them in their own writing.

BEYOND THE BOOK

Research Project: Rising Waters

Isle de Jean Charles is one community being impacted by rising sea levels, but there are many more communities in danger. Break students into small groups and ask them to:

- Identify another coastal community or island being impacted by rising sea levels.
- Research the impact of rising sea levels on the geographic location, people's lifestyle and customs, access to services (e.g., hospitals and schools), food sources, and work.
- Explore how the community they selected is dealing with their changing environment.
- Create a multimedia presentation to present their research to the class.
- Present their findings in a formal group presentation.

To reflect, ask students:

- What similarities did you notice about the different locations and the impact of rising sea levels?
- How are communities dealing with these changes? What creative solutions are people developing?
- Many locations in the United States (e.g., New Orleans, San Francisco, Miami, Manhattan) are extremely vulnerable to rising sea levels. How can highly populated cities deal with this threat?

The Vanishing Island

Skill: Greek and Latin Affixes and Roots

Use the Checklist to analyze Greek and Latin Affixes and Roots in "The Vanishing Island." Refer to the sample student annotations about Greek and Latin Affixes and Roots in the text.

••• CHECKLIST FOR GREEK AND LATIN AFFIXES AND ROOTS

In order to identify Greek and Latin affixes and roots, note the following:

- ✓ the root
- ✓ the prefix and/or suffix

To use common, grade-appropriate Greek or Latin affixes and roots as clues to the meaning of a word, use the following questions as a guide:

- ✓ Can I identify the root of this word? Should I look in a dictionary or other resource?
- ✓ What is the meaning of the root?
- ✓ Can I identify the prefix and/or suffix of this word? Should I look in a dictionary or other resource?
- ✓ What is the meaning of the prefix and/or suffix?
- ✓ Does this affix change the word's part of speech?
- ✓ How do the word parts work together to define the word's meaning and part of speech?

Reading & Writing Companion | 21

Skill: Greek and Latin Affixes and Roots

Introduce the Skill

Watch the Concept Definition video and read the following definition with your students.

A **root** is the basic part of a word that gives the word its meaning. An **affix** is a word part that is added to a root. Affixes can change the word's meaning or its part of speech. **Prefixes** are affixes added to the beginning of a word, and **suffixes** are added to the end of a word.

For example, the word *acid* is the root in the word *acidic*. The suffix *-ic* changes the word *acid* from a noun to an adjective.

Many words in English come from ancient Greek and Latin. Knowing the meanings of Greek and Latin affixes and roots can often help readers figure out the meanings of unfamiliar words.

⚙ TURN AND TALK

1. What are some of your favorite words? Why do you like these words?

2. What word parts can be added to the beginnings or ends of those words to create new words? For example, the word *script*, meaning "something written," can be changed to *transcript, manuscript,* or *description.*

ELL SPEAKING FRAMES

- One of my favorite words is ____. I like this word because ____.
- A word part that is added to the beginning of the word is ____. This changes the ____.
- A word part that is added to the end of the word is ____. This changes the ____.

V SKILL VOCABULARY

root / la raíz *noun* the most basic part of a word that gives a word its meaning

affix / el afijo *noun* a word part added to a root that can change the word's part of speech or meaning

prefix / el prefijo *noun* an affix added to the beginning of a word COGNATE

suffix / el sufijo *noun* an affix attached to the end of a word; may change the spelling of the base word depending on the suffix COGNATE

Your Turn

Ask students to complete the Your Turn activity.

QUESTION 1

A. Incorrect. The context does not support this meaning.

B. Incorrect. The word *marina* is not used as a verb.

C. Incorrect. Neither the context nor the root supports this meaning.

D. Correct. Both the context and the root support this meaning.

QUESTION 2

A. Incorrect. The context does not support this meaning.

B. Correct. Both the context and the root support this meaning.

C. Incorrect. Neither the context nor the root supports this meaning.

D. Incorrect. Neither the context nor the root supports this meaning.

QUESTION 3

A. Correct. The context and the root support this meaning.

B. Incorrect. The context and the root do not support this meaning.

C. Incorrect. The context does not support this meaning.

D. Incorrect. The context does not support this meaning.

QUESTION 4

A. Incorrect. The context and the root do not support this meaning.

B. Incorrect. The context and the root do not support this meaning.

C. Correct. The context and root support this meaning.

D. Incorrect. While the root *port* means "carry," the context does not support this meaning.

The Vanishing Island

Skill: Greek and Latin Affixes and Roots

Reread paragraphs 15 and 21 of "The Vanishing Island." Then, using the Checklist on the previous page, answer the multiple-choice questions below.

↻ YOUR TURN

> **marina** mar•in•a \mə ˈrē-nə\
> **Origin:** from the Latin root *mar* meaning "sea"
>
> **local** loc•al \lō-kəl\
> **Origin:** from the Latin root *loc* meaning "place"
>
> **quiet** qui•et \kwī-ət\
> **Origin:** from the Latin root *qui* meaning "rest"
>
> **transport** trans•port \tran(t)s-pôrt\
> **Origin:** from the Latin root *trans* meaning "across" and *port* meaning "carry"
>
> **misdeed** mis•deed \mis-dēd\
> **Origin:** from the Greek root *mis* meaning "bad"

1. Based on its context and root, what is the most likely meaning of *marina*?

   ○ A. an island
   ○ B. to go swimming
   ○ C. a group of sailors
   ○ D. a dock in the water

2. Based on its context and root, what is the most likely meaning of *local*?

   ○ A. below
   ○ B. nearby
   ○ C. healthy
   ○ D. well-known

3. Based on its context and root, what is the most likely meaning of *quiet*?

   ○ A. calm
   ○ B. noisy
   ○ C. alive
   ○ D. asleep

4. Based on the Greek or Latin root and context, which of the words listed above best completes the following sentence?
   The men were on trial for several _____, including carrying money out of the country.

   ○ A. locals
   ○ B. marinas
   ○ C. misdeeds
   ○ D. transports

The Vanishing Island

Skill: Media

Use the Checklist to analyze Media in "The Vanishing Island." Refer to the sample student annotations about Media in the text.

••• CHECKLIST FOR MEDIA

In order to identify the advantages and disadvantages of using different media, note the following:

- ✓ the features of each medium, such as print or digital text, video, and multimedia

- ✓ how different media present a particular topic, idea, or historical event—such as World War II or the first moon landing—and can include diaries, eyewitness accounts, films, books, news and feature articles, photographs, and so on

- ✓ which details are stressed in each type of media presentation

- ✓ how readers and historians compare and contrast accounts in different media as they analyze and interpret events

- ✓ the reliability of each medium

- ✓ when presentations contradict each other

To evaluate the advantages and disadvantages of using different media to present a particular topic or idea, ask the following questions:

- ✓ What are the advantages and disadvantages of using different media to present a particular topic or idea?

- ✓ Which account of the event or topic is better supported by objective facts?

- ✓ Is an eyewitness account of an event more valuable than a film or book about the same subject? Why or why not?

Reading & Writing Companion   23

V SKILL VOCABULARY

media / los medios **noun** the plural form of the word medium; a means of sending a communication to an intended audience

medium / el medio **noun** a form of communication, such as television, the Internet, and radio COGNATE

Skill: Media

Introduce the Skill

Watch the Concept Definition video and read the following definition with your students.

Media is the plural form of the word *medium*. A **medium** is a means of sending a communication to an intended audience. Throughout most of human history, people communicated through three main media: speech, writing, and visual arts such as drawing, painting, and sculpture. But in the 19th century, media options suddenly exploded. The invention of photography, and then the telegraph and the telephone, changed the world. Within a century radio, motion pictures, and television followed.

Stories and ideas change as they are translated from one medium to another. A dialogue between two characters in a novel, for example, becomes very different when it is delivered by actors in a film—with close-ups, sound effects such as music, and other elements unique to the medium of film itself.

Today, new media are being invented at a much faster pace than ever before, and each of these forms of online communication has its own "language" and creates its own experience.

TURN AND TALK

1. What types of media have you used?

2. Do you like it when something you read combines text with other media like visuals? Why or why not?

 SPEAKING FRAMES

- I have used ____.
- I (do / do not) like text with other media.
- Other media like visuals (are / are not) helpful because ____.

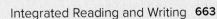

Your Turn

Ask students to complete the Your Turn activity.

QUESTION 1

A. Correct. The text feature of the print medium is the boldface heading "Eight Generations of History."

B. Incorrect. The boldface heading "Eight Generations of History" does not support this inference.

C. Incorrect. The boldface heading "Eight Generations of History" does not support this inference.

D. Incorrect. The boldface heading "Eight Generations of History" does not support this inference.

QUESTION 2

A. Incorrect. The photograph does not give information about Jean Lafitte.

B. Incorrect. The photograph does not show how the island has changed.

C. Correct. The photograph provides information about how people once lived on the island, such as their houses and clothes and how many children they might have.

D. Incorrect. The photograph does not give information about why the land was once declared uninhabitable.

QUESTION 3

A. Incorrect. This is not an accurate explanation of the difference between the two types of media.

B. Correct. Both the print text and the visual photograph help the reader understand the author's key ideas.

C. Incorrect. This is not a main advantage of including both types of media.

D. Incorrect. This is not a main advantage of including both types of media.

The Vanishing Island

Skill:
Media

Reread paragraphs 20–22 of "The Vanishing Island." Then, using the Checklist on the previous page, answer the multiple-choice questions below.

 YOUR TURN

1. Based on a text feature of the print medium in this excerpt, the reader can identify that the section is about—

   ○ A. the tribe's experiences on the island.
   ○ B. Native American traditions.
   ○ C. possible places for relocation.
   ○ D. environmental factors that affect the island.

2. The photograph in this excerpt provides information about—

   ○ A. Jean Lafitte.
   ○ B. how the island has changed.
   ○ C. how people on the island lived.
   ○ D. why the land was "uninhabitable."

3. The main advantage to including both types of media is that—

   ○ A. the photograph gives readers information that printed text cannot possibly give.
   ○ B. the two types of media work together to provide a clear idea and explanation for the reader's benefit.
   ○ C. it shows that the author did extensive research on the subject and is a reliable source of information.
   ○ D. the photograph helps break up the printed words on the page and makes it appear more readable.

Close Read

Reread "The Vanishing Island." As you reread, complete the Skills Focus questions below. Then use your answers and annotations from the questions to help you complete the Write activity.

SKILLS FOCUS

1. The Latin root *duc* means "to lead." Identify a word with this root, and explain how the meaning of the root helps you understand the meaning of the word in context.

2. Identify a detail in the text that is clarified by a visual media item. Explain how the visual item deepens your understanding of the author's ideas.

3. For visual media items, what are some possible advantages and disadvantages of including them with the text? Be specific in your response and cite at least two examples for each situation.

4. Identify specific textual evidence that shows how relocation is a good way for the tribe to preserve their unique heritage. Explain your response.

5. Identify an example from some type of medium in "The Vanishing Island" of a risk members of the tribe took and explain why they took that chance.

✏ WRITE

INFORMATIONAL: Based on the information in the article, what makes people care so deeply about this "vanishing island" that nothing can induce them to leave? Why do people still continue to inhabit it and work so hard for its cultural survival? Use evidence from the text, including different media, to support your understanding of the reading.

Reading & Writing Companion **25**

Close Read

Skills Focus

QUESTION 1: Greek and Latin Affixes and Roots

See paragraph 18.

QUESTION 2: Media

See paragraph 27.

QUESTION 3: Media

See paragraph 20.

QUESTION 4: Textual Evidence

See paragraphs 51 and 52.

QUESTION 5: Connect to Essential Question

See paragraph 22.

✓ CHECK FOR SUCCESS

If students struggle to respond to Skills Focus question 1, ask them the following questions:

1. What word do you see with *duc* in paragraph 18?

2. How is "to lead" part of the word's meaning?

Writer's Notebook

Give students time to reflect on how "The Vanishing Island" connects to the unit's essential question: "Why do we take chances?" by freewriting in their Writer's Notebooks.

ELL Beginning & Intermediate

Read aloud the unit's essential question: "Why do we take chances?" Encourage students to draw their reflections or allow students to write in their native language. Circulate the room, prompting students for their thoughts as they respond orally or through pantomime.

Advanced & Advanced High

Allow students to share their reflections orally in pairs or small groups before freewriting.

Collaborative Conversation

 SCAFFOLDS

Break students into collaborative conversation groups to discuss the Close Read prompt. Ask students to use the StudySyncTV episode as a model for their discussion. Remind them to reference their Skills Focus annotations in their discussion.

Based on the information in the article, what makes people care so deeply about this "vanishing island" that nothing can induce them to leave? Why do people still continue to inhabit it and work so hard for its cultural survival? Use evidence from the text, including different media, to support your understanding of the reading.

Use the scaffolds below to differentiate instruction for your **ELL** English Language Learners and **A** Approaching grade-level learners.

ELL **BEGINNING, INTERMEDIATE** Use the discussion guide and speaking frames to facilitate the discussion with support from the teacher.

ADVANCED, ADVANCED HIGH Use the discussion guide and speaking frames to facilitate the discussion in mixed-level groups.

A **APPROACHING** Use the discussion guide to facilitate the discussion in mixed-level groups.

APPROACHING
ADVANCED, ADVANCED HIGH
BEGINNING, INTERMEDIATE

Discussion Guide	Speaking Frames
1. Which key details explain an important idea?	• ____ is a key detail. • It helps develop the author's ideas because ____.
2. What printed text explains an important idea?	• ____ is important text. • It helps develop the author's ideas because ____.
3. Which visual media explain an important idea?	• ____ is an important visual. • It helps develop the author's ideas because ____.
4. How do the key details and different media work together to tell why people stay on the island?	• The key details and different media work together to explain ____.

Review Prompt and Rubric

Before students begin writing, review the writing prompt and rubric with the class.

INFORMATIONAL: Based on the information in the article, what makes people care so deeply about this "vanishing island" that nothing can induce them to leave? Why do people still continue to inhabit it and work so hard for its cultural survival? Use evidence from the text, including different media, to support your understanding of the reading.

 PROMPT GUIDE

- Which key details explain an important idea?
- What printed text explains an important idea?
- Which visual media explain an important idea?

- How do the key details and different media work together to tell why people stay on the island?

Score	Media	Language and Conventions
4	The writer clearly analyzes and explains how different media support their ideas. The writer provides exemplary analysis, using relevant evidence from the text.	The writer demonstrates a consistent command of grammar, punctuation, and usage conventions. Although minor errors may be evident, they do not detract from the fluency or the clarity of the writing.
3	The writer analyzes and explains how different media support their ideas. The writer provides sufficient analysis, using relevant evidence from the text most of the time.	The writer demonstrates an adequate command of grammar, punctuation, and usage conventions. Although some errors may be evident, they create few (if any) disruptions in the fluency or clarity of the writing.
2	The writer begins to analyze or explain how different media support their ideas, but the analysis is incomplete. The writer uses relevant evidence from the text only some of the time.	The writer demonstrates a partial command of grammar, punctuation, and usage conventions. Some distracting errors may be evident, at times creating minor disruptions in the fluency or clarity of the writing.
1	The writer attempts to analyze or explain how different media support their ideas, but the analysis is not successful. The writer uses little or no relevant evidence from the text.	The writer demonstrates little or no command of grammar, punctuation, and usage conventions. Serious and persistent errors create disruptions in the fluency of the writing and sometimes interfere with meaning.
0	The writer does not provide a relevant response to the prompt or does not provide a response at all.	Serious and persistent errors overwhelm the writing and interfere with the meaning of the response as a whole, making the writer's meaning impossible to understand.

Write

Ask students to complete the writing assignment using textual evidence to support their answers.

Use the scaffolds below to differentiate instruction for your **ELL** English Language Learners and **A** Approaching grade-level learners.

ELL **BEGINNING** With the help of the word bank, write a response using paragraph frame 1.

INTERMEDIATE With the help of the word bank, write a response using paragraph frames 1 and 2.

ADVANCED, ADVANCED HIGH Write a response of differentiated length using the sentence starters.

A **APPROACHING** Write a response of differentiated length using the sentence starters.

| BEGINNING | ADVANCED, ADVANCED HIGH |
| INTERMEDIATE | APPROACHING |

Word Bank	Paragraph Frame 1	Paragraph Frame 2	Sentence Starters
Indian Removal Act photographs culture heading history	The residents of Isle de Jean Charles care about the island because of its ____. Printed text, such as the ____ "Eight Generations of History," provides information about the island's people. Visual media, such as ____, show the generations that lived there before them. Key details, such as information about the ____, show that the island has kept them safe. Tribe members worry that their ____ will disappear along with the island.	Many tribe members feel like the island is ____. Even though only two dozen people remain on the island, they want to stay because ____. A key detail in the text that supports this is Text that supports this is ____. A visual that develops this is ____.	• People care about the island because . . . • People stayed on the island even after . . . because . . . • A key detail in the text that explains this is . . . • Text that supports this idea is . . . • A visual that supports this idea is . . .

Peer Review

Students should submit substantive feedback to two peers using the review instructions below.

- How well does this response answer the prompt?
- How well does the writer support his or her ideas with details and examples from the text?
- Does the writer identify media that also support his or her ideas?
- What did the writer do well in this response? What does the writer need to work on?

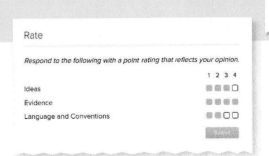

SENTENCE FRAMES

- You were able to (completely / partly / almost) answer the prompt because ____.
- You could answer the prompt more completely by ____.
- You supported the idea of ____ with the detail of ____.

- You identified at least one example of printed text that ____.
- You identified at least one visual media item that ____.
- One idea that needs more support is ____.
- My favorite part of your response is ____ because ____.

A Night to Remember

INFORMATIONAL TEXT
Walter Lord
1955

Introduction

studysync tv

Walter Lord interviewed scores of *Titanic* survivors to create a powerful account of the ship's sinking in the calm, frigid North Atlantic on April 14, 1912. In this passage, we hear a variety of reactions at the beginning of the disaster, from the first sighting of an iceberg by the ship's lookout to the mysterious jolt heard and felt by crew members and passengers alike, each observer interpreting the impact differently.

In this excerpt, *Titanic* survivors recount their varied impressions when the ship collided with the iceberg. The quartermaster remembered seeing ice crystals flashing in the lights outside; when the ship passed the iceberg, he initially thought it was a large sailboat. Below deck, the stewards heard the impact as a grinding sound, which they thought was a broken propeller blade. Consequently, they were looking forward to spending a few days in port while the ship would be repaired. The night baker was upset because the impact knocked over a tray of rolls he was preparing for the morning. Some passengers said it sounded like a wave striking the hull. Others stated that it was like rolling over "a thousand marbles," while some claimed that it reminded them of the San Francisco earthquake in 1906. However, none of them suspected what an awful night they had in store.

 Proficiency-leveled summaries and summaries in multiple languages are available digitally.

🔊 Audio and audio text highlighting are available with this text.

COMPARING WITHIN AND ACROSS GENRES

 Read together, this excerpt from *A Night to Remember* and President Ronald Reagan's "Address to the Nation on the Explosion of the Space Shuttle *Challenger*" will allow students to analyze what happens when a big risk has a negative outcome.

Access Complex Text

LEXILE: 1050L   WORD COUNT: 1,147

The following areas may be challenging for students, particularly 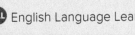 English Language Learners and Ⓐ Approaching grade-level learners.

Prior Knowledge	Organization	Specific Vocabulary
• Students may not know the significance of the *Titanic*. There were over 2,000 passengers—who were organized by class, or type of ticket— and crew members. There were too few lifeboats, and a passenger's gender and class of ticket affected who survived.	• The text retells one event from the points of view of several passengers and crew members. Students may need help tracking the shifts in point of view as they read the text.	• Nautical terms, such as *knots, bow, starboard,* and *stern,* may present a challenge to some readers. Remind students to use a dictionary to define unfamiliar words.

 SCAFFOLDS   ENGLISH LANGUAGE LEARNERS   Ⓐ APPROACHING GRADE LEVEL   BEYOND GRADE LEVEL

These icons identify differentiation strategies and scaffolded support for a variety of students. See the digital lesson plan for additional differentiation strategies and scaffolds.

Instructional Path

The print teacher's edition includes essential point-of-use instruction and planning tools. Complete lesson plans and program documents appear in your digital teacher account.

Independent Read: A Night to Remember

Objectives: After reading the text, students will write a short response that demonstrates their understanding of the text through a personal connection.

Independent Read

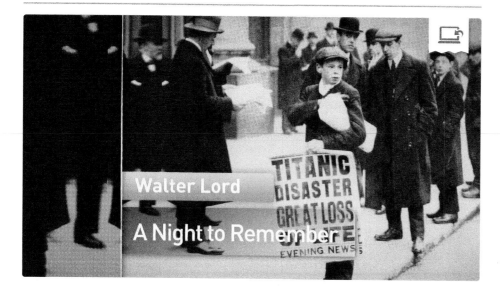

Walter Lord
A Night to Remember

Introduce the Text

As a class, watch the video preview ▶ and have students read the introduction in pairs to make connections to the video preview.

- What two words would you use to describe this video?

- What is one prediction you can make about the text you're going to read?

> **ELL SPEAKING FRAMES**
> - Two words I would use to describe it are ____.
> - I think the text will ____. I think this because ____.
> - I predict that there will be ____. I believe this because ____.

Entry Point

As students prepare to read *A Night to Remember*, share the following information with them to provide context.

✓ In the early 1900s, passenger ships gave travelers a way to cross the Atlantic. One of these ships was an enormous luxury liner called the *Titanic*. Due to its design, many people thought that this ship could not sink.

✓ On its maiden voyage, however, the *Titanic* hit an iceberg. There were about 2,200 people on the ship, and over 1,500 people died. The majority of deaths occurred among the crew and the third-class passengers.

✓ The author of this text is Walter Lord (1917–2002). In the mid-20th century, he took a new approach to recording history in this book: He gathered and shared stories from people who survived the tragedy. This is now called a documentary style of writing.

"It was almost 11:40 P.M. on Sunday, the 14th of April, 1912."

from Chapter: "Another Belfast Trip"

1 High in the crow's-nest[1] of the New White Star Liner *Titanic,* Lookout Frederick Fleet peered into a dazzling night. It was calm, clear and bitterly cold. There was no moon, but the cloudless sky blazed with stars. The Atlantic was like polished plate glass; people later said they had never seen it so smooth.

2 This was the fifth night of the *Titanic's* maiden voyage to New York, and it was already clear that she was not only the largest but also the most **glamorous** ship in the world. Even the passengers' dogs were glamorous. John Jacob Astor had along his Airedale Kitty. Henry Sleeper Harper, of the publishing family, had his prize Pekingese Sun Yat-sen. Robert W. Daniel, the Philadelphia banker, was bringing back a champion French bulldog just purchased in Britain. Clarence Moore of Washington also had been dog-shopping, but the 50 pairs of English foxhounds he bought for the Loudoun Hunt weren't making the trip.

3 That was all another world to Frederick Fleet. He was one of six lookouts carried by the *Titanic,* and the lookouts didn't worry about passenger problems. They were the "eyes of the ship," and on this particular night Fleet had been warned to watch especially for icebergs.

4 So far, so good. On duty at 10 o'clock . . . a few words about the ice problem with Lookout Reginald Lee, who shared the same watch . . . a few more words about the cold . . . but mostly just silence, as the two men stared into the darkness.

5 Now the watch was almost over, and still there was nothing unusual. Just the night, the stars, the biting cold, the wind that whistled through the rigging as the *Titanic* raced across the calm, black sea at 22 1/2 knots[2]. It was almost 11:40 P.M. on Sunday, the 14th of April, 1912.

6 Suddenly Fleet saw something directly ahead, even darker than the darkness. At first it was small (about the size, he thought, of two tables put together), but every second it grew larger and closer. Quickly Fleet banged the crow's-nest

---

1. **crow's-nest** a platform on a ship's mast or in a high place used for lookout
2. **knots** nautical miles

Reading & Writing Companion **27**

SELECTION VOCABULARY

glamorous / glamoroso/a ***adjective*** extremely attractive; excitingly attractive COGNATE

Analyze Vocabulary Using Context Clues

As students read the text, ask them to make predictions about each bold vocabulary word based on the context clues in the sentence.

✓ CHECK FOR SUCCESS

If students are unable to determine the meaning of one or more bolded vocabulary words, project the Checklist from the Grade 8 Context Clues lesson with the class. After revisiting, guide students as they make predictions about the bold word in paragraph 9 using the following routine:

- Is the word a noun, a verb, an adjective, or an adverb?
- What is described as "detached" in this paragraph?
- Is it a positive or negative description?

TURN AND TALK

Have students discuss their original vocabulary predictions with a neighbor. Come to a consensus as a class before confirming their definitions.

TEXT TALK

What was the weather and water like on the night the Titanic sank?

See paragraph 1: It was a cold, clear, and cloudless night. The water was calm and smooth.

NOTES

bell three times, the warning of danger ahead. At the same time he lifted the phone and rang the bridge.

7 "What did you see?" asked a calm voice at the other end.

8 "Iceberg right ahead," replied Fleet.

9 "Thank you," acknowledged the voice with curiously **detached** courtesy. Nothing more was said.

10 For the next 37 seconds, Fleet and Lee stood quietly side by side, watching the ice **draw** nearer. Now they were almost on top of it, and still the ship didn't turn. The berg towered wet and glistening far above the forecastle deck, and both men braced themselves for a crash. Then, miraculously, the bow began to swing to port. At the last second the stem shot into the clear, and the ice glided swiftly by along the starboard side. It looked to Fleet like a very close shave.

11 At this moment Quartermaster George Thomas Rowe was standing watch on the after bridge. For him too, it had been an uneventful night—just the sea, the stars, the biting cold. As he paced the deck, he noticed what he and his mates called "Whiskers 'round the Light"—tiny splinters of ice in the air, fine as dust, that gave off **myriads** of bright colors whenever caught in the glow of the deck lights.

12 Then suddenly he felt a curious motion break the steady rhythm of the engines. It was a little like coming alongside a dock wall rather heavily. He glanced forward—and stared again. A windjammer,³ sails set, seemed to be passing along the starboard side. Then he realized it was an iceberg, towering perhaps 100 feet above the water. The next instant it was gone, drifting astern into the dark.

13 Meanwhile, down below in the First Class dining saloon on D Deck, four other members of the *Titanic's* crew were sitting around one of the tables. The last diner had long since departed, and now the big white Jacobean⁴ room was empty except for this single group. They were dining-saloon stewards, indulging in the time-honored pastime of all stewards off duty—they were gossiping about their passengers.

14 Then, as they sat there talking, a faint grinding jar seemed to come from somewhere deep inside the ship. It was not much, but enough to break the conversation and rattle the silver that was set for breakfast next morning.

15 Steward James Johnson felt he knew just what it was. He recognized the kind of shudder a ship gives when she drops a propeller blade, and he knew this sort of mishap meant a trip back to the Harland & Wolff Shipyard at Belfast—with plenty of free time to enjoy the hospitality of the port.

3. **windjammer** a type of large sailing ship for passengers or cargo
4. **Jacobean** design or literature from Britain during the reign of King James IV (1567–1625)

TEXT TALK

What did Fleet do when he spotted an iceberg?

See paragraphs 6–9: He rings a warning bell and calls the bridge to report the iceberg ahead of the ship.

On which side of the ship did the iceberg hit the *Titanic*?

See paragraph 10: The iceberg hit the starboard side of the ship.

What did Steward James Johnson think happened to the *Titanic*?

See paragraph 15: Johnson thought the ship had dropped a propeller blade.

 SELECTION VOCABULARY

detached / indiferente **adjective** unemotional; unconcerned

  • What is described as "detached" in this paragraph?
  • Is it a positive or negative description?

draw / avanzar **verb** to move to one side COGNATE

• What is happening to the ship in this paragraph? Where might it draw?
• What does the amount of time that Fleet and Lee wait suggest about the ship's movement?

myriads / la miríada **noun** large numbers; multitudes COGNATE

  • What is there myriads of in this paragraph?
  • What do the myriads help describe?

NOTES

16 Somebody near him agreed and sang out cheerfully, "Another Belfast trip!"

17 In the galley just to the stern, Chief Night Baker Walter Belford was making rolls for the following day. (The honor of baking fancy pastry was reserved for the day shift.) When the jolt came, it **impressed** Belford more strongly than Steward Johnson—perhaps because a pan of new rolls clattered off the top of the oven and scattered about the floor.

18 The passengers in their cabins felt the jar too, and tried to connect it with something familiar. Marguerite Frolicher, a young Swiss girl accompanying her father on a business trip, woke up with a start. Half-asleep, she could think only of the little white lake ferries at Zurich making a sloppy landing. Softly she said to herself, "Isn't it funny . . . we're landing!"

19 Major Arthur Godfrey Peuchen, starting to undress for the night, thought it was like a heavy wave striking the ship. Mrs. J. Stuart White was sitting on the edge of her bed, just reaching to turn out the light, when the ship seemed to roll over "a thousand marbles." To Lady Cosmo Duff Gordon, waking up from the jolt, it seemed "as though somebody had drawn a giant finger along the side of the ship." Mrs. John Jacob Astor thought it was some mishap in the kitchen.

20 It seemed stronger to some than to others. Mrs. Albert Caldwell pictured a large dog that had a baby kitten in its mouth and was shaking it. Mrs. Walter B. Stephenson recalled the first **ominous** jolt when she was in the San Francisco earthquake—then decided this wasn't that bad. Mrs. E. D. Appleton felt hardly any shock at all, but she noticed an unpleasant ripping sound . . . like someone tearing a long, long strip of calico.[5]

21 The jar meant more to J. Bruce Ismay, Managing Director of the White Star Line, who in a festive mood was going along for the ride on the *Titanic's* first trip. Ismay woke up with a start in his deluxe suite on B Deck—he felt sure the ship had struck something, but he didn't know what.

Excerpted from *A Night to Remember* by Walter Lord, published by Bantam Books.

---

5. **calico** a type of rough fabric of woven cotton

✏ WRITE

PERSONAL RESPONSE: How do the reactions of the *Titanic* passengers affect your feelings, such as sympathy, about the collision? How does reading these personal reactions help you better understand what happened? Be sure to use evidence to support your response.

Reading & Writing Companion **29**

TEXT TALK

Where was Marguerite Frolicher when the *Titanic* hit the iceberg? What did she think was happening?

See paragraph 18: She was in her cabin. She thought the boat was landing.

What did J. Bruce Ismay believe caused the jar?

See paragraph 21: He thought the ship had struck something.

The ship was described as "glamorous," but it had a devastating end. Do you think the expectations of the ship made the tragedy that much more shocking for the passengers? Why or why not?

Answers will vary.

B Ask each Beyond grade-level student to write one additional discussion question. Then have one or two students facilitate a discussion, using their questions to guide the conversation.

V SELECTION VOCABULARY

impressed / impresionar *verb* to create a strong effect; to have a forceful impact COGNATE

ELL
- Who does the jolt impress?
- What smaller words can you see in *impress*?

ominous / ominoso/a *adjective* threatening; suggesting that something bad will happen COGNATE

ELL
- What word does *ominous* describe?
- What previous event is the character describing?

Reading Comprehension OPTIONAL

Have students complete the digital reading comprehension questions ✅ when they finish reading.

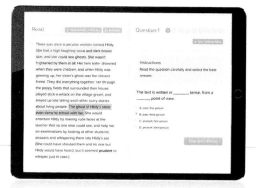

ANSWER KEY

QUESTION 1: D	**QUESTION 5:** D	**QUESTION 9:** D
QUESTION 2: B	**QUESTION 6:** B	**QUESTION 10:**
QUESTION 3: C	**QUESTION 7:** A	*See chart.*
QUESTION 4: C	**QUESTION 8:** C	

First	Second	Third	Fourth
Lookouts Fleet and Lee prepare themselves mentally for a possible crash into the iceberg.	Quartermaster George Thomas Rowe paces the deck.	In the galley, Night Baker Belford notices the jolt more than Steward Johnson in the dining area.	Passengers Peuchen, White, Gordon, and Astor use metaphors to describe the iceberg's impact upon the ship.

Connect and Extend OPTIONAL

CONNECT TO EXTENDED WRITING PROJECT

Students can use *A Night to Remember* as a resource when writing their informational essays. Have students use Walter Lord's style of reporting the events as an inspiration for their own writing.

BEYOND THE BOOK

Art: A Google Doodle Tribute to the *Titanic*

Students will design a Google Doodle to be displayed on April 14 to remember the *Titanic*. Students should include details from *A Night to Remember* in their Google Doodle. They can create pieces of artwork with moveable parts to demonstrate how it should be animated or use an online design tool to create their Google Doodle.

StudySyncTV

Project the StudySyncTV episode ▶ and pause at the following times to prompt discussion:

0:12 What do you think it would feel like to be in the middle of the ocean at night with the stars providing the only light you can see?

0:24 What would you do if you were a passenger and you felt the impact?

0:36 What do you predict the passengers and crew did when the *Titanic* began to sink?

Collaborative Conversation

SCAFFOLDS

Post the writing prompt to generate a discussion in small groups. Ask students to first break down the prompt before they discuss relevant ideas and textual evidence. Ask students to use the StudySyncTV episode as a model for their discussion.

How do the reactions of the *Titanic* passengers affect your feelings, such as sympathy, about the collision? How does reading these personal reactions help you better understand what happened? Be sure to use evidence to support your response.

Use the scaffolds below to differentiate instruction for your **ELL** English Language Learners and **A** Approaching grade-level learners.

ELL **BEGINNING, INTERMEDIATE** Use the <u>discussion guide</u> and <u>speaking frames</u> to facilitate the discussion with support from the teacher.

ADVANCED, ADVANCED HIGH Use the <u>discussion guide</u> and <u>speaking frames</u> to facilitate the discussion in mixed-level groups.

A **APPROACHING** Use the <u>discussion guide</u> to facilitate the discussion in mixed-level groups.

APPROACHING
ADVANCED, ADVANCED HIGH
BEGINNING, INTERMEDIATE

Discussion Guide	Speaking Frames
1. How do you feel when you read the reactions of the *Titanic* passengers?	• I feel ____ and ____.
2. Which person did you feel sympathy for?	• I felt sympathy for ____ because ____.
3. What do you know about the disaster from reading the personal reactions?	• From reading the reactions I know ____.

Review Prompt and Rubric

Before students begin writing, review the writing prompt and rubric with the class.

PERSONAL RESPONSE: How do the reactions of the *Titanic* passengers affect your feelings, such as sympathy, about the collision? How does reading these personal reactions help you better understand what happened? Be sure to use evidence to support your response.

 PROMPT GUIDE

- What feelings do you have when you read the reactions of the *Titanic* passengers?
- What do you learn from reading the reactions?

- What evidence from the text can you include to help explain your feelings and what you learned?

Score	Personal Response	Language and Conventions
4	The writer clearly explains his or her personal feelings about the text, using relevant evidence from the text as needed.	The writer demonstrates a consistent command of grammar, punctuation, and usage conventions. Although minor errors may be evident, they do not detract from the fluency or the clarity of the writing.
3	The writer sufficiently explains his or her personal feelings about the text, using relevant evidence from the text most of the time.	The writer demonstrates an adequate command of grammar, punctuation, and usage conventions. Although some errors may be evident, they create few (if any) disruptions in the fluency or clarity of the writing.
2	The writer begins to explain his or her personal feelings about the text, but the explanation is incomplete. The writer uses relevant evidence from the text only some of the time.	The writer demonstrates a partial command of grammar, punctuation, and usage conventions. Some distracting errors may be evident, at times creating minor disruptions in the fluency or clarity of the writing.
1	The writer attempts to explain his or her personal feelings about the text, but the explanation is not successful. The writer uses little or no relevant evidence from the text.	The writer demonstrates little or no command of grammar, punctuation, and usage conventions. Serious and persistent errors create disruptions in the fluency of the writing and sometimes interfere with meaning.
0	The writer does not provide a relevant response to the prompt or does not provide a response at all.	Serious and persistent errors overwhelm the writing and interfere with the meaning of the response as a whole, making the writer's meaning impossible to understand.

Write

Ask students to complete the writing assignment using textual evidence to support their answers.

Use the scaffolds below to differentiate instruction for your **ELL** English Language Learners and **A** Approaching grade-level learners.

ELL **BEGINNING** With the help of the <u>word bank</u>, write a response using <u>paragraph frame 1</u>.

INTERMEDIATE With the help of the <u>word bank</u>, write a response using <u>paragraph frames 1 and 2</u>.

ADVANCED, ADVANCED HIGH Write a response of differentiated length using the <u>sentence starters</u>.

A **APPROACHING** Write a response of differentiated length using the <u>sentence starters</u>.

BEGINNING		ADVANCED, ADVANCED HIGH
INTERMEDIATE		APPROACHING

Word Bank	Paragraph Frame 1	Paragraph Frame 2	Sentence Starters
lookout danger collision iceberg imagine	Reading the reactions of the *Titanic* passengers makes me feel like I actually got to talk to the real people. I can more easily ____ what it was like for them to experience the disaster, so I better understand what happened. I feel sympathy for them because I know what actually happened to them. For example, Frederick Fleet was a ____ on the *Titanic* who first saw the ____. The ship turned at the last minute, and Fleet thought the *Titanic* had avoided a ____. I feel sympathy for Fleet because he did not understand the ____ that he was in.	Another passenger who was on the *Titanic* during the crash was ____. He reacted by ____. Reading that helps me ____. He thought ____. Reading about his experience, I feel ____ because he ____.	• Reading the reactions of the *Titanic* passengers makes me feel . . . • I can more easily imagine what it was like for them to . . . • I feel sympathy for them because . . . • For example . . .

Peer Review

Students should submit substantive feedback to two peers using the review instructions below.

- How well does this response answer the prompt?
- Which of the author's comments inspired you to think differently about the text?
- What did the writer do well in this response? What does the writer need to work on?

Rate

Respond to the following with a point rating that reflects your opinion.

	1 2 3 4
Ideas	▪▪▪▫
Evidence	▪▪▪▪
Language and Conventions	▪▪▫▫

Submit

ELL **A** **SENTENCE FRAMES**

- You were able to (completely / partly / almost) answer the prompt because ____.
- You could answer the prompt more completely by ____.
- You supported the idea of ____ with the detail of ____.
- One idea that needs more support is ____.
- I thought differently about the text after reading ____.
- My favorite part of your response is ____.

No Risk, No Reward

Address to the Nation on the Explosion of the Space Shuttle *Challenger*

INFORMATIONAL TEXT
Ronald Reagan
1986

Introduction

On January 28, 1986, millions of Americans watched on live TV as the Space Shuttle *Challenger* violently exploded just 73 seconds after takeoff, killing all seven people on board. It was the tenth mission for *Challenger*, but the first scheduled to carry an ordinary citizen into space, a teacher from New Hampshire named Christa McAuliffe. That evening, President Ronald Reagan (1911–2004) addressed the nation, including the many school children who witnessed the disaster, and lauded the bravery of the fallen crew.

On January 28, 1986, U.S. President Reagan preempted his State of the Union speech to address the nation. Earlier that morning, the space shuttle *Challenger* exploded during its nationally televised launch, killing everyone on board. Reagan began by praising the crew members, who knew the risks yet courageously went ahead with the mission. He also tried to console their family members with the reminder that the nation was thinking of them. As the launch was televised in schools across the country, Reagan also spoke to the American children, explaining that the *Challenger* crew were pioneers and discovery is undertaken by the brave, not the fainthearted. Praising all the men and women who work at NASA, Reagan concluded his speech by affirming that the space program would proceed with future missions, and the journey of discovery would continue.

ELL Proficiency-leveled summaries and summaries in multiple languages are available digitally.

🔊 Audio and audio text highlighting are available with this text.

COMPARING WITHIN AND ACROSS GENRES

 What happens when a big risk has a negative outcome? In the wake of the *Challenger* explosion, President Ronald Reagan speaks to a shocked and grieving nation about the crew who gave their lives for science and why space exploration is worth the risk.

Access Complex Text

LEXILE: 780L   **WORD COUNT:** 651

The following areas may be challenging for students, particularly **ELL** English Language Learners and **A** Approaching grade-level learners.

Genre	Purpose	Prior Knowledge
• The text is a speech, a public statement meant to be heard and seen. A speech reflects the speaker's point of view. • In the speech, President Reagan uses the pronoun *we* to indicate not only himself and the First Lady, but also all Americans.	• The speech contains a eulogy, or memorial speech, of the astronauts who died, as well as reassurances to the nation's children. • One role of the president is to speak to the nation in times of crisis or tragedy.	• Students may not be familiar with NASA and the U.S. space program, from the first flights to the space shuttle missions. • Reagan ends his speech with a quote from John Gillespie Magee, Jr., a pilot who was killed during a flight in 1941.

SCAFFOLDS   **ELL ENGLISH LANGUAGE LEARNERS**   **A APPROACHING GRADE LEVEL**   **B BEYOND GRADE LEVEL**

These icons identify differentiation strategies and scaffolded support for a variety of students. See the digital lesson plan for additional differentiation strategies and scaffolds.

Instructional Path

First Read: Address to the Nation on the Explosion of the Space Shuttle *Challenger*

Objectives: After an initial reading and discussion of the Presidential address, students will be able to identify and restate the text's key ideas and details.

Skill: Summarizing

Objectives: After rereading and discussing a model of close reading, students will be able to determine how to write an objective summary of a text.

Skill: Informational Text Structure

Objectives: After rereading and discussing a model of close reading, students will be able to analyze how multiple organizational patterns within a text help develop the thesis.

Close Read: Address to the Nation on the Explosion of the Space Shuttle *Challenger*

Objectives: After engaging in a close reading and discussion of the text, students will be able to analyze how different structures of the text help to effectively communicate information.

Progress Monitoring

Opportunities to Learn	Opportunities to Demonstrate Learning	Opportunities to Reteach
Summarizing		
⚙ Skill: Summarizing	⚙ Skill: Summarizing • Your Turn ▢ Close Read • Skills Focus • Write	⚙ Spotlight Skill: Summarizing
Informational Text Structure		
⚙ Skill: Informational Text Structure	⚙ Skill: Informational Text Structure • Your Turn ▢ Close Read • Skills Focus • Write	⚙ Unit 6 Skill: Informational Text Structure - Blood, Toil, Tears and Sweat ⚙ Unit 6 Skill: Informational Text Structure - Nobel Prize Acceptance Speech ⚙ Spotlight Skill: Informational Text Structure

First Read

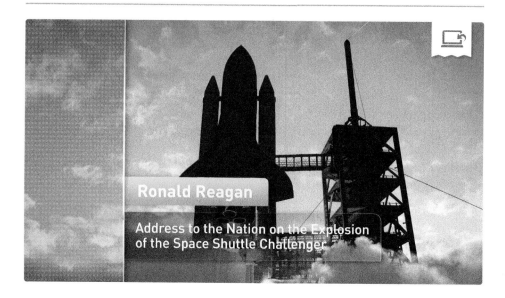

Ronald Reagan

Address to the Nation on the Explosion of the Space Shuttle Challenger

Introduce the Text

As a class, watch the video preview ▶ and have students read the introduction in pairs to make connections to the video preview.

To activate prior knowledge and experiences, ask students:

- What part of the video stood out to you the most?

- What kind of speech are you about to read? How can you tell?

ELL SPEAKING FRAMES

- The ____ in the video makes me think ____.
- The video shows ____. This makes me wonder ____.
- I think the text will ____. I think this because ____.
- I predict that there will be ____. I believe this because ____.

Entry Point

As students prepare to read "Address to the Nation on the Explosion of the Space Shuttle *Challenger*," share the following information with them to provide context.

✓ NASA launched the space shuttle *Challenger* on the morning of January 28, 1986, but it exploded 73 seconds after liftoff. The *Challenger* was carrying six crew members and one passenger, and they all lost their lives.

✓ The passenger was a teacher named Christa McAuliffe, and NASA had selected her to be the first teacher in space. As a result, many students were watching the launch.

✓ Ronald Reagan delivered a speech about the *Challenger* disaster later that evening. It was written by speechwriter Peggy Noonan, and it was meant for an audience of all ages. The speech was widely acclaimed, and it became one of Reagan's most historic speeches.

"We're still pioneers. They, the members of the *Challenger* crew, were pioneers."

January 28, 1986

NOTES

1 Ladies and gentlemen, I'd planned to speak to you tonight to report on the state of the Union,[1] but the events of earlier today have led me to change those plans. Today is a day for mourning and remembering. Nancy and I are pained to the core by the tragedy of the shuttle *Challenger*. We know we share this pain with all of the people of our country. This is truly a national loss.

2 Nineteen years ago, almost to the day, we lost three astronauts in a terrible accident on the ground. But we've never lost an astronaut in flight; we've never had a tragedy like this. And perhaps we've forgotten the courage it took for the crew of the shuttle. But they, the *Challenger* Seven, were aware of the dangers, but overcame them and did their jobs brilliantly. We mourn seven heroes: Michael Smith, Dick Scobee, Judith Resnik, Ronald McNair, Ellison Onizuka, Gregory Jarvis, and Christa McAuliffe. We mourn their loss as a nation together.

Five astronauts and two payload specialists make up the STS 51-L crew, scheduled to fly aboard the Space Shuttle *Challenger* in January of 1986. Crew members are (left to right, front row) astronauts Michael J. Smith, Francis R. (Dick) Scobee, and Ronald E. McNair; and (left to right, back row) Ellison S. Onizuka, Sharon Christa McAuliffe, Gregory Jarvis, and Judith A. Resnik.

3 For the families of the seven, we cannot bear, as you do, the full impact of this tragedy. But we feel the loss, and we're thinking about you so very much. Your loved ones were daring and brave, and they had that special **grace,** that special spirit that says, "Give me a challenge, and I'll meet it with joy." They had a hunger to explore the universe and discover its truths. They wished to serve, and they did. They served all of us. We've grown used to wonders in

1. **state of the Union** Reagan had previously planned to deliver the State of the Union, an annual speech given by U.S. presidents before Congress on general topics

Reading & Writing Companion **31**

Skill: Summarizing

Reagan calls members of the Challenger crew pioneers. Although we have become used to the idea of space, we must remember we are all still pioneers. The Challenger crew wished to serve and met the challenge with joy. We feel their loss.

SELECTION VOCABULARY

grace / la gentileza *noun* polite and pleasant behavior

horizon / el horizonte *noun* the limit of possibility or knowledge COGNATE

ELL
- Whose horizons are described in this paragraph?
- What does "the process of exploration and discovery" help us see?

Analyze Vocabulary Using Context Clues

In paragraph 3, focus on the sentence that uses the word *grace*. Point out these context clues:

1. First, I notice who the sentence is about—"your loved ones"—which means the astronauts who died.

2. I see that *grace* was something "your loved ones" had, and that it was "that special spirit."

3. I think *grace* means a special quality of someone's personality, such as the ability to welcome challenges.

Summarizing

What does the reader notice Reagan talking about in the third paragraph?

Reagan talks about the seven members of the *Challenger* crew and the grace, bravery, and special spirit they possessed.

TEXT TALK

What event led to this speech?

See the Introduction and paragraph 1: The space shuttle *Challenger* exploded, killing seven astronauts.

Who were the astronauts killed in the *Challenger* disaster?

See paragraph 2: The astronauts were Michael Smith, Dick Scobee, Judith Resnik, Ronald McNair, Ellison Onizuka, Gregory Jarvis, and Christa McAuliffe.

How did the president explain the disaster to the schoolchildren of America?

See paragraph 4: He explains that risk and danger are part of the process of exploration and discovery, which is why the astronauts were brave.

Informational Text Structure

How does the reader use signal words to identify a secondary structure?

The reader recognizes that the word *like* suggests a comparison, and a compare-and-contrast text structure is used in the last two paragraphs. This reinforces a key concept about the nature and perils of exploration.

TEXT TALK

What does President Reagan promise will happen with the space program?

See paragraph 5: He promises that the program will continue and expand.

What coincidence does President Reagan talk about?

See paragraph 6: The explorer Sir Francis Drake died on his ship on the same day 390 years before; he was dedicated to exploration.

What did the *Challenger* explosion teach the nation? What lessons were learned from the tragedy?

Answers will vary.

Address to the Nation on the Explosion of the Space Shuttle *Challenger*

NOTES

this century. It's hard to dazzle us. But for 25 years the United States space program has been doing just that. We've grown used to the idea of space, and perhaps we forget that we've only just begun. We're still pioneers. They, the members of the *Challenger* crew, were pioneers.

4 And I want to say something to the schoolchildren of America who were watching the live coverage of the shuttle's takeoff. I know it is hard to understand, but sometimes painful things like this happen. It's all part of the process of exploration and discovery. It's all part of taking a chance and expanding man's **horizons**. The future doesn't belong to the fainthearted; it belongs to the brave. The *Challenger* crew was pulling us into the future, and we'll continue to follow them.

5 I've always had great faith in and respect for our space program, and what happened today does nothing to diminish it. We don't hide our space program. We don't keep secrets and cover things up. We do it all up front and in public. That's the way freedom is, and we wouldn't change it for a minute. We'll continue our quest in space. There will be more shuttle flights and more shuttle crews and, yes, more volunteers, more civilians, more teachers in space. Nothing ends here; our hopes and our journeys continue. I want to add that I wish I could talk to every man and woman who works for NASA or who worked on this mission and tell them: "Your dedication and **professionalism** have moved and impressed us for decades. And we know of your **anguish**. We share it."

Skill:
Informational
Text Structure

In the second-to-last paragraph, Reagan mentions Sir Francis Drake. He was an ocean explorer who died at sea 390 years ago. Here Reagan uses a compare-and-contrast text structure to compare the *Challenger* crew to another explorer.

6 There's a **coincidence** today. On this day 390 years ago, the great explorer Sir Francis Drake died aboard ship off the coast of Panama. In his lifetime the great frontiers were the oceans, and an historian later said, "He lived by the sea, died on it, and was buried in it." Well, today we can say of the *Challenger* crew: Their dedication was, like Drake's, complete.

7 The crew of the space shuttle *Challenger* honored us by the manner in which they lived their lives. We will never forget them, nor the last time we saw them, this morning, as they prepared for their journey and waved goodbye and "slipped the surly bonds of earth" to "touch the face of God."

V SELECTION VOCABULARY

professionalism / el profesionalismo *noun* skill and competence COGNATE

 ELL
- What smaller word do you see in *professionalism*?
- Who is described as having professionalism in this paragraph?

anguish / la angustia *noun* severe suffering or distress COGNATE

 ELL
- How did the people at NASA feel after the explosion?
- Is the word positive or negative?

coincidence / la coincidencia *noun* two things that happen by chance at the same time or place COGNATE

 ELL
- What two events happened on January 28?
- Did the two events happen by chance or by human planning?

Reading Comprehension OPTIONAL

Have students complete the digital reading comprehension questions ✔ when they finish reading.

ANSWER KEY

QUESTION 1: A	**QUESTION 5:** A	**QUESTION 9:**
QUESTION 2: A	**QUESTION 6:** C	*See first chart.*
QUESTION 3: D	**QUESTION 7:** C	**QUESTION 10:**
QUESTION 4: C	**QUESTION 8:** B	*See second chart.*

Excerpt	Significance
". . . as they prepared for their journey and waved goodbye and 'slipped the surly bonds of earth' . . .'"	Quoting a poem as an elegy to the astronauts
"We don't hide our space program. We don't keep secrets and cover things up."	Calling out the USSR and their way of governing
"Their dedication was, like Drake's, complete."	Comparing the astronauts to the European explorers from centuries ago
". . . but the events of earlier today have led me to change those plans."	Canceling a major national address

Synonym	Word
dignity	grace
suffering	anguish
chance happening	coincidence
competence	professionalism

Connect and Extend

CONNECT TO EXTENDED WRITING PROJECT

Students can use "Address to the Nation on the Explosion of the Space Shuttle *Challenger*" as a resource when writing their informational essays. Students may consider ways to structure their own writing.

BEYOND THE BOOK

Writing: Obituaries for *Challenger* Astronauts

Break students into seven groups and give each group the name of one of the people who died in the 1986 *Challenger* explosion: Michael Smith, Dick Scobee, Judith Resnik, Ronald McNair, Ellison Onizuka, Gregory Jarvis, or Christa McAuliffe.

Ask students to:

- Research the person's life to learn about his/her family, work, and accomplishments.
- Read examples of obituaries in the local paper or online.
    > How long is the average obituary?
    > What types of details and information do obituaries contain about people who have died?
- Write an obituary announcing the astronaut's death and celebrating his/her life and accomplishments.

Allow each group to read their obituary for the class.

Then discuss the following:

- What did these individuals have in common?
- After learning more about them, how does this change the way you think about the 1986 *Challenger* explosion?

Think Questions

Circulate as students answer Think Questions independently. Scaffolds for these questions are shown on the opposite page.

QUESTION 1: Textual Evidence

The *Challenger* explosion was significant because seven astronauts died and they were the first astronauts to die after takeoff. President Reagan said, "We've never lost an astronaut in flight; we've never had a tragedy like this." Also, the *Challenger* tragedy was significant because a teacher, Christa McAuliffe, was one of the astronauts who died.

QUESTION 2: Textual Evidence

President Reagan calls the astronauts "the *Challenger* Seven." He describes the astronauts as brave and willing to take risks. The President said they "were aware of the dangers, but overcame them and did their jobs brilliantly."

QUESTION 3: Textual Evidence

President Reagan is proud of the space program because it is a symbol of freedom, and he wants the United States to continue to explore space. He promises, "There will be more shuttle flights and more shuttle crews and, yes, more volunteers, more civilians, more teachers in space."

QUESTION 4: Context Clues

The horizon is the farthest distance you can see, the boundary between the earth and the sky. Reagan uses *horizons* to mean the boundaries of human knowledge. "Expanding man's *horizons*" means expanding our knowledge through "the process of exploration and discovery."

QUESTION 5: Greek and Latin Affixes and Roots

An *incident* is something that happens. So *coincidence* must mean things that happen together, such as at the same time or place. Also, coincidences happen just by chance. For example, in this case, two tragedies happened to take place on the same date: the death of Sir Francis Drake and the deaths of seven astronauts.

First Read

Read "Address to the Nation on the Explosion of the Space Shuttle *Challenger*." After you read, complete the Think Questions below.

THINK QUESTIONS

1. Refer to one or more details from the text to support your understanding of the significance of the *Challenger* tragedy. What words and phrases in the first two paragraphs indicate this significance?

2. How does President Reagan describe the astronauts? Use details from the text to write two or three sentences that summarize his description.

3. Write two or three sentences explaining how President Reagan feels about the space program. What details does he offer to support his ideas? Cite evidence from the text to support your answer.

4. Use context to determine the meaning of the word **horizons** as it is used in this speech. Write your definition of *horizons* here and tell how you found it.

5. Remembering that the Latin prefix *co-* means "together," use the context clues provided in the passage to determine the meaning of **coincidence**. Write your definition of *coincidence* here and tell how you got it.

Copyright © BookheadEd Learning, LLC

Reading & Writing Companion   33

Think Questions

Use the scaffolds below to differentiate instruction for your **ELL** ELL English Language Learners and **A** Approaching grade-level learners.

ELL **BEGINNING** Write a response using the underline{word bank} and sentence frames.

INTERMEDIATE Write a response using the underline{sentence frames}.

ADVANCED, ADVANCED HIGH Write a response using the underline{Text-Dependent Question Guide}.

A **APPROACHING** Write a response using the underline{Text-Dependent Question Guide}.

| | INTERMEDIATE | APPROACHING |
| BEGINNING | | ADVANCED, ADVANCED HIGH |

Word Bank	Sentence Frames	Text-Dependent Question Guide
NASA *Challenger* discovery loss	The president talked about "the tragedy of the _____. *Challenger*." The president said, "We mourn seven _____." The president called the tragedy a national _____.	1. • What did the president mean by "the events of earlier today"? • How many astronauts died in the *Challenger* tragedy? • Who is mourning the deaths of the astronauts?
time space	The president referred to the astronauts as the _____ Seven. The president said that the members of the crew were _____.	2. • What group name does the president give to the astronauts? • What word does the president use to describe "the members of the *Challenger* crew"?
program shuttle heroes ideas pioneers	President Reagan had "great faith in and respect for our space _____." The president said, "We'll continue our quest in _____." The president said, "I wish I could talk to every man and woman who works for _____."	3. • What does President Reagan have "great faith in and respect for"? • How will we "continue our quest"? • Who does the president wish he could talk to?
	Horizons are the limits of our _____. The president said, "It's all part of the process of exploration and _____."	4. • Read: "It's all part of taking a chance and expanding man's **horizons**." • When you expand your view, or horizons, what happens to your mind? • What process is "expanding man's horizons" a part of?
	Coincidence means "two events that happen by chance at the same _____."	5. • Read: "There's a **coincidence** today. On this day 390 years ago, the great explorer Sir Francis Drake died aboard ship off the coast of Panama." • What event happened 390 years earlier on the same day as the *Challenger* disaster? • Were the two events planned so they would happen on the same day?

Skill: Summarizing

Introduce the Skill

Watch the Concept Definition video and read the following definition with your students.

When you **summarize** a text, you briefly state the main points and most important details in your own words. Summarizing can help you organize, explain, and remember concepts in an informational text or the events that take place in a story.

To summarize, you must decide what is most important as you read. Ask the basic questions: *who, what, when, where, why,* and *how.* Using your own words, write your answers to these questions from an **objective** point of view, without inserting your own feelings and opinions.

Summarizing is sometimes confused with paraphrasing. When you **paraphrase**, you do not condense a text to its most important details. Instead, you restate the entire text in your own words. A summary is much shorter than the original text, while a paraphrase may be the same length as the original text.

TURN AND TALK

1. Think about your favorite book or movie. Can you describe who did what, where, when, why, and how without including your thoughts and feelings about it?

2. Why is it important to leave out our thoughts and feelings when we summarize?

ELL SPEAKING FRAMES

- The [book / movie] took place in ___.
- In [book or movie title], the main character was ___ and in the [book / movie] they ___.
- The reason the main character did what they did was to ___.
- It is important to leave out our thoughts and feelings when we summarize because ___.

Address to the Nation on the Explosion of the Space Shuttle *Challenger*

Skill:
Summarizing

Use the Checklist to analyze Summarizing in "Address to the Nation on the Explosion of the Space Shuttle *Challenger*." Refer to the sample student annotations about Summarizing in the text.

••• CHECKLIST FOR SUMMARIZING

In order to determine how to write an objective summary of a text, note the following:

- ✓ in a nonfiction text, examine the details, making notations in a notebook or graphic organizer
  - ask basic questions such as *who, what, when, where, why,* and *how*
  - identify what each of the details describe or have in common
  - determine what central or main idea ties all the information together
- ✓ use the main idea as the topic sentence of the summary
- ✓ stay objective and do not add your own personal thoughts, judgments, or opinions to the summary

To provide an objective summary of a text, consider the following questions:

- ✓ What are the answers to basic *who, what, where, when, why,* and *how* questions in works of nonfiction?
- ✓ Have I determined what each of the details have in common and what central or main idea ties them together?
- ✓ In what order should I put the main ideas and most important details in a work of nonfiction to make my summary clear and logical?
- ✓ Is my summary objective, or have I added my own thoughts, judgments, and personal opinions?

V SKILL VOCABULARY

summarize / resumir **verb** to restate briefly the most important points in a text

objective / objetivo/a **adjective** undistorted by emotion or personal bias COGNATE

paraphrase / parafrasear **verb** to restate the author's words in your own words COGNATE

Skill:
Summarizing

Reread paragraph 5 of "Address to the Nation on the Explosion of the Space Shuttle *Challenger*." Then, using the Checklist on the previous page, answer the multiple-choice questions below.

YOUR TURN

1. This question has two parts. First, answer Part A. Then, answer Part B.

   Part A: What is the main idea of paragraph 5?

   ○ A. It is important to keep the space program hidden from the public.
   ○ B. NASA will continue with their space exploration program.
   ○ C. President Reagan wants to talk to everyone at NASA who worked on this mission.
   ○ D. More teachers will be in space one day.

   Part B: Which two details from the paragraph support your answer to Part A?

   ○ A. "We don't hide our space program" and "we know of your anguish."
   ○ B. "We don't hide our space program" and "we don't keep secrets and cover things up."
   ○ C. "There will be more shuttle flights and more shuttle crews and, yes, more volunteers, more civilians, more teachers in space" and "nothing ends here; our hopes and our journeys continue."
   ○ D. "We do it all up front and in public" and "we know of your anguish."

2. In paragraph 5, what is the important link between Reagan's statements about the space program and the people who work at NASA that supports the main idea and should be included in a summary?

   ○ A. President Reagan says that we don't hide our space program, and we don't keep secrets and cover things up.
   ○ B. Reagan states that there will be more shuttle flights and more shuttle crews, more volunteers, more civilians, and more teachers in space.
   ○ C. Reagan says that "our journeys continue," and this is supported by his statements that he has great faith in the space program, and that the professionalism and dedication of the people who work at NASA have impressed us for decades.
   ○ D. President Reagan says that he has to talk to every man and woman who works for NASA or this mission about hiding the space program so tragedies like *Challenger* do not happen again.

Reading & Writing
Companion   **35**

Your Turn

Ask students to complete the Your Turn activity.

QUESTION 1

Part A

A. Incorrect. Reagan says that the United States doesn't hide its space program and we don't keep secrets or cover things up.

B. Correct. The entire paragraph is about the importance of continuing the space program.

C. Incorrect. This is only one detail from the paragraph that supports the main idea.

D. Incorrect. This is only one detail from the paragraph that supports the main idea.

Part B

A. Incorrect. These phrases do not support the idea of continuing the space program.

B. Incorrect. These phrases do not support the idea of continuing the space program.

C. Correct. These statements support the idea that the NASA space program will continue.

D. Incorrect. These phrases do not support the idea of continuing the space program.

QUESTION 2

A. Incorrect. This is not a link between his two statements related to the continuation of the space program.

B. Incorrect. This is an important detail, but it does not specifically refer to the link between his opening statement and his opinion of the employees at NASA.

C. Correct. These details support the fact that he feels the space program should continue despite the *Challenger* tragedy, and they should be included in a summary.

D. Incorrect. Reagan does say that he wants to talk to everyone at NASA, but he does not want to "hide" the space program.

Skill: Informational Text Structure

Introduce the Skill

Watch the Concept Definition video ▶ and read the following definition with your students.

Text structure refers to the organizational pattern authors of nonfiction use to present information. Some of the most common informational text structures include **sequential**, **problem and solution**, **cause and effect**, and **comparison and contrast**. In a sequential text structure, authors present information about events or steps in a process, in the order in which they take or have taken place. Writers who specialize in history or science topics often use a cause and effect text structure to explain how or why something happened. Many authors use a compare and contrast text structure to present information about things that are different but have something in common, such as two points of view on a subject. Or a writer may present a problem or a series of problems, and offers solutions on how to solve them.

Authors may also use text structure to organize information about multiple topics, or use more than one organizational pattern within the same text.

 TURN AND TALK

1. What is one informational text you've read recently?

2. What kind of text structures did the author use?

> **ELL SPEAKING FRAMES**
> - One informational text I read recently is ____.
> - The author used a ____ structure.
> - This text structure helped the author develop the key concept that ____.

Address to the Nation on the Explosion of the Space Shuttle *Challenger*

Skill:
Informational Text Structure

Use the Checklist to analyze Informational Text Structure in "Address to the Nation on the Explosion of the Space Shuttle *Challenger*." Refer to the sample student annotations about Informational Text Structure in the text.

••• CHECKLIST FOR INFORMATIONAL TEXT STRUCTURE

In order to determine the structure of a specific paragraph in a text, note the following:

✓ details and signal words that reveal the text structure in a paragraph of the text

✓ a key concept in the paragraph that is revealed by the text structure the author has chosen to organize the text

✓ particular sentences in the paragraph and the role they play in defining and refining a key concept

To analyze in detail the structure of a specific paragraph in a text, including the role of particular sentences in developing and refining a key concept, consider the following questions:

✓ What is the structure of the paragraph?

✓ Which sentences in the paragraph reveal the text structure the author is using?

✓ What role do these sentences play in developing and refining a key concept?

 SKILL VOCABULARY

text structure / la estructura del texto *noun* the order or pattern a writer uses to organize ideas or events COGNATE

sequential text structure / la estructura secuencial del texto *noun* a text structure in which events or steps are presented in the order in which they have taken place COGNATE

problem and solution text structure / el problema y la solución *noun* a text structure that identifies a problem and offers a solution COGNATE

Address to the Nation on the Explosion of the Space Shuttle *Challenger*

Skill:
Informational Text Structure

Reread paragraph 3 of "Address to the Nation on the Explosion of the Space Shuttle *Challenger*." Then, using the Checklist on the previous page, answer the multiple-choice questions below.

YOUR TURN

1. The primary text structure in paragraph 3 is—

   ○ A. description.
   ○ B. cause and effect.
   ○ C. problem and solution.
   ○ D. compare and contrast.

2. The author develops this text structure by—

   ○ A. using the word *but* to identify differences.
   ○ B. discussing change over time to describe a solution to a problem.
   ○ C. starting many of the clauses with similar phrases to describe or define the qualities of two groups.
   ○ D. describing two groups' feelings after the *Challenger* disaster to develop its effect.

3. This text structure helps develop the author's thesis by—

   ○ A. developing the key concept that the disaster was a great loss because the astronauts had families.
   ○ B. developing the key concept that the disaster was a great loss because it was the end result of decades of research.
   ○ C. developing the key concept that the disaster was a great loss because many Americans were saddened by the disaster.
   ○ D. developing the key concept that the disaster was a great loss because Americans lost a group of special people who were willing to take on an important challenge for their country.

SkillsTV

Project the SkillsTV episode and pause at the following times to prompt discussion:

0:34 How do the students use the title to help them understand the text?

1:38 How do the students use textual evidence to recognize a change in text structure?

2:06 How do the students use textual evidence to understand the purpose of a change in text structure?

Your Turn

Ask students to complete the Your Turn activity.

QUESTION 1

A. Correct. Reagan describes or defines the qualities of the *Challenger* astronauts and the nation they served.

B. Incorrect. Although Reagan mentions the effect of the *Challenger* disaster, cause and effect is not the primary organizational pattern in the paragraph.

C. Incorrect. Reagan does not identify a problem or solution in this paragraph.

D. Incorrect. Compare and contrast is not the primary organizational pattern in the paragraph.

QUESTION 2

A. Incorrect. Reagan's use of the word does not develop the primary organizational pattern.

B. Incorrect. The idea or key concept of change does not develop the primary organizational pattern.

C. Correct. Reagan starts many of the clauses with *they* and a verb that describe the astronauts' qualities or actions. Then he uses *we* to discuss Americans in a similar manner.

D. Incorrect. Reagan's description of feelings is not the primary organizational pattern in the paragraph.

QUESTION 3

A. Incorrect. Reagan's description of the astronauts and other Americans emphasizes that their deaths are a loss to the families and to the nation.

B. Incorrect. Reagan does not discuss the research involved in creating and launching the *Challenger* shuttle.

C. Incorrect. Reagan's structure emphasizes the astronauts' contributions rather than Americans' feelings after the disaster.

D. Correct. Emphasizing the astronauts' qualities and contributions to an important program helps develop the significance of the loss for the nation.

Close Read

Skills Focus

QUESTION 1: Informational Text Structure

See paragraph 6: President Reagan notes that Sir Francis Drake died on the same day as the astronauts on *Challenger*. By comparing the astronauts to Sir Francis Drake, he is suggesting that the astronauts are great explorers, and it makes losing them seem more significant and tragic.

QUESTION 2: Summarizing

See paragraph 5: Reagan believes that the space program is something to be proud of and a representation of freedom in the United States. Even after the *Challenger* tragedy, Reagan makes a point to say that we as a country will continue to explore space, which emphasizes his support of the space program.

QUESTION 3: Connect to Essential Question

See paragraph 2: Space exploration is dangerous and can cost an astronaut his or her life, but astronauts take the risk because they are courageous and committed to their jobs.

Address to the Nation on the Explosion of the Space Shuttle *Challenger*

Close Read

Reread "Address to the Nation on the Explosion of the Space Shuttle *Challenger*." As you reread, complete the Skills Focus questions below. Then use your answers and annotations from the questions to help you complete the Write activity.

SKILLS FOCUS

1. Identify examples of compare-and-contrast structure in the text. Explain how these comparisons help develop the thesis, or central message, in Reagan's speech.

2. Identify Reagan's stance on the space program. Write one or two sentences summarizing his message.

3. Identify details in the text that show the risks of the space program. Explain why astronauts are willing to take chances and explore space.

✏ WRITE

COMPARATIVE: In "Address to the Nation on the Explosion of the Space Shuttle *Challenger*," President Reagan addresses the public about a national tragedy. In *A Night to Remember*, the tragedy is recounted through interviews with various people who experienced the *Titanic's* crash. How do the different structures of the texts help to effectively communicate information regarding the tragedies? Are there advantages or disadvantages to the structure of either text? Which one do you prefer? Cite specific examples from the text to explain which structure better helps to effectively communicate information and make the author's point.

Writer's Notebook

Connect to Essential Question: Give students time to reflect on how "Address to the Nation on the Explosion of the Space Shuttle *Challenger*" connects to the unit's essential question "Why do we take chances?" by freewriting in their Writer's Notebooks.

 Beginning & Intermediate

Read aloud the unit's essential question: "Why do we take chances?" Encourage students to draw their connections or allow students to write in their native language. Circulate the room, prompting students for their thoughts as they respond orally or through pantomime.

 Advanced & Advanced High

Allow students to share their reflections orally in pairs or small groups before freewriting.

Collaborative Conversation

Break students into collaborative conversation groups to discuss the Close Read prompt. Ask students to use the StudySyncTV episode as a model for their discussion. Remind them to reference their Skills Focus annotations in their discussion.

In "Address to the Nation on the Explosion of the Space Shuttle *Challenger*," President Reagan addresses the public about a national tragedy. In *A Night to Remember*, the tragedy is recounted through interviews with various people who experienced the *Titanic's* crash. How do the different structures of the texts help to effectively communicate information regarding the tragedies? Are there advantages or disadvantages to the structure of either text? Which one do you prefer? Cite specific examples from the texts to explain which structure better helps to effectively communicate information and make the author's point.

Use the scaffolds below to differentiate instruction for your **ELL** ELL English Language Learners and **A** Approaching grade-level learners.

ELL **BEGINNING, INTERMEDIATE** Use the <u>discussion guide</u> and <u>speaking frames</u> to facilitate the discussion with support from the teacher.

ADVANCED, ADVANCED HIGH Use the <u>discussion guide</u> and <u>speaking frames</u> to facilitate the discussion in mixed-level groups.

A **APPROACHING** Use the <u>discussion guide</u> to facilitate the discussion in mixed-level groups.

APPROACHING
ADVANCED, ADVANCED HIGH
BEGINNING, INTERMEDIATE

Discussion Guide	Speaking Frames
1. What is one type of text structure that Reagan uses in the speech?	• In paragraph ____ (number), Reagan uses ____ text structure.
2. How does this text structure help communicate information?	• Reagan uses this text structure to communicate ____.
3. What is one type of text structure that Lord uses in the excerpt?	• In paragraph ____ (number), Lord uses a ____ text structure.
4. How does this text structure help communicate information?	• Lord uses this text structure to communicate ____.

Review Prompt and Rubric

Before students begin writing, review the writing prompt and rubric with the class.

Comparative: In "Address to the Nation on the Explosion of the Space Shuttle *Challenger*," President Reagan addresses the public about a national tragedy. In *A Night to Remember*, the tragedy is recounted through interviews with various people who experienced the *Titanic's* crash. How do the different structures of the texts help to effectively communicate information regarding the tragedies? Are there advantages or disadvantages to the structure of either text? Which one do you prefer? Cite specific examples from the texts to explain which structure better helps to effectively communicate information and make the author's point.

ELL **PROMPT GUIDE**

A
- What types of text structures do Reagan and Lord use?
- How does the use of these text structures help to communicate information?

- What are the advantages and disadvantages of using these text structures?

Score	Informational Text Structure	Language and Conventions
4	The writer clearly analyzes and explains the author's use of informational text structure. The writer provides exemplary analysis, using relevant evidence from the text.	The writer demonstrates a consistent command of grammar, punctuation, and usage conventions. Although minor errors may be evident, they do not detract from the fluency or the clarity of the writing.
3	The writer analyzes and explains the author's use of informational text structure. The writer provides sufficient analysis, using relevant evidence from the text most of the time.	The writer demonstrates an adequate command of grammar, punctuation, and usage conventions. Although some errors may be evident, they create few (if any) disruptions in the fluency or clarity of the writing.
2	The writer begins to analyze or explain the author's use of informational text structure, but the analysis is incomplete. The writer uses relevant evidence from the text only some of the time.	The writer demonstrates a partial command of grammar, punctuation, and usage conventions. Some distracting errors may be evident, at times creating minor disruptions in the fluency or clarity of the writing.
1	The writer attempts to analyze or explain the author's use of informational text structure, but the analysis is not successful. The writer uses little or no relevant evidence from the text.	The writer demonstrates little or no command of grammar, punctuation, and usage conventions. Serious and persistent errors create disruptions in the fluency of the writing and sometimes interfere with meaning.
0	The writer does not provide a relevant response to the prompt or does not provide a response at all.	Serious and persistent errors overwhelm the writing and interfere with the meaning of the response as a whole, making the writer's meaning impossible to understand.

Write

Ask students to complete the writing assignment using textual evidence to support their answers.

Use the scaffolds below to differentiate instruction for your **ELL** English Language Learners and **A** Approaching grade-level learners.

ELL **BEGINNING** With the help of the <u>word bank</u>, write a response using <u>paragraph frame 1</u>.

INTERMEDIATE With the help of the <u>word bank</u>, write a response using <u>paragraph frames 1 and 2</u>.

ADVANCED, ADVANCED HIGH Write a response of differentiated length using the <u>sentence starters</u>.

A **APPROACHING** Write a response of differentiated length using the <u>sentence starters</u>.

| BEGINNING | | ADVANCED, ADVANCED HIGH |
| INTERMEDIATE | | APPROACHING |

Word Bank	Paragraph Frame 1	Paragraph Frame 2	Sentence Starters
sequential order explanation depends compare and contrast	____ was one text structure used in "Address to the Nation on the Explosion of the Space Shuttle *Challenger*." This structure effectively communicated why the *Challenger* explosion was tragic by comparing it to another hardship in exploration. The ____ text structure used in *A Night to Remember* effectively communicated what it was like to be on the *Titanic* the night it sank. Compare-and-contrast text structure has the advantage of explaining the explosion by connecting it to other tragedies, but a disadvantage is that the information it communicates ____ on comparing it to another event. Sequential text structure has the advantage of providing a detailed ____ of the events, but it forces the writer to tell the story of what happened in ____.	I think ____ text structure is ____ because ____.	• The compare and contrast text structure used in . . . • The sequential text structure used in . . . • Compare and contrast text structure has the advantage of . . . • Sequential text structure has the advantage of . . . • I prefer the . . . structure of . . .

Peer Review

Students should submit substantive feedback to two peers using the instructions below.

- How well does this response answer the prompt?
- How well does the writer support his or her ideas with details from the text?
- What did the writer do well in this response? What does the writer need to work on?

Rate

Respond to the following with a point rating that reflects your opinion.

	1 2 3 4
Ideas	■ ■ ■ □
Evidence	■ ■ ■ ■
Language and Conventions	■ ■ □ □

Submit

ELL
A **SENTENCE FRAMES**

- You were able to (completely / partly / almost) answer the prompt.
- You supported the idea of ____ with the detail of ____.

- One idea that needs more support is ____.
- My favorite part of your response is ____.

A Kenyan Teen's Discovery:

Let There Be Lights to Save Lions

INFORMATIONAL TEXT
Nina Gregory
2013

Introduction

H aving roamed the lands of present-day Kenya and Tanzania for thousands of years, the Maasai tribe had long coexisted with the region's lion population. But now, the lion population is in sharp decline—and their next-door neighbors are a big reason why. Richard Turere is one of those neighbors, a thirteen-year-old inventor who lives among the Maasai near Nairobi National Park, which hosts many of the endangered lions of Kenya. Living in such close proximity, some lions have begun to prey on the livestock owned by locals like Richard's family. A struggle has emerged between the locals and the encroaching lions, resulting in deaths of a highly threatened and endangered species (there are fewer than 2,000 lions remaining in Kenya). In this article and its accompanying video, explore how young Richard devised an inventive way to save both livestock and lions from harm.

In 2013, Richard Turere, a 13-year-old inventor from Kenya, was invited to give a TED Talk to explain how he created a way to prevent lions from attacking livestock. Richard lives near the Nairobi National Park, a sanctuary for endangered lions in close proximity to surrounding farms. Richard explains that cows are kept in sheds in the evenings, which makes them easy prey. In an effort to protect livestock, many local farmers resorted to killing lions, and as a result, only an estimated 2,000 lions remain in the region. One night, Richard realized that lions are scared of flashlights. This led him to create a system he named Lion Lights, which uses flashing lights to mimic human activity. Richard's system has worked so well that many of his neighbors asked him to build one for them. Currently, Lion Lights are employed throughout Kenya.

 ELL Proficiency-leveled summaries and summaries in multiple languages are available digitally.

🔊 Audio and audio text highlighting are available with this text.

CONNECT TO ESSENTIAL QUESTION

Why do we take chances?

What happens when protecting one group of animals puts another group of animals at risk? This informational text and video show how Richard Turere drew inspiration from this problem.

Access Complex Text

LEXILE: 950L   WORD COUNT: 502

The following areas may be challenging for students, particularly **ELL** English Language Learners and **A** Approaching grade-level learners.

Connection of Ideas	Purpose	Organization
• Readers synthesize information from the video and article to better understand the importance of Richard's invention.	• The text is from a news source, and it gives information about a real person and real events. • The author's purpose is to explain how Richard got his idea and invented his Lion Lights.	• The text shows a cause and effect. The cause is the conflict between humans and lions. The effect is Richard's invention. • Clues such as "from ages 6 to 9" and "one night" show chronological order.

 SCAFFOLDS   **ELL** ENGLISH LANGUAGE LEARNERS   **A** APPROACHING GRADE LEVEL   **B** BEYOND GRADE LEVEL

These icons identify differentiation strategies and scaffolded support for a variety of students. See the digital lesson plan for additional differentiation strategies and scaffolds.

Instructional Path

The print teacher's edition includes essential point-of-use instruction and planning tools. Complete lesson plans and program documents appear in your digital teacher account.

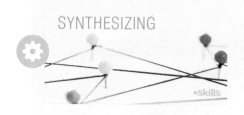

Skill: Synthesizing

Objectives: After reading and discussing a model, students will be able synthesize information from multiple texts to create new understanding in order to improve reading comprehension.

First Read: A Kenyan Teen's Discovery: Let There Be Lights to Save Lions

Objectives: After an initial reading and discussion of the informational text and viewing of the video, students will be able to identify and restate the text's key ideas and details.

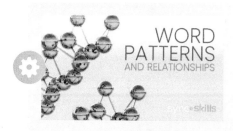

Skill: Media

Objectives: After rereading and discussing a model of close reading, students will be able to analyze and evaluate characteristics, purpose, advantages, and disadvantages of different types of media.

Skill: Word Patterns and Relationships

Objectives: After rereading and discussing a model of close reading, students will be able to analyze word patterns and relationships to better understand vocabulary in a text.

Close Read: A Kenyan Teen's Discovery: Let There Be Lights to Save Lions

Objectives: After engaging in a close reading and discussion of the text, students will be able to analyze the use and advantages and disadvantages of different mediums to convey information in a short written response.

Blast: Now, That's an Idea

Objectives: After exploring background information and research links about a topic, students will respond to a question with a 140-character response.

Progress Monitoring

Opportunities to Learn	Opportunities to Demonstrate Learning	Opportunities to Reteach

Synthesizing

⚙ Skill: Synthesizing	💬 First Read • Read and Annotate	⚙ Spotlight Skill: Synthesizing

Media

⚙ Skill: Media	⚙ Skill: Media • Your Turn 💬 Close Read • Skills Focus • Write	⚙ Unit 3 Skill: Media - The Call of the Wild ⚙ Unit 4 Skill: Media - Across Five Aprils ⚙ Spotlight Skill: Media

Word Patterns and Relationships

⚙ Skill: Word Patterns and Relationships	⚙ Skill: Word Patterns and Relationships • Your Turn	⚙ Unit 4 Skill: Word Patterns and Relationships - Blind ⚙ Spotlight Skill: Word Patterns and Relationships

First Read

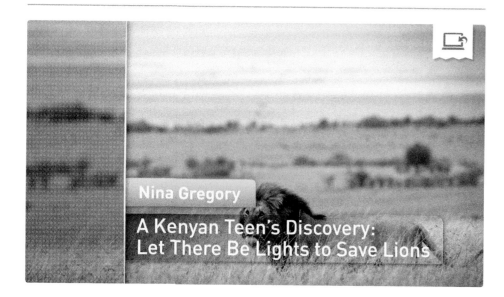

Nina Gregory

**A Kenyan Teen's Discovery:
Let There Be Lights to Save Lions**

Introduce the Text

As a class, watch the video preview ▶ and have students read the introduction in pairs to make connections to the video preview.

To activate prior knowledge and experiences, ask students:

- What image was your favorite from the video? Why?

- How do the images, words, and music in the video connect to the information in the introduction?

ELL SPEAKING FRAMES

- The ____ in the video makes me think ____.
- The video shows ____. This makes me wonder ____.
- I think the text will ____. I think this because ____.
- I predict that there will be ____. I believe this because ____.

Entry Point

As students prepare to read "A Kenyan Teen's Discovery: Let There Be Lights to Save Lions," share the following information with them to provide context.

✓ The Maasai live in the Great Rift Valley of East Africa, which is also the location of the Serengeti, the Maasai Mara, and other extensive areas of savanna (grassland) that have been set aside to preserve African wildlife, including lions, elephants, cheetahs, zebras, and hippos.

✓ The Maasai lead a semi-nomadic life, herding their cattle in this semi-arid land according to the seasonal rains. Since formal education of children was established, adults have taken over the main responsibility of herding the cattle, with boys resuming the job only when school is out, such as weekends.

✓ TED Talks are free online lectures given on a wide range of topics by experts in their fields. Lists of TED Talks that are especially interesting and beneficial to middle-school students are also available online.

"A light went on inside him and an idea was born."

NOTES

1   One of the talks from the TED stage in Long Beach, Calif., this week came from Richard Turere, an inventor. He is a Maasai from Kenya. And he's 13.

2   "From ages 6 to 9, I started looking after my father's cows," Richard says. "I'd take them out in the morning and bring them back in the evening. We put them in a small cow shed at night," and that's when the trouble would start. Lions would jump in the shed and kill the cows, which are enclosed and an easy target.

3   Lions are the top tourist attraction to Kenya, especially in the Nairobi National Park, which is near where Richard lives. Lions are also considered **critically** endangered in Kenya.

Skill:
Media

According to the video I saw, killing lions can also be cultural. However, this seems to be the bigger problem. The article and the video showing the lions and livestock offer a variety of ways to understand why Richard's invention is so important.

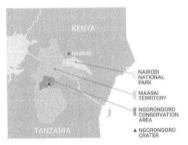

Map showing Maasai Territory, Nairobi National Park area, Ngorongoro Conservation Area, and Ngorongoro Crater.*
*Approximate sizes of areas and locations.

KENYA
- NAIROBI
- NAIROBI NATIONAL PARK
- MAASAI TERRITORY
- NGORONGORO CONSERVATION AREA
- ▲ NGORONGORO CRATER
TANZANIA

4   The Kenya Wildlife Service estimates there are just 2,000 lions left in the country. One of the main causes of their demise, "is that people kill them in **retaliation** for lions attacking their livestock," says Paula Kahumbu, executive director of Wildlife Direct, a wildlife **conservation** organization in Africa.

Copyright © BookheadEd Learning, LLC

40   Reading & Writing Companion

Analyze Vocabulary Using Context Clues

In paragraph 3, focus on the sentence that uses the word *critically*. Point out these context clues:

1.   First, I notice the word *critical* inside the word *critically*. It means "near a turning point or crisis."

2.   When I read the sentence again, I think that the danger to lions is close to a crisis.

3.   This meaning fits because the text is about stopping the killing of endangered lions.

Media

How does the student relate the video to the article?

The student says that seeing the livestock in the video increased his understanding of the need for Richard's invention discussed in the article.

TEXT TALK

How did Richard learn lions were killing cows?

See paragraph 2: Richard was caring for cows and knew lions killed cows by jumping in the shed at night.

What put lions in Kenya in danger?

See paragraph 4: People were killing them because lions attacked their livestock.

V SELECTION VOCABULARY

critically / críticamente *adverb* in a serious manner

retaliation / la represalia *noun* action taken in return for being hurt

ELL
- What is happening to the lions?
- Why are people taking action?

conservation / la preservación *noun* protection of the natural environment

ELL
- What does Paula Kahumbu do as part of Wildlife Direct?
- How does that give you a clue to the meaning of *conservation*?

Word Patterns and Relationships

What was the relationship that the reader used in the second annotation, and why?

The reader used an synonym/antonym relationship to eventually determine the meaning of the word *crisis*.

Skills Focus

QUESTION 2: Summarizing

Richard Turere saw that lions are scared of people's moving flashlights. He used spare parts and a solar panel to create an invention that protects cows from lions with moving lights.

TEXT TALK

What did Paula Kahumbu study?

See paragraph 5: She studied the conflict between lions and humans.

How did Richard discover lions are afraid of moving lights?

See paragraph 7: One night Richard walked around with a flashlight and made the discovery.

What did Richard invent?

See paragraphs 7–9: He invented Lion Lights. They act like a person walking around with a flashlight.

---

5 She has been studying the **conflict** between humans and lions, and her work led her to Richard. In one week, she **monitored** over 50 cases where lions attacked livestock. "It's a very, very serious problem," she says.

6 Her work studying the problem led her to Richard.

7 One night he was walking around with a flashlight and discovered the lions were scared of a moving light. A light went on inside him and an idea was born.

8 Three weeks and much tinkering later, Richard had invented a system of lights that flash around the cow shed, **mimicking** a human walking around with a flashlight. His system is made from broken flashlight parts and an indicator box from a motorcycle.

9 "The only thing I bought was a solar panel," which charges a battery that supplies power to the lights at night, Richard says. He calls the system Lion Lights.

10 "There have been a lot of efforts to try to protect the lions," Kahumbu says. "It's a crisis and everyone is looking for a solution. One idea was land leases, another was lion-proof fences. And basically no one even knew that Richard had already come up with something that worked."

11 His simple solution was so successful, his neighbors heard about it and wanted Lion Lights, too. He installed the lights for them and for six other homes in his community. From there, the lights spread and are now being used all around Kenya. Someone in India is trying them out for tigers. In Zambia and Tanzania they're being used, as well.

12 To get to the TED stage, Richard traveled on an airplane for the first time in his life. He says he has a lot to tell his friends about when he goes back home, and among the scholars and prize winners, scientists and poets, what impressed him the most on his trip was something he saw at the nearby Aquarium of the Pacific: "It was my first time seeing a shark. I've never seen a shark."

Skill:
Word Patterns and Relationships

Kahumbu says protecting lions is a crisis and everyone is looking for a solution. An antonym for *solution* is *problem*. But this seems like more than just a problem as there have been so many efforts to solve it. So, a crisis must mean an emergency.

Reading & Writing Companion 41

SELECTION VOCABULARY

conflict / el conflicto **noun** a state of opposition between persons, ideas, or interests; a disagreement COGNATE

- Who is in "conflict"?
- Why is the conflict a problem?

monitor / monitorear **verb** to check, track, and observe COGNATE

- What was "monitored" in a week?
- How does that give you a clue to the meaning of *monitor*?

mimic / imitar **verb** to copy or imitate

- What did Richard discover about the lions?
- How do the words around *mimicking* help you understand its meaning?

Reading Comprehension OPTIONAL

Have students complete the digital reading comprehension questions ✓ when they finish reading.

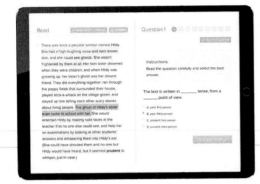

ANSWER KEY

QUESTION 1: D	**QUESTION 5:** D	**QUESTION 9:**
QUESTION 2: A	**QUESTION 6:** C	*See first chart.*
QUESTION 3: C	**QUESTION 7:** B	**QUESTION 10:**
QUESTION 4: A	**QUESTION 8:** B	*See second chart.*

First	Second	Third	Fourth
A conflict begins between locals who own livestock and the lions that attack the livestock, resulting in more lion deaths.	Richard notices that the lions are afraid of his flashlight when he is out walking at night.	Using his idea and the materials around him, Richard invents Lion Lights to keep the lions away from livestock.	Richard's invention becomes so popular that his neighbors and people in other countries use them as well.

Synonym	Word
protection	conservation
revenge	retaliation
seriously	critically
struggle	conflict
observed	monitored
copying	mimicking

Connect and Extend OPTIONAL

CONNECT TO EXTENDED WRITING PROJECT

Students can use "A Kenyan Teen's Discovery: Let There Be Lights to Save Lions" as a mentor text for their Extended Writing Project. They may use the text as a resource for their informational essays.

BEYOND THE BOOK

Infographic: Man vs. Nature

Conflicts between people and nature are increasing as humans infringe on land that has belonged to other animals. Students will select another example of this conflict between human beings and animals to research. They will transform this research into a dynamic infographic designed to raise awareness about this man-versus-nature conflict.

Ask students to:

- Clearly identify the conflict between humans and animals they want to research.
- Research this conflict to find out more about it.
  - > Where is this conflict taking place?
  - > What is causing the conflict?
  - > In what way are humans and/or animals threatened?
  - > What damage has already been done?
  - > What are possible solutions to this conflict?
- Design an infographic that identifies the conflict and location, provides visual data to show the impact of the conflict, and communicates a clear call to action. Infographics can be done on paper or online.

Once students have posted their infographics in class or online, allow students to do a gallery walk to see what their peers have created.

To reflect, ask students:

- Which infographics were most effective at communicating information?

Think Questions

Circulate as students answer Think Questions independently. Scaffolds for these questions are shown on the opposite page.

QUESTION 1: Textual Evidence

Richard's invention works well because it imitates "a human walking around with a flashlight." Richard discovered that lions are afraid of a moving light. His Lion Lights frighten the lions away from livestock without hurting them.

QUESTION 2: Textual Evidence

Richard did not buy a lot of expensive things to create Lion Lights because he used old parts from flashlights and a motorcycle. The only thing he bought was a solar panel to power the lights at night when the lions attack the livestock.

QUESTION 3: Textual Evidence

Paula Kahumbu, the executive director of Wildlife Direct, says, "There have been a lot of efforts to try to protect the lions." She mentions the idea of land leases and the idea of fences that would keep the lions out. Richard's solution was successful because it was simple and not expensive to make.

QUESTION 4: Context Clues; Greek and Latin Affixes and Roots

I think *conservation* must mean "saving or guarding resources." The word is used to describe an organization that is concerned about lions being killed. The organization wants to save or protect animals that are in danger of becoming extinct.

QUESTION 5: Context Clues

I think *retaliation* must mean "hurting someone because they have hurt you." The context clues in the sentence support this meaning. People are killing lions because lions are killing their livestock. The people need their livestock because it is their livelihood. They take out their revenge on the lions.

A Kenyan Teen's Discovery: Let There Be Lights to Save Lions

First Read

Read "A Kenyan Teen's Discovery: Let There Be Lights to Save Lions." After you read, complete the Think Questions below.

THINK QUESTIONS

1. Why does Richard's invention work so well? How does it keep the lions away from the livestock without harming them? Use specific evidence from the text to support your answer.

2. What items did Richard use to create his invention? Did he have to buy a lot of expensive equipment? Why or why not?

3. Before Richard's idea became known, what were some of the other ideas people had to keep the lions from attacking livestock? Cite specific examples from the text.

4. The root *serv* comes from the Latin word *servare*, meaning "to save or guard." With this in mind, write a definition of **conservation** in your own words, indicating any words or phrases that helped you understand.

5. Use context clues to find the meaning of the word **retaliation** as it is used in paragraph 4. Write your own definition of *retaliation*, identifying any context clues that helped you unlock the meaning of the word.

42   Reading & Writing Companion   Please note that excerpts and passages in the StudySync® library and this workbook are intended as touchstones to generate interest in an author's work. The excerpts and passages do not substitute for the reading of entire texts, and StudySync® strongly recommends that students seek out and purchase the whole literary or informational work in order to experience it as the author intended. Links to online resellers are available in our digital library. In addition, complete works may be ordered through an authorized reseller by filling out and returning to StudySync® the order form enclosed in this workbook.

Think Questions

Use the scaffolds below to differentiate instruction for your **ELL** English Language Learners and **A** Approaching grade-level learners.

ELL **BEGINNING** Write a response using the <u>word bank</u> and <u>sentence frames</u>.

INTERMEDIATE Write a response using the <u>sentence frames</u>.

ADVANCED, ADVANCED HIGH Write a response using the <u>Text-Dependent Question Guide</u>.

A **APPROACHING** Write a response using the <u>Text-Dependent Question Guide</u>.

| | INTERMEDIATE | APPROACHING |
| BEGINNING | | ADVANCED, ADVANCED HIGH |

Word Bank	Sentence Frames	Text-Dependent Question Guide
fences hurting human motorcycle wildlife lions saving scare solar panel revenge parts simple	Richard's invention works well because the flashing lights act like a ____ walking around with a flashlight. The lights ____ the lions away. The invention saves the cows without hurting the ____.	1. • What is Richard's invention? • How does the invention work? • Why doesn't the invention harm lions?
	Richard uses old flashlight ____ and an indicator box from a ____. His invention was not expensive because he only bought a ____.	2. • What things does Richard use for his Lion Lights? • What does Richard buy? • Was the invention expensive to make?
	Before Richard's invention, people tried land leases and ____. Richard's invention was better because it was ____ and didn't cost much to make.	3. • Why was it important to keep the lions from attacking livestock? • What other ideas did people try? • Why was Richard's invention better than the other ideas?
	Conservation describes a ____ organization. This gives me a clue that *conservation* means "____ wildlife."	4. • Read: "One of the main causes of their demise 'is that people kill them in retaliation for lions attacking their livestock,' says Paula Kahumbu, executive director of Wildlife Direct, a wildlife **conservation** organization in Africa." • What does *servare* mean? • What does *conservation* describe in this sentence? • What does that tell me about the meaning of the word *conservation*?
	Retaliation means "taking ____." The people are ____ the lions because the lions are attacking their livestock.	1. • Read: " . . . people kill them in **retaliation** for lions attacking their livestock . . . " • What are the lions doing? • Is *retaliation* a reward or revenge?

Skill: Media

Introduce the Skill

Watch the Concept Definition video ▶ and read the following definition with your students.

Media is the plural form of the word *medium*. A **medium** is a means of sending a communication to an intended audience. Throughout most of human history, people communicated through three main media: speech, writing, and visual arts such as drawing, painting, and sculpture. But in the 19th century, media options suddenly exploded. The invention of photography, and then the telegraph and the telephone, changed the world. Within a century radio, motion pictures, and television followed.

Stories and ideas change as they are translated from one medium to another. A dialogue between two characters in a novel, for example, becomes very different when it is delivered by actors in a film—with close-ups, sound effects such as music, and other elements unique to the medium of film itself.

Today, new media are being invented at a much faster pace than ever before, and each of these forms of online communication has its own "language" and creates its own experience.

TURN AND TALK

1   What types of media have you used?

2   Do you like it when something you read combines text with other media, such as visuals? Why or why not?

Skill:
Media

Use the Checklist to analyze Media in "A Kenyan Teen's Discovery: Let There Be Lights to Save Lions." Refer to the sample student annotations about Media in the text.

••• CHECKLIST FOR MEDIA

In order to identify the purpose of information and the advantages and disadvantages of presenting it in different forms of media, note the following:

✓   the features of each medium, such as print or digital text, video, and multimedia

✓   how the medium contributes to the information in the text

✓   how the same information can be treated, or presented, in more than one medium, including visually, quantitatively, or orally

✓   how different media present a particular topic, idea, or historical event and can include diaries, eyewitness accounts, films, books, news and feature articles, or photographs

✓   which details are emphasized or absent in each medium and the reasons behind these choices

✓   how readers and historians compare and contrast accounts in different media as they analyze and interpret events

✓   the reliability of each medium, including specific words and images that can help you identify the motive or motives behind a video, oral, quantitative, or written work

To evaluate the advantages and disadvantages of using different media to present a particular topic or idea and analyze the purpose of presenting information in diverse formats, ask the following questions:

✓   What are the advantages and disadvantages of using different media to present a particular topic or idea?

✓   What was the purpose behind the creation of this video, speech, book, or article?

✓   What were the motives behind its presentation? How do you know?

V   SKILL VOCABULARY

medium / el medio **noun** a form of communication, such as television, the Internet, and radio COGNATE

media / los medios **noun** the plural form of the word *medium*; a means of sending a communication to an intended audience

Kenyan Teen's Discovery: Let There Be Lights to Save Lions

Skill:
Media

Watch the video clips from "Inside Africa" on the StudySync site as indicated for each question. Then, using the Checklist on the previous page, answer the multiple-choice questions below.

YOUR TURN

1. Watch from the beginning of the video to 00:24. Both types of media—video and audio—of the Maasai man and his herd are intended to—

   ○ A. provide background information about Maasai life.
   ○ B. emphasize threats to cattle in the region.
   ○ C. show that the cattle suffer during seasonal changes.
   ○ D. show the distance the cattle travel.

2. Watch the video from 03:47 to 04:13. The interaction of visual and audio in the video clip in the explanation of the lion-killing ritual is intended to—

   ○ A. suggest that lion hunting is dangerous.
   ○ B. show that it is difficult to kill a lion.
   ○ C. emphasize the symbolic importance of the ritual.
   ○ D. explain why the ritual has been outlawed in the region.

3. The main advantage of using both digital text and the video clip is to make sure that the reader—

   ○ A. knows where the region is located and what the land looks like.
   ○ B. is provided with background knowledge about Kenyan culture.
   ○ C. understands the key ideas of the lion problem and its solution.
   ○ D. grasps how Richard Turere's invention works.

Copyright © BookheadEd Learning, LLC

44 Reading & Writing Companion

Your Turn

Ask students to complete the Your Turn activity.

QUESTION 1

A. Correct. The purpose of the video clip is to give background information about Maasai practices.

B. Incorrect. The video clip does not focus on threats to cattle in the region.

C. Incorrect. The video clip does not suggest that the cattle suffer during seasonal changes.

D. Incorrect. This video clip does not show any distance measurements.

QUESTION 2

A. Incorrect. The clip is not intended to suggest that lion killing is dangerous.

B. Incorrect. The clip is not intended to show how difficult it is to kill a lion.

C. Correct. The camera's focus on the lions and the spear tip, combined with the audio explanation of the ritual, emphasizes its symbolic importance.

D. Incorrect. The clip is not intended to explain why the ritual has been outlawed in the region.

QUESTION 3

A. Incorrect. The location and appearance of the region are not the main advantages of using both types of media.

B. Incorrect. Both kinds of media were not used to provide background about Kenyan culture.

C. Correct. The digital text article and the video, taken together, enable a reader to better understand the lion problem and Richard Turere's solution.

D. Incorrect. Both kinds of media were not used to show how the invention works.

Skill: Words Patterns and Relationships

Introduce the Skill

Watch the Concept Definition video and read the following definition with your students.

Understanding how words relate to other words is an important part of creating meaning in both reading and writing, and it can also help build vocabulary. **Cause/effect** is a relationship where one thing is the result of the other. For example, if someone is described as a catalyst for change, the reader can infer that *catalyst* means someone who causes change to happen. **Part/whole** is a relationship in which a part of something is compared to the whole. For example, the knowledge that a gearshift is a mechanism that is part of a whole automobile can help a reader define *gearshift* as well as *mechanism*. **Item/category** is a relationship in which a word can be seen to belong to larger category. For example, categorizing poodles, beagles, and schnauzers as canines shows that *canine* is another word for *dog*. Recognizing **word patterns** is another way to help you determine a word's meaning and part of speech, as when *analyze* becomes *analysis*.

Skill: Word Patterns and Relationships

Use the Checklist to analyze Word Patterns and Relationships in "A Kenyan Teen's Discovery: Let There Be Lights to Save Lions." Refer to the sample student annotations about Word Patterns and Relationships in the text.

••• CHECKLIST FOR WORD PATTERNS AND RELATIONSHIPS

In order to determine the relationship between specific words to better understand each one, note the following:

- ✓ any unfamiliar words in the text
- ✓ surrounding words and phrases to better understand word meanings or any possible relationships between words
- ✓ examples of part/whole, item/category, or other relationships between words, such as cause/effect, analogies, or synonym/antonym relationships
- ✓ ways that the specific words relate to each other

To analyze the relationship between specific words to better understand each one, consider the following questions:

- ✓ Are these words related to each other in some way? How?
- ✓ What kind of relationship do these words have?
- ✓ How can I use the relationship between two or more specific words to better understand each of the words?
- ✓ Can any of these words be defined by identifying a synonym/antonym or cause/effect relationship?

TURN AND TALK

1. What are two words that come to mind when you think about word relationships?

2. What are ways in which the two words are related?

ELL SPEAKING FRAMES

- Two words that I think of when I think about word relationships are ___ and ___.
- The two words are related ___.
- The two words have a ___ relationship.

SKILL VOCABULARY

cause / la causa *noun* something that brings about an action or effect COGNATE

effect / el efecto *noun* a result; that which has been brought about COGNATE

part / la parte *noun* a piece or fragment of something COGNATE

whole / el todo *noun* a complete unit or entity

A Kenyan Teen's Discovery: Let There Be Lights to Save Lions

Skill: Word Patterns and Relationships

Reread paragraphs 5–9 of "A Kenyan Teen's Discovery: Let There Be Lights to Save Lions." Then, using the Checklist on the previous page, answer the multiple-choice questions below.

YOUR TURN

1. The word *light* appears twice in the paragraph 7. How is the meaning of the word in the first sentence different from the way the word is used in the second sentence of the paragraph?

   ○ A. In the first sentence the world *light* means "something that is moving," and in the second sentence it refers to the beginnings of an idea.

   ○ B. In the first sentence the word *light* means "illumination that makes things visible," and in the second sentence it refers to Richard shining the flashlight on himself.

   ○ C. In the first sentence the word *light* means "illumination that makes things visible," and in the second sentence it refers to the beginnings of an idea.

   ○ D. In the first sentence the word *light* means "something that comes out of a flashlight," and in the second sentence it refers to the beginnings of an idea.

2. How does the relationship between the two meanings of the word *light* help you to better understand how the author uses the word to create and highlight meaning in the text?

   ○ A. The first meaning of the word *light* helps Richard to make a discovery about the lions and their behavior because he is using a flashlight. The meaning of the word in the second sentence refers to the idea that Richard had to solve a problem.

   ○ B. The meanings of the word *light* and the way they are used are related because in the first sentence, *light* means actual illumination that Richard uses to see the lions in the darkness. In the second sentence it means the light Richard uses to see something within himself.

   ○ C. The meanings are related because one refers to the flashlight Richard uses while walking around at night, and the other indicates that Richard has a light within him, or an idea, to help him "see" a solution to his problem.

   ○ D. The meaning of the word *light* and the way the word is used in the first and second sentences are related. In the first sentence it means the actual illumination that makes things visible. In the second sentence it is used in a symbolic way to refer to a sudden idea. While not an actual light, it indicates that Richard has a light within him, or an idea, to help him "see" a solution.

Copyright © BookheadEd Learning, LLC

SKILL VOCABULARY

item / el elemento ***noun*** one part or component of a group or collection

category / la categoría ***noun*** a collection of things that share a common quality COGNATE

word pattern / el patrón de las palabras ***noun*** the changes in a word depending on usage, as with the verb *analyze* and the noun *analysis*

Your Turn

Ask students to complete the Your Turn activity.

QUESTION 1

A. Incorrect. Although Richard is moving the source of the light around by using a flashlight, the definition of *light* in the first sentence is not "something that moves or is moving."

B. Incorrect. The word *light* in the second sentence does not mean that a light is shining on Richard. This is a description of how Richard is using the flashlight and not a definition for the word.

C. Correct. The definition of *light* in the first sentence means illumination, as from the sun or a light bulb, that makes things visible. The second definition means a symbolic light.

D. Incorrect. The fact that light, or illumination, comes out of a flashlight is not a definition for the word *light* because it can come from many different sources.

QUESTION 2

A. Incorrect. This does not explain how the meanings of the two words are related.

B. Incorrect. Richard does not use an actual light to see the solution to the problem.

C. Incorrect. A flashlight creates light, but it is not related to the meaning of the word *light* as it is used in the first sentence.

D. Correct. The two uses of the word are related because *light* means illumination that makes things visible, yet it can also be used in a symbolic way to mean an idea or realization that points the way out of the "darkness" of a troubling problem.

Close Read

Skills Focus

QUESTION 1: Media

See paragraph 3: The article says that Richard Turere lives near Nairobi National Park. The map shows me exactly where this national park is, so including it is an advantage to the reader.

QUESTION 2: Summarizing

See paragraphs 7–9.

QUESTION 3: Media

See paragraph 10: The text explains that people have tried lots of different methods to protect lions. The video shows footage from the Ngorongoro Conservation Area, which helps protect lions. The video helps me understand how giving lions their own land helps protect them.

QUESTION 4: Connect to Essential Question

See paragraph 11: Richard's invention helps people in many places. This shows that creating something new is worth taking a chance because you never know who will benefit from your efforts.

A KENYAN TEEN'S DISCOVERY
LET THERE BE LIGHTS TO SAVE LIONS

Close Read

Reread "A Kenyan Teen's Discovery: Let There Be Lights to Save Lions" and rewatch the video "Inside Africa" on the StudySync site. As you reread, complete the Skills Focus questions below. Then use your answers and annotations from the questions to help you complete the Write activity.

◎ SKILLS FOCUS

1. Identify a detail from the article that is clarified by the map. Explain the advantage of including the map to convey information.

2. Identify evidence that shows how Richard Turere's invention works. Write a two-sentence summary of his process.

3. Identify a detail from the article that is developed by the video. Explain the advantage of including the video to understand this information.

4. How and why did Richard Turere take a chance with the creation of his invention? What was risky about this venture? How did his invention impact his community once it was introduced?

✏ WRITE

INFORMATIONAL: How do the video and the text work together to introduce and explain the impact of Richard Turere's invention? What are the advantages and disadvantages of using these different media in the article? Cite evidence from both the text and the video in your response.

Copyright © BookheadEd Learning, LLC

Reading & Writing Companion   47

Writer's Notebook

Connect to Essential Question: Give students time to reflect on how "A Kenyan Teen's Discovery: Let There Be Lights to Save Lions" and the video clip from "Inside Africa" connect to the unit's essential question "Why do we take chances?" by freewriting in their Writer's Notebooks.

ELL Beginning & Intermediate

Read aloud the unit's essential question: "Why do we take chances?" Encourage students to draw their connections or allow students to write in their native language. Circulate the room, prompting students for their thoughts as they respond orally or through pantomime.

ELL Advanced & Advanced High

Allow students to share their reflections orally in pairs or small groups before freewriting.

Collaborative Conversation

Break students into collaborative conversation groups to discuss the Close Read prompt. Ask students to use the StudySyncTV episode as a model for their discussion. Remind them to reference their Skills Focus annotations in their discussion.

How do the video and the text work together to introduce and explain the impact of Richard Turere's invention? What are the advantages and disadvantages of using these different media in the article? Cite evidence from both the text and the video in your response.

Use the scaffolds below to differentiate instruction for your ⓔ English Language Learners and ⒶApproaching grade-level learners.

ⓔ **BEGINNING, INTERMEDIATE** Use the <u>discussion guide</u> and <u>speaking frames</u> to facilitate the discussion with support from the teacher.

ADVANCED, ADVANCED HIGH Use the <u>discussion guide</u> and <u>speaking frames</u> to facilitate the discussion in mixed-level groups.

Ⓐ **APPROACHING** Use the <u>discussion guide</u> to facilitate the discussion in mixed-level groups.

APPROACHING
ADVANCED, ADVANCED HIGH
BEGINNING, INTERMEDIATE

Discussion Guide	Speaking Frames
1. How does the text provide information about the impact of Richard Turere's invention?	• The text gives information about ____. • This helps me understand ____.
2. How does the video provide information about the impact of Richard Turere's invention?	• The video gives information about ____. • This helps me understand ____.
3. What are the advantages and disadvantages of using these different media in the text?	• One advantage of using these different media is ____. • A disadvantage of using these different media is ____.

Review Prompt and Rubric

Before students begin writing, review the writing prompt and rubric with the class.

INFORMATIONAL: How do the video and the text work together to introduce and explain the impact of Richard Turere's invention? What are the advantages and disadvantages of using these different media in the article? Cite evidence from both the text and the video in your response.

ELL

A

PROMPT GUIDE

- How does the text introduce and explain the impact of Richard Turere's invention?
- What information does the video provide that shows the impact of Richard Turere's invention?

- How do the text and video work together to convey information?
- What are the advantages and disadvantages of using these different media in the text?

Score	Media	Language and Conventions
4	The writer clearly analyzes and explains information from different media and the advantages and disadvantages of using them. The writer provides exemplary analysis, using relevant evidence from the text and video.	The writer demonstrates a consistent command of grammar, punctuation, and usage conventions. Although minor errors may be evident, they do not detract from the fluency or the clarity of the writing.
3	The writer analyzes and explains information from different media and the advantages and disadvantages of using them. The writer provides sufficient analysis, using relevant evidence from the text and video most of the time.	The writer demonstrates an adequate command of grammar, punctuation, and usage conventions. Although some errors may be evident, they create few (if any) disruptions in the fluency or clarity of the writing.
2	The writer begins to analyze or explain information from different media and the advantages and disadvantages of using them, but the analysis is incomplete. The writer uses relevant evidence from the text and video only some of the time.	The writer demonstrates a partial command of grammar, punctuation, and usage conventions. Some distracting errors may be evident, at times creating minor disruptions in the fluency or clarity of the writing.
1	The writer attempts to analyze or explain information from different media and the advantages and disadvantages of using them, but the analysis is not successful. The writer uses little or no relevant evidence from the text and video.	The writer demonstrates little or no command of grammar, punctuation, and usage conventions. Serious and persistent errors create disruptions in the fluency of the writing and sometimes interfere with meaning.
0	The writer does not provide a relevant response to the prompt or does not provide a response at all.	Serious and persistent errors overwhelm the writing and interfere with the meaning of the response as a whole, making the writer's meaning impossible to understand.

Write

Ask students to complete the writing assignment using textual evidence to support their answers.

Use the scaffolds below to differentiate instruction for your **ELL** English Language Learners and **A** Approaching grade-level learners.

ELL **BEGINNING** With the help of the <u>word bank</u>, write a response using <u>paragraph frame 1</u>.

INTERMEDIATE With the help of the <u>word bank</u>, write a response using <u>paragraph frames 1 and 2</u>.

ADVANCED, ADVANCED HIGH Write a response of differentiated length using the <u>sentence starters</u>.

A **APPROACHING** Write a response of differentiated length using the <u>sentence starters</u>.

| BEGINNING | | ADVANCED, ADVANCED HIGH |
| INTERMEDIATE | | APPROACHING |

Word Bank	Paragraph Frame 1	Paragraph Frame 2	Sentence Starters
cows Maasai lions both saves	The text introduces Richard Turere's invention to protect his family's ____. The video shows a conservation area to protect ____. It explains that both cattle and lions are vital to ____ culture. Together the media show that saving ____ animals is important which is an advantage of using both media. Just one medium would be a disadvantage because the message would not be as strong. The impact of Richard's invention is that it ____ these animals' lives.	An important text detail is ____. An important visual element is ____. An important audio element is ____. Together, these details work together to emphasize that ____.	• The text gives information about . . . • An example of this is . . . This shows the impact of the invention by . . . • The video builds on this idea by . . . • One advantage of using both media is . . . • A disadvantage of using both media is . . . • This helps me understand the impact of the invention because . . .

Peer Review

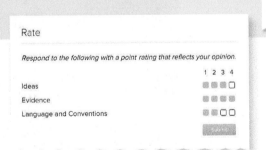

Students should submit substantive feedback to two peers using the instructions below.
- How well does this response answer the prompt?
- How well does the writer support his or her ideas?
- How well does the writer explain the advantages and disadvantages of using the different media?

Rate

Respond to the following with a point rating that reflects your opinion.

	1 2 3 4
Ideas	▪▪▪☐
Evidence	▪▪▪▪
Language and Conventions	▪▪☐☐

Submit

ELL **A** **SENTENCE FRAMES**
- You were able to (completely / partly / almost) ____ answer the prompt.
- You supported the idea of ____ with the detail of ____.
- One idea that needs more support is ____.
- You explained the advantages and disadvantages ____.

Mother to Son

POETRY
Langston Hughes
1922

Introduction

African American poet Langston Hughes (1902–1967) is one of the best-known poets of the Harlem Renaissance, a cultural and intellectual movement that began in the 1920s and resulted in the production of African American literature, art, and music that challenged racism and promoted progressive politics, such as racial and social integration. In Hughes's poem "Mother to Son," the speaker is a mother who draws on her own experiences to teach her son about perseverance.

In this poem, the speaker is a mother giving advice to her son. Using an extended metaphor of ascending a staircase, the mother explains how her life has not been easy. She begins by saying that her journey has "been no crystal stair," describing her staircase as filled with splinters and torn-up floorboards. Her metaphoric climb continues as she turns blind corners and moves through darkened sections. Despite the difficulties, she reminds her son to not turn back or sit down, which she asserts would be even more difficult. She concludes by saying that she is still climbing, even though life is hard.

 Proficiency-leveled summaries and summaries in multiple languages are available digitally.

 Audio and audio text highlighting are available with this text.

COMPARING WITHIN AND ACROSS GENRES

Read with the poem "Learning to Read" and *Narrative of the Life of Frederick Douglass, An American Slave*, Langston Hughes's classic poem "Mother to Son" invites students to compare and contrast the risks taken by African Americans.

Access Complex Text

LEXILE: N/A   WORD COUNT: 99

The following areas may be challenging for students, particularly **ELL** English Language Learners and **A** Approaching grade-level learners.

Prior Knowledge	Sentence Structure	Connection of Ideas
• Students should know that Hughes was an African American poet associated with the Harlem Renaissance, an arts movement during the 1920s that sought to express African Americans' experiences.	• Sentences written in dialect may challenge readers. Several lines do not follow the rules of standard grammar (e.g., "ain't been no") and may include contractions and other words spelled as they would be pronounced by the speaker, such as *I'se* and *kinder*. • Students may need guidance following the author's free verse style, including his use of punctuation (e.g., colon, dashes) to connect and emphasize ideas in the lines of the poem.	• Understanding the poem's extended metaphor, which compares life to a staircase, is key to determining the theme.

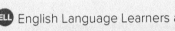

SCAFFOLDS   **ENGLISH LANGUAGE LEARNERS**   **APPROACHING GRADE LEVEL**   **BEYOND GRADE LEVEL**

These icons identify differentiation strategies and scaffolded support for a variety of students. See the digital lesson plan for additional differentiation strategies and scaffolds.

Instructional Path

The print teacher's edition includes essential point-of-use instruction and planning tools
Complete lesson plans and program documents appear in your digital teacher account

Independent Read: Mother to Son

Objectives: After reading the text, students will demonstrate their understanding of metaphor by writing a short, personal response.

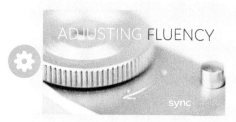

Skill: Adjusting Fluency

Objectives: Adjust fluency when reading grade-level text, based on the reading purpose.

DIGITAL ONLY

Independent Read

Introduce the Text

As a class, watch the video preview ▶ and have students read the introduction in pairs to make connections to the video preview.

- How do the images, words, and music in this video make you feel?

- How do the images, words, and music in the video connect to the information in the introduction?

- How do you think this poem will make you feel?

Entry Point

As students prepare to read "Mother to Son," share the following information with them to provide context.

✓ Langston Hughes (1902–1967) was a poet, novelist, playwright, and columnist. He was among the first poets to use jazz rhythms and urban African American dialect in his poems. His literary works reflect his passionate efforts for racial equality and social justice.

"Well, son, I'll tell you:
Life for me ain't been no crystal stair."

Analyze Vocabulary Using Context Clues

As students read the text, ask them to make predictions about each bold vocabulary word based on the context clues in the sentence.

1 Well, son, I'll tell you:
2 Life for me ain't been no **crystal** stair.
3 It's had tacks in it,
4 And **splinters,**
5 And boards torn up,
6 And places with no carpet on the floor—
7 Bare.
8 But all the time
9 I'se been a-climbin' on,
10 And reachin' **landin's,**
11 And turnin' corners,
12 And sometimes goin' in the dark
13 Where there ain't been no light.
14 So, boy, don't you turn back.
15 Don't you set down on the steps
16 'Cause you finds it's kinder hard.
17 Don't you fall now—
18 For I'se still goin', honey,
19 I'se still climbin',
20 And life for me ain't been no crystal stair.

TEXT TALK

To what does the speaker compare life?

See line 2: She compares life to a staircase, which for her is not like crystal.

What images does the speaker use to describe stairs?

See lines 3–7: She describes the stairs as worn out and full of splinters.

How does the speaker describe the way she moves on the stairs?

See lines 9–12: She describes herself as climbing, reaching landings, turning corners, and going on in the dark.

What does the speaker tell her son to do?

See lines 14–17: She tells him not to stop climbing, not to sit down, and not to fall.

Reading & Writing Companion **49**

V SELECTION VOCABULARY

crystal / el cristal **adjective** having qualities like crystal, or glassware that is very clear and that suggests elegance COGNATE

 • What object does the speaker describe as "crystal"?
• What comparison does the speaker make between her life and this object? How does she describe her life?

splinter / la astilla **noun** a small, thin, sharp bit of wood that has broken off from a larger board

 • What shape is the staircase in?
• What else does the stair have?

Mother to Son

✏ WRITE

PERSONAL RESPONSE: The mother of the poem's title shows sympathy for her son, but she does not let him dwell on defeat. What did you think about the mother's advice in "Mother to Son"? What kind of advice have you received from an adult in your life? What kind of a metaphor could you use to share the advice with a friend?

Ⅴ SELECTION VOCABULARY

landin's (landing) / el descanso **noun** a wide, flat place between sections of stairs in a staircase

- How does the speaker get to "landin's"?
- What does she do after she reaches these landings?

Reading Comprehension OPTIONAL

Have students complete the digital reading comprehension questions ✓ when they finish reading.

ANSWER KEY

QUESTION 1: B

QUESTION 2: C

QUESTION 3: A

QUESTION 4: D

QUESTION 5:

See chart.

Mother Says of Herself	Mother Says to Son
"Life for me ain't been no crystal stair."	"Don't you set down on the steps"
"And sometimes goin' in the dark"	"Don't you fall now—"

Connect and Extend OPTIONAL

CONNECT TO EXTENDED WRITING PROJECT

Students can find inspiration from the poem "Mother to Son" when writing their informational essays. Have students relate Langston Hughes's metaphor to the challenges real people may face.

BEYOND THE BOOK

Art: Visual Metaphor for Life

Langston Hughes's poem "Mother to Son" compares life to a staircase to teach about perseverance. Students will create their own visual metaphors about life to teach an important life lesson.

Ask students to:

- Imagine you are going to give a younger sibling, family member, or friend advice about life.
  - > What is the most important lesson you have learned?
  - > What piece of advice would you want to give someone you care about?
- As Hughes does in his poem, select an object that can be used to represent life's ups and downs.
- Create a visual metaphor using the artistic medium of your choice (e.g., papier-mâché, clay, paint) to reveal this life lesson.
- Write a 20-line poem that articulates this life lesson and weaves in details from your visual metaphor.

Host a gallery walk for parents and student to show off the students' artwork and poems.

To reflect, ask students:

- How did you decide what metaphor to use?
- Did creating the visual metaphor make the poem easier to write?

Collaborative Conversation

SCAFFOLDS

Post the writing prompt to generate a discussion in small groups. Ask students to first break down the prompt before they discuss relevant ideas and textual evidence.

The mother of the poem's title shows sympathy for her son, but she does not let him dwell on defeat. What did you think about the mother's advice in "Mother to Son"? What kind of advice have you received from an adult in your life? What kind of a metaphor could you use to share the advice with a friend?

Use the scaffolds below to differentiate instruction for your **ELL** English Language Learners and **A** Approaching grade-level learners.

ELL **BEGINNING, INTERMEDIATE** Use the discussion guide and speaking frames to facilitate the discussion with support from the teacher.

ADVANCED, ADVANCED HIGH Use the discussion guide and speaking frames to facilitate the discussion in mixed-level groups.

A **APPROACHING** Use the discussion guide to facilitate the discussion in mixed-level groups.

APPROACHING

ADVANCED, ADVANCED HIGH

BEGINNING, INTERMEDIATE

Discussion Guide	Speaking Frames
1. What did you think about the mother's advice in "Mother to Son"?	• I think the mother's advice (is / is not) good because ____.
2. What kind of advice have you received from an adult in your life?	• I have received advice from ____. (He / she) told me ____.
3. What kind of a metaphor could you use to share the advice with a friend?	• I can use the metaphor of ____ to share this advice with a friend.

Review Prompt and Rubric

Before students begin writing, review the writing prompt and rubric with the class.

PERSONAL RESPONSE: The mother of the poem's title shows sympathy for her son, but she does not let him dwell on defeat. What did you think about the mother's advice in "Mother to Son"? What kind of advice have you received from an adult in your life? What kind of a metaphor could you use to share the advice with a friend?

PROMPT GUIDE

- What did you think about the mother's advice in "Mother to Son"?
- What kind of advice have you received from an adult in your life?

- What kind of a metaphor could you use to share the advice with a friend?

Score	Personal Response	Language and Conventions
4	The writer clearly explains his or her personal connection to the text, using relevant evidence from the text as needed.	The writer demonstrates a consistent command of grammar, punctuation, and usage conventions. Although minor errors may be evident, they do not detract from the fluency or the clarity of the writing.
3	The writer sufficiently explains his or her personal connection to the text, using relevant evidence from the text most of the time.	The writer demonstrates an adequate command of grammar, punctuation, and usage conventions. Although some errors may be evident, they create few (if any) disruptions in the fluency or clarity of the writing.
2	The writer begins to explain his or her personal connection to the text, but the explanation is incomplete. The writer uses relevant evidence from the text only some of the time.	The writer demonstrates a partial command of grammar, punctuation, and usage conventions. Some distracting errors may be evident, at times creating minor disruptions in the fluency or clarity of the writing.
1	The writer attempts to explain his or her personal connection to the text, but the explanation is not successful. The writer uses little or no relevant evidence from the text.	The writer demonstrates little or no command of grammar, punctuation, and usage conventions. Serious and persistent errors create disruptions in the fluency of the writing and sometimes interfere with meaning.
0	The writer does not provide a relevant response to the prompt or does not provide a response at all.	Serious and persistent errors overwhelm the writing and interfere with the meaning of the response as a whole, making the writer's meaning impossible to understand.

Write

 SCAFFOLDS

Ask students to complete the writing assignment using textual evidence to support their answers.

Use the scaffolds below to differentiate instruction for your **ELL** English Language Learners and **A** Approaching grade-level learners.

ELL **BEGINNING** With the help of the <u>word bank</u>, write a response using <u>paragraph frame 1</u>.

INTERMEDIATE With the help of the <u>word bank</u>, write a response using <u>paragraph frames 1 and 2</u>.

ADVANCED, ADVANCED HIGH Write a response of differentiated length using the <u>sentence starters</u>.

A **APPROACHING** Write a response of differentiated length using the <u>sentence starters</u>.

	BEGINNING INTERMEDIATE		ADVANCED, ADVANCED HIGH APPROACHING
Word Bank	**Paragraph Frame 1**	**Paragraph Frame 2**	**Sentence Starters**
flying a kite grandmother persevere wise follow my dreams	In "Mother to Son," the mother tells her son to ____. I think that this advice is ____. I have received advice from my ____. (He / she) told me to ____. I would use the metaphor of ____ to share this advice with a friend.	When you persevere, you stick to a goal even though ____. In my metaphor, sticking to a goal is represented by ____. The challenges come when ____. If you stick to your goal, ____.	• The mother tells her son to . . . • I think that this advice is . . . because . . . • I have received advice from . . . • (He / she) told me to . . . • To share this advice with a friend, I would use the metaphor of . . . • In this metaphor, . . . would represent . . .

Peer Review

Students should submit substantive feedback to two peers using the review instructions below.

- How well does this response answer the prompt?
- Which of the author's comments inspired you to think differently about the text?
- What did the writer do well in this response? What does the writer need to work on?

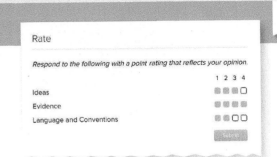

Rate

Respond to the following with a point rating that reflects your opinion.

	1	2	3	4
Ideas	■	■	■	○
Evidence	■	■	■	■
Language and Conventions	■	■	○	○

Submit

 SENTENCE FRAMES

- You were able to (completely / partly / almost) answer the prompt.
- You could answer the prompt more completely by ____.

- I thought differently about the text after reading ____.
- My favorite part of your response is ____.

Learning to Read

POETRY
Frances Ellen Watkins Harper
1854

Introduction

Born a free woman in Baltimore, Frances Ellen Watkins Harper (1825–1911) is known by some as the mother of African American journalism. Harper experienced commercial success as a poet and novelist, and she is credited with establishing the tradition of African American protest poetry. Harper also helped enslaved people escape along the Underground Railroad and was a well-known public speaker and civil rights activist. In the poem "Learning to Read," she animates her real-life experiences talking to newly-freed enslaved people. "Learning to Read" is told from the perspective of a woman who fights to earn her education late in life.

Sixty-year-old Chloe opens this poem by recounting how teachers in the North set up schools in the South, but the Southern masters did not want enslaved people to read because they understood that knowledge would give them power. Nonetheless, the enslaved people were able to learn covertly. The speaker's uncle, Caldwell, hid pages of a book under his hat, and an enslaved person named Ben learned to read by eavesdropping on the master's children while they were taking lessons. When Chloe had an opportunity to learn how to read, people told her that she was too old. Chloe felt like she had no time to waste and wanted to learn how to read the Bible. By the end of the poem, she has learned how to read, and she describes feeling like a queen in her little cabin.

 Proficiency-leveled summaries and summaries in multiple languages are available digitally.

 Audio and audio text highlighting are available with this text.

COMPARING WITHIN AND ACROSS GENRES

In her poem "Learning to Read," poet Frances Ellen Watkins Harper uses biblical allusions and details of life after the Civil War to recount the joys and complications of education. Along with "Mother to Son" and *Narrative of the Life of Frederick Douglass, An American Slave,* students will continue to explore the African American experience through this text.

Access Complex Text

LEXILE: N/A **WORD COUNT:** 258

The following areas may be challenging for students, particularly **ELL** English Language Learners and **A** Approaching grade-level learners.

Prior Knowledge	Specific Vocabulary	Connection of Ideas
• The poem is set in the South during the Civil War. Students may be unfamiliar with the history of slavery in America. It is especially important for students to understand that enslaved people were forbidden from reading by slaveholders.	• Terms related to the Civil War era—such as *Rebs* and *Yankees*—may challenge readers. Remind students to use context clues or a reference work to learn the meaning of unfamiliar terms. • Some dialect or expressions of the time may need explanation.	• Some readers may not immediately connect the poem's allusions to the Bible. Direct students who have trouble explaining the connections among *Bible, hymns,* and *Testament* to a relevant reference source.

 SCAFFOLDS   **ELL ENGLISH LANGUAGE LEARNERS** **A APPROACHING GRADE LEVEL** **B BEYOND GRADE LEVEL**

These icons identify differentiation strategies and scaffolded support for a variety of students. See the digital lesson plan for additional differentiation strategies and scaffolds.

Instructional Path

The print teacher's edition includes essential point-of-use instruction and planning tools. Complete lesson plans and program documents appear in your digital teacher account.

Independent Read: Learning to Read

Objectives: Students will closely read the text in order to participate in a collaborative conversation in response to a prompt and write a reflection on participation in the discussion.

Independent Read

Frances Ellen Watkins Harper

Learning to Read

Introduce the Text

As a class, watch the video preview ▶ and have students read the introduction in pairs to make connections to the video preview.

- What is one prediction you can make about the poem you're going to read?

- How do you think this poem will make you feel?

ELL SENTENCE FRAMES

- I think the text will ____. I think this because ____.
- I predict that there will be ____. I believe this because ____.

Entry Point

As students prepare to read "Learning to Read," share the following information with them to provide context.

✓ Frances Ellen Watkins Harper (1825–1911) was an avid reader, a pioneering writer, and an active abolitionist. She was born free in Baltimore and worked to end slavery by helping enslaved people escape on the Underground Railroad. She also taught at a school, delivered speeches, and wrote articles in anti-slavery newspapers. Harper became known as the "mother of African American journalism."

✓ Before the end of the Civil War, it had been illegal to educate enslaved people in many southern states. After the war, local groups of African Americans and several aid organizations set out to establish schools for learners of all ages in the southern states. However, many white Southerners still resisted efforts to educate people who had been enslaved.

"Knowledge didn't agree with slavery—
'Twould make us all too wise."

NOTES

1 Very soon the **Yankee** teachers
2   Came down and set up school;
3 But, oh! how the **Rebs** did hate it,—
4   It was agin' their rule.

5 Our masters always tried to hide
6   Book learning from our eyes;
7 Knowledge didn't agree with slavery—
8   'Twould make us all too wise.

9 But some of us would try to steal
10   A little from the book.
11 And put the words together,
12   And learn by **hook or crook**.

13 I remember Uncle Caldwell,
14   Who took pot liquor fat
15 And greased the pages of his book,
16   And hid it in his hat.

17 And had his master ever seen
18   The **leaves** upon his head,
19 He'd have thought them greasy papers,
20   But nothing to be read.

21 And there was Mr. Turner's Ben,
22   Who heard the children spell,
23 And picked the words right up by heart,
24   And learned to read 'em well.

25 Well, the Northern folks kept sending
26   The Yankee teachers down;
27 And they stood right up and helped us,
28   Though Rebs did **sneer** and frown.

52 Reading & Writing Companion

V SELECTION VOCABULARY

yankee / yanqui *noun* someone who supported the North during the Civil War COGNATE

reb / el/la confederado/a *noun* someone who supported the Confederacy during the Civil War

ELL
• Who are the Rebs in this stanza?
• Does the speaker describe the Rebs positively or negatively?

Analyze Vocabulary Using Context Clues

As students read the text, ask them to make predictions about each bold vocabulary word based on the context clues in the sentence.

✓ **CHECK FOR SUCCESS**

If students are unable to determine the meaning of one or more bolded vocabulary words, project the Checklist from the Grade 8 Context Clues lesson with the class. After revisiting, guide students as they make predictions about the bold word in line 1 using the following routine:

• Is the word a noun, a verb, an adjective, or an adverb?
• Who are the *Yankees* in this stanza?
• Where are the *Yankees* coming from? Where are they going?

TEXT TALK

Who is this narrator and in what time period does the narrator live?

See lines 1–4: The speaker begins by talking about "Yankee teachers" and "Rebs," so it is the time of the Civil War. The narrator must live in the South.

What inference can you make about the speaker's background in the second stanza?

See lines 5 and 7: The speaker was an enslaved person, since she refers to "masters" and "slavery."

How does Uncle Caldwell hide the pages he reads?

See lines 16–18: He hides them in his hat.

Why is it that formerly enslaved people are learning to read at this time, according to the speaker?

See lines 25–27: The Northerners who won the war are coming down to the South to teach them.

Prepare for Advanced Courses

Use the activity below to differentiate instruction for your B Beyond grade-level learners.

Direct students to reread lines 29–44.

Ask students: What kind of voice does the poet create in the speaker, and how does she do it?

Answers will vary; sample answer: The rhythm of the poem is regular and very strong, and this gives the speaker's voice strength. The speaker describes a journey from her decision to learn to read to getting "a pair of glasses." She then goes "straight to work" and "never stopped" until she could read the Bible. The rhythm and details show her steady determination to succeed.

29 And I longed to read my Bible,
30   For precious words it said;
31 But when I begun to learn it,
32   Folks just shook their heads,

33 And said there is no use trying,
34   Oh! Chloe, you're too late;
35 But as I was rising sixty,
36   I had no time to wait.

37 So I got a pair of glasses,
38   And straight to work I went,
39 And never stopped till I could read
40   The hymns and Testament.[1]

41 Then I got a little cabin
42   A place to call my own—
43 And I felt independent
44   As the queen upon her throne.

Frances Harper (1825–1911), African-American poet, abolitionist, novelist, lecturer, and womens rights advocate

---

1. **Testament** the Christian bible is split into two Testaments, Old and New

WRITE

DISCUSSION: It's often said that "knowledge is power." The speaker of the poem presents the reason enslaved people were not allowed to learn to read: "Knowledge didn't agree with slavery— / 'Twould make us all too wise." Discuss these ideas and your response to the poem.

TEXT TALK

Why do people think it's too late for the speaker to learn to read?

See lines 32–36: She is sixty, so people tell her it is too late for her to learn.

Why did so many Southerners oppose formerly enslaved people learning how to read? What does that tell you about discrimination in the South around the time of the Civil War?

Answers will vary.

V SELECTION VOCABULARY

by hook or crook / como sea *phrase* by any possible way

ELL
- What is done "by hook or crook" in this stanza?
- Is it easy or difficult to do?

leaf / la hoja *noun* page in a book

ELL
- Where are the "leaves" in this stanza?
- How does the master feel about the leaves?

sneer / burlarse *verb* to smile meanly

ELL
- Who is "sneering" in this stanza?
- What makes them sneer?

Reading Comprehension OPTIONAL

Have students complete the digital reading comprehension questions ✅ when they finish reading.

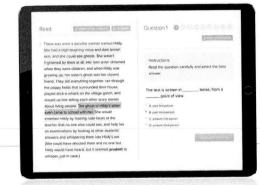

ANSWER KEY

QUESTION 1: C

QUESTION 2: D

QUESTION 3: C

QUESTION 4: D

QUESTION 5:

See chart.

First	Second	Third	Fourth
Uncle Caldwell greases the book pages with fat.	Ben learns to read after listening to children spell words.	The speaker gets a pair of glasses and learns to read the Bible.	The speaker gets a cabin of her own.

Connect and Extend OPTIONAL

CONNECT TO EXTENDED WRITING PROJECT

Students can find inspiration from the poem "Learning to Read" when writing their informational essays. Have students reflect on Frances Ellen Watkins Harper's details about risk-taking and reward.

BEYOND THE BOOK

Analysis: Rap as Modern Day Protest Poetry

Frances Ellen Watkins Harper is credited with establishing the tradition of African American protest poetry. This poetry was designed to shine a light on the struggles and inequalities that African Americans face in society. Similarly, modern day rap continues to emphasize the inequalities among races and in socioeconomic status in America.

Ask students to:

- Select a rap song that they believe is a modern example of protest poetry. [Note: Teachers can provide a list of songs to ensure the language is appropriate.]

- Analyze the lyrics of the song to identify the specific racial and socioeconomic inequalities identified in this song. Think about the following questions:

  > What specific inequalities does the artist identify in this song?

  > What is causing these inequalities?

  > How can these inequalities be corrected?

  > Why do you think this song qualifies as "protest poetry"?

Once students have selected their song and written an analytical paragraph, put them into small groups to discuss the songs they selected and why they believe they are examples of modern day protest poetry. They should use the questions above to guide their conversation.

Collaborative Conversation

Post the writing prompt to generate a discussion in small groups. Ask students to first break down the prompt before they discuss relevant ideas and textual evidence.

It's often said that "knowledge is power." The speaker of the poem presents the reason enslaved people were not allowed to learn to read: "Knowledge didn't agree with slavery— / 'Twould make us all too wise." Discuss these ideas and your response to the poem

Use the scaffolds below to differentiate instruction for your **ELL** English Language Learners and **A** Approaching grade-level learners.

ELL **BEGINNING, INTERMEDIATE** Use the <u>discussion guide</u> and <u>speaking frames</u> to facilitate the discussion with support from the teacher.

ADVANCED, ADVANCED HIGH Use the <u>discussion guide</u> and <u>speaking frames</u> to facilitate the discussion in mixed-level groups.

A APPROACHING Use the <u>discussion guide</u> to facilitate the discussion in mixed-level groups.

APPROACHING
ADVANCED, ADVANCED HIGH
BEGINNING, INTERMEDIATE

Discussion Guide	Speaking Frames
1. Do you think knowledge is power? Why or why not?	• I think knowledge (is / is not) power because ____.
2. Why would being able to read make someone more knowledgeable?	• I think being able to read makes someone more knowledgeable because ____.
3. Why do you think enslaved people were not allowed to read?	• I think enslaved people were not allowed to read because ____.
4. What do you think would be able to happen if enslaved people were allowed to become more knowledgeable?	• If enslaved people were allowed to become more knowledgeable ____.

Review Prompt and Rubric

Before students begin writing, review the writing prompt and rubric with the class.

REFLECTION: As you write, make sure to

- evaluate how well everyone followed the rules when making decisions affecting the group
- evaluate your own participation in the discussion
- reflect on how well you posed questions that connected the ideas of several speakers and responded to others' questions and comments with relevant evidence, observations, and ideas

PROMPT GUIDE

- What does "knowledge is power" mean?
- Where do you see the idea of knowledge in the poem? Where do you see the idea of power in the poem?

- What did the poem make you feel about knowledge and power?

Score	Reflection	Language and Conventions
4	The writer clearly reflects on how well he or she posed questions that connected the ideas of several speakers and responded to others' questions and comments, and also clearly reflects on his or her own participation. The writer consistently refers to specific examples from the discussion.	The writer demonstrates a consistent command of grammar, punctuation, and usage conventions. Although minor errors may be evident, they do not detract from the fluency or the clarity of the writing.
3	The writer reflects on how well he or she posed questions that connected the ideas of several speakers and responded to others' questions and comments, and also reflects on his or her own participation. The writer refers to specific examples from the discussion most of the time.	The writer demonstrates an adequate command of grammar, punctuation, and usage conventions. Although some errors may be evident, they create few (if any) disruptions in the fluency or clarity of the writing.
2	The writer begins to reflect on how well he or she posed questions that connected the ideas of several speakers and responded to others' questions and comments, and also begins to reflect on his or her own participation. The writer refers to specific examples from the discussion some of the time.	The writer demonstrates a partial command of grammar, punctuation, and usage conventions. Some distracting errors may be evident, at times creating minor disruptions in the fluency or clarity of the writing.
1	The writer attempts to reflect on how well he or she posed questions that connected the ideas of several speakers and responded to others' questions and comments, and also attempts to reflect on as well as his or her own participation. The writer refers to few, if any examples from the discussion.	The writer demonstrates little or no command of grammar, punctuation, and usage conventions. Serious and persistent errors create disruptions in the fluency of the writing and sometimes interfere with meaning.
0	The writer does not provide a relevant response to the prompt or does not provide a response at all.	Serious and persistent errors overwhelm the writing and interfere with the meaning of the response as a whole, making the writer's meaning impossible to understand.

Write

Ask students to complete the writing assignment using textual evidence to support their answers.

Use the scaffolds below to differentiate instruction for your **ELL** English Language Learners and **A** Approaching grade–level learners.

ELL **BEGINNING** With the help of the <u>word bank</u>, write a response using <u>paragraph frame 1</u>.

INTERMEDIATE With the help of the <u>word bank</u>, write a response using <u>paragraph frames 1 and 2</u>.

ADVANCED, ADVANCED HIGH Write a response of differentiated length using the <u>sentence starters</u>.

A **APPROACHING** Write a response of differentiated length using the <u>sentence starters</u>.

BEGINNING / INTERMEDIATE			ADVANCED, ADVANCED HIGH / APPROACHING
Word Bank	**Paragraph Frame 1**	**Paragraph Frame 2**	**Sentence Starters**
knowledge average slavery good gain freedom reading power	My discussion group talked about ____. I think my group did a(n) ____ job connecting to each other's ideas. I think this because ____. I added to the discussion by ____.	One person said that reading helps people ____ knowledge, and another person said people with knowledge have ____. I asked "what would happen if ____ people had more power?" This led to our group to talking about enslaved people fighting for their ____ with their new power.	• My discussion group talked about . . . • I think my group did a(n) . . . job . . . • I added to the discussion by . . . • One person said . . . • Another person said . . . • This led to our group to talking about . . .

Peer Review

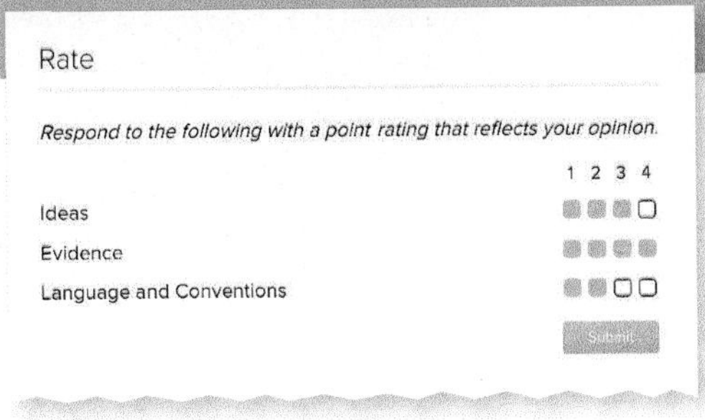

Students should submit substantive feedback to two peers using the review instructions below.

- How well does the writer refer to specific examples from the discussion?
- What does the writer do well in this reflection? What does the writer need to work on?

Rate

Respond to the following with a point rating that reflects your opinion.

	1	2	3	4
Ideas	■	■	■	○
Evidence	■	■	■	■
Language and Conventions	■	■	○	○

Submit

ELL

SENTENCE FRAMES

A
- The writer does a ___ job referring to specific examples from the discussion.

- The writer does ___ well in this reflection.
- The writer need to work on ___.

Narrative of the Life of Frederick Douglass, An American Slave

INFORMATIONAL TEXT
Frederick Douglass
1845

Introduction

Published in 1845, *Narrative of the Life of Frederick Douglass, An American Slave* describes Douglass's journey from slavery to freedom. This great American orator provides a factual account of his struggle to educate and free himself and others from the oppression of his times. The memoir's vivid descriptions of life as an enslaved person played a key role in fueling the abolitionist movement in the North prior to the Civil War. In the following excerpt from the middle of the text, Douglass overcomes the odds against him, procuring the assistance of others in teaching himself to read despite laws prohibiting slaves from learning such skills.

In this excerpt from Frederick Douglass's autobiography, he recounts how he struggled to learn to read and write while he was enslaved. While living with Master Hugh, the master's mistress started to teach Douglass how to read, but then she took on the views of her husband—it was dangerous for slaves to have access to knowledge—and she stopped. Douglass found willing teachers in the white children he would encounter around the neighborhood. When he was sent on errands, Douglass would trade bread in return for reading lessons. At 12 years old, Douglass found a life-changing book that depicted a conversation between an enslaved man and his master, in which the enslaved man convinced the master to set him free. Douglass explained that this book gave voice to feelings that he did not know how to express.

 Proficiency-leveled summaries and summaries in multiple languages are available digitally.

 Audio and audio text highlighting are available with this text.

COMPARING WITHIN AND ACROSS GENRES

 In the powerful memoir *Narrative of the Life of Frederick Douglass, An American Slave*, Douglass recounts how he came to learn to read and write, the risks involved, and the powerful impact this learning had on his life.

Access Complex Text

LEXILE: 1010L   **WORD COUNT:** 945

The following areas may be challenging for students, particularly **ELL** English Language Learners and **A** Approaching grade-level learners.

Prior Knowledge	Sentence Structure	Genre
• Frederick Douglass was born into slavery around 1820. He escaped and became a notable writer and abolitionist. • Douglass alludes to the speeches of Richard Brinsley Sheridan, who argued for the freedom of the Irish from British rule.	• The language in the selection is complex. Douglass uses long sentences with many clauses. Students may benefit from breaking these long sentences into smaller parts.	• *Narrative of the Life of Frederick Douglass, An American Slave* is a memoir that tells of the author's experiences. Remind students that the selection is part of a longer work. • Douglass uses first-person point of view to tell his story.

SCAFFOLDS   **ENGLISH LANGUAGE LEARNERS**   **A** **APPROACHING GRADE LEVEL**   **BEYOND GRADE LEVEL**

These icons identify differentiation strategies and scaffolded support for a variety of students. See the digital lesson plan for additional differentiation strategies and scaffolds.

Instructional Path

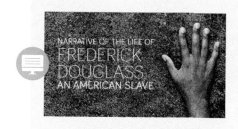

First Read: Narrative of the Life of Frederick Douglass

Objectives: After an initial reading and discussion of the excerpt, students will be able to identify and restate the text's key ideas and details.

Skill: Informational Text Elements

Objectives: After rereading and discussing a model of close reading, students will be able to analyze how an author makes connections between individuals, events, and ideas through various informational text elements.

Skill: Figurative Language

Objectives: After rereading and discussing a model of close reading, students will be able to determine the meaning of figures of speech in a text.

Close Read: Narrative of the Life of Frederick Douglass

Objectives: After engaging in a close reading and discussion of the text, students will be able to analyze informational text elements and figurative language in a short, written response.

Progress Monitoring

Opportunities to Learn	Opportunities to Demonstrate Learning	Opportunities to Reteach
Informational Text Elements		
⚙ Skill: Informational Text Elements	⚙ Skill: Informational Text Elements • Your Turn 🗐 Close Read • Skills Focus • Write	⚙ Unit 5 Skill: Informational Text Elements - Parallel Journeys ⚙ Unit 5 Skill: Informational Text Elements - Long Walk to Freedom ⚙ Spotlight Skill: Informational Text Elements
Figurative Language		
⚙ Skill: Figurative Language	⚙ Skill: Figurative Language • Your Turn 🗐 Close Read • Complete Vocabulary Chart • Skills Focus • Write	⚙ Spotlight Skill: Figurative Language

First Read

Frederick Douglass

Narrative of the Life of Frederick Dou...

Introduce the Text

As a class, watch the video preview ▶ and have students read the introduction in pairs to make connections to the video preview.

To activate prior knowledge and experiences, ask students:

- How does the information in this video connect to what you already know?

- Why do you think it's important to learn about this person?

ELL SPEAKING FRAMES

- The ____ in the video makes me think ____.
- The video shows ____. This makes me wonder ____.
- I think the text will ____. I think this because ____.
- I predict that there will be ____. I believe this because ____.

Entry Point

As students prepare to read *Narrative of the Life of Frederick Douglass*, share the following information with them to provide context.

✓ Frederick Douglass (1818–1895) was an abolitionist and U.S. diplomat. He was originally named "Frederick Augustus Washington Bailey," and he was born into slavery in Tuckahoe, Maryland. He secretly managed to learn to read and write, even though it was illegal for him to be educated at the time. He then escaped from slavery, changed his last name, and became a leading abolitionist. Douglass was famous for his exceptional writing and speaking skills.

✓ Douglass first published *Narrative of the Life of Frederick Douglass, An American Slave* in 1845. It was one of Douglass's responses to anyone who doubted that such an eloquent speaker could have been enslaved. The book was widely read in the United States and Europe.

"The silver trump of freedom had roused my soul to eternal wakefulness."

from Chapter VII

1   I lived in Master Hugh's family about seven years. During this time, I succeeded in learning to read and write. In accomplishing this, I was compelled to resort to various stratagems.[1] I had no regular teacher. My mistress, who had kindly commenced to instruct me, had, in compliance with the advice and direction of her husband, not only ceased to instruct, but had set her face against my being instructed by any one else. It is due, however, to my mistress to say of her, that she did not adopt this course of treatment immediately. She at first lacked the depravity indispensable to shutting me up in mental darkness. It was at least necessary for her to have some training in the exercise of irresponsible power, to make her equal to the task of treating me as though I were a brute.

2   My mistress was, as I have said, a kind and tender-hearted woman; and in the simplicity of her soul she commenced, when I first went to live with her, to treat me as she supposed one human being ought to treat another. In entering upon the duties of a slaveholder, she did not seem to perceive that I sustained to her the relation of a mere chattel, and that for her to treat me as a human being was not only wrong, but dangerously so. Slavery proved as injurious to her as it did to me. When I went there, she was a pious, warm, and tender-hearted woman. There was no sorrow or suffering for which she had not a tear. She had bread for the hungry, clothes for the naked, and comfort for every mourner that came within her reach. Slavery soon proved its ability to divest her of these heavenly qualities. Under its influence, the tender heart became stone, and the lamblike disposition gave way to one of tiger-like fierceness. The first step in her downward course was in her ceasing to instruct me. She now commenced to practise her husband's precepts. She finally became even more violent in her opposition than her husband himself. She was not satisfied with simply doing as well as he had commanded; she seemed anxious to do better. Nothing seemed to make her more angry than to see me with a newspaper. She seemed to think that here lay the danger. I have had her rush at me with a face made all up of fury, and snatch from me a newspaper, in a manner that fully revealed her apprehension. She was an

Skill: Figurative Language

A lamb and a tiger remind me of the lamb and the lion in the Bible. The allusion continues as Douglass describes how his mistress changes from having kind and generous qualities to having a hardened heart and the fierceness of a tiger.

1. **stratagems** plans or strategies

Reading & Writing Companion   **55**

Analyze Vocabulary Using Context Clues

In paragraph 4, focus on the sentence that uses the word *bestow*. Point out these context clues:

1.   First, I notice that the word *bestow* follows the helping verb phrase "used to." That tells me that *bestow* is a verb.

2.   When I read the sentence again, I notice the verb *give*. I think this is a synonym. I read the sentence again using the word *give* in place of *bestow*.

3.   It fits within the context of the sentence, in which Douglass describes how he and the children gave each other help.

Figurative Language

What does the reader notice about the way that the mistress is described?

The reader notices that she is described as turning from a lamb to a tiger, which the reminds the reader of an allusion to lions and lambs in the Bible.

TEXT TALK

How did Douglass's mistress treat him?

See paragraphs 1 and 2: At first, she treated him well and began to teach him to read, but later, she was unkind and prevented him from learning.

Informational Text Elements

How does the reader identify the connections between the individuals in paragraph 2 and paragraph 4?

The reader explains that Douglass's mistress and the white boys are all key figures in his quest for knowledge.

Skills Focus

QUESTION 2: Central or Main Idea

Douglass points out how unfair it is that he has to be enslaved for life when the other boys would be "free" when they grew up. This textual evidence develops Douglass's thesis that slavery was an extremely unfair system.

TEXT TALK

How did Douglass continue learning to read on his own?

See paragraph 4: Douglass continued learning to read by trading bread to poor white boys in exchange for lessons.

Narrative of the Life of Frederick Douglass, An American Slave

NOTES

apt woman; and a little experience soon demonstrated, to her satisfaction, that education and slavery were incompatible with each other.

3   From this time I was most narrowly watched. If I was in a separate room any considerable length of time, I was sure to be suspected of having a book, and was at once called to give an account of myself. All this, however, was too late. The first step had been taken. Mistress, in teaching me the alphabet, had given me the *inch*, and no precaution could prevent me from taking the ell.[2]

○ 4   The plan which I adopted, and the one by which I was most successful, was that of making friends of all the little white boys whom I met in the street. As many of these as I could, I converted into teachers. With their kindly aid, obtained at different times and in different places, I finally succeeded in learning to read. When I was sent of errands, I always took my book with me, and by going one part of my errand quickly, I found time to get a lesson before my return. I used also to carry bread with me, enough of which was always in the house, and to which I was always welcome; for I was much better off in this regard than many of the poor white children in our neighborhood. This bread I used to **bestow** upon the hungry little urchins, who, in return, would give me that more valuable bread of knowledge. I am strongly tempted to give the names of two or three of those little boys, as a testimonial of the gratitude and affection I bear them; but **prudence** forbids;— not that it would injure me, but it might embarrass them; for it is almost an unpardonable offence to teach slaves to read in this Christian country. It is enough to say of the dear little fellows, that they lived on Philpot Street, very near Durgin and Bailey's ship-yard. I used to talk this matter of slavery over with them. I would sometimes say to them, I wished I could be as free as they would be when they got to be men. "You will be free as soon as you are twenty-one, but I am a slave for life! Have not I as good a right to be free as you have?" These words used to trouble them; they would express for me the liveliest sympathy, and **console** me with the hope that something would occur by which I might be free.

Skill: Informational Text Elements

Earlier in the text, Douglass's mistress refused to teach him anymore, so he had to find another way to learn to read. The mistress became cruel, but these white boys are helpful. The white boys and the mistress are connected because they are key to Douglass's ability to read.

5   I was now about twelve years old, and the thought of being a slave for life began to **bear** heavily upon my heart. Just about this time, I got hold of a book entitled "The Columbian Orator." Every opportunity I got, I used to read this book. Among much of other interesting matter, I found in it a dialogue between a master and his slave. The slave was represented as having run away from his master three times. The dialogue represented the conversation which took place between them, when the slave was retaken the third time. In this dialogue, the whole argument in behalf of slavery was brought forward by the master, all of which was disposed of by the slave. The slave was made to say some very smart as well as impressive things in reply to his

---

2. *ell* (archaic) a six hand-width measurement used in textile-making

---

SELECTION VOCABULARY

bestow / otorgar **verb** to give

prudence / la prudencia **noun** good judgment that helps a person avoid problems COGNATE

ELL • What does "prudence" forbid Douglass from doing?
• Would the consequences of that action be positive or negative?

console / consolar **verb** to comfort COGNATE

ELL • How does the word *sympathy* give a clue about *console*?
• How does the word *hope* give a clue about *console*?

bear / pesar **verb** to be oppressive, to weigh down

ELL • How does Douglass feel in this part of the text?
• What nearby word describes *bear*? Is it positive or negative?

NOTES

master—things which had the desired though unexpected effect; for the conversation resulted in the voluntary emancipation of the slave on the part of the master.

6   In the same book, I met with one of Sheridan's mighty speeches on and in behalf of Catholic emancipation. These were choice documents to me. I read them over and over again with unabated interest. They gave tongue to interesting thoughts of my own soul, which had frequently flashed through my mind, and died away for want of utterance. The moral which I gained from the dialogue was the power of truth over the conscience of even a slaveholder. What I got from Sheridan was a bold denunciation of slavery, and a powerful vindication of human rights.

7   The reading of these documents enabled me to utter my thoughts, and to meet the arguments brought forward to sustain slavery; but while they relieved me of one difficulty, they brought on another even more painful than the one of which I was relieved. The more I read, the more I was led to abhor and detest my enslavers. I could regard them in no other light than a band of successful robbers, who had left their homes, and gone to Africa, and stolen us from our homes, and in a strange land reduced us to slavery. I loathed them as being the meanest as well as the most wicked of men. As I read and contemplated the subject, behold! that very discontentment which Master Hugh had predicted would follow my learning to read had already come, to torment and sting my soul to unutterable **anguish.** As I writhed under it, I would at times feel that learning to read had been a curse rather than a blessing. It had given me a view of my wretched condition, without the remedy. It opened my eyes to the horrible pit, but to no ladder upon which to get out. In moments of agony, I envied my fellow-slaves for their stupidity. I have often wished myself a beast. I preferred the condition of the meanest reptile to my own. Any thing, no matter what, to get rid of thinking! It was this everlasting thinking of my condition that tormented me. There was no getting rid of it. It was pressed upon me by every object within sight or hearing, animate or inanimate. The silver trump of freedom had roused my soul to eternal wakefulness. Freedom now appeared, to disappear no more forever. It was heard in every sound, and seen in every thing. It was ever present to torment me with a sense of my wretched condition. I saw nothing without seeing it, I heard nothing without hearing it, and felt nothing without feeling it. It looked from every star, it smiled in every calm, breathed in every wind, and moved in every storm.

8   I often found myself regretting my own existence, and wishing myself dead; and but for the hope of being free, I have no doubt but that I should have killed myself, or done something for which I should have been killed. While in this state of mind, I was eager to hear any one speak of slavery. I was a ready listener. Every little while, I could hear something about the abolitionists. It

Reading & Writing Companion   57

Skills Focus

QUESTION 4: Figurative Language

Douglass uses this metaphor to express his feelings about being enslaved and not knowing how to free himself. This comparison shows that he feels trapped and that he wants to gain his freedom. This helps me understand why he is so committed to learning. He sees it as a tool to gain his freedom.

Skills Focus

QUESTION 3: Informational Text Elements

A problem that Douglass has is that knowing about freedom while being enslaved makes him feel depressed. He talks about his depression just before introducing the abolitionists, which signifies that they are important to the "hope of being free."

TEXT TALK

What did Douglass learn about that gave him hope?

See paragraph 8: Douglass felt hopeful after learning about abolition and abolitionists.

What did the Irishmen tell Douglass to do?

See paragraph 8: The Irishmen told Douglass that he should escape to the North.

SELECTION VOCABULARY

anguish / la angustia **noun** severe suffering or distress   COGNATE

ELL
• How do the words *sting* and *torment* give clues about *anguish*?
• What other nearby words describe *anguish*? Are they positive or negative?

Prepare for Advanced Courses

Use the activity below to differentiate instruction for your **B** Beyond grade-level learners.

Look at the word *abolition* in paragraph 8.

"...it was spoken of as the fruit of abolition. *Hearing the word in this connection very often, I set about learning what it meant. The dictionary afforded me little or no help. I found it was "the act of abolishing;" but then I did not know what was to be abolished."*

Ask students to examine the word abolition. An abolitionist is someone who wanted to end slavery. The Latin root *abolere* means "destroy." Have students discuss the meaning and transformation of the word. Ask students: How does Douglass feel about the use of the word *abolition*? Do you think he would feel differently had he known the meaning?

NOTES

American orator, editor, author, abolitionist, and former enslaved person Frederick Douglass (1818–1895) edits a journal at his desk, late 1870s.

was some time before I found what the word meant. It was always used in such connections as to make it an interesting word to me. If a slave ran away and succeeded in getting clear, or if a slave killed his master, set fire to a barn, or did any thing very wrong in the mind of a slaveholder, it was spoken of as the fruit of *abolition.* Hearing the word in this connection very often, I set about learning what it meant. The dictionary afforded me little or no help. I found it was "the act of abolishing;" but then I did not know what was to be abolished. Here I was perplexed. I did not dare to ask any one about its meaning, for I was satisfied that it was something they wanted me to know very little about. After a patient waiting, I got one of our city papers, containing an account of the number of petitions from the north, praying for the abolition of slavery in the District of Columbia, and of the slave trade between the States. From this time I understood the words *abolition* and *abolitionist,* and always drew near when that word was spoken, expecting to hear something of importance to myself and fellow-slaves. The light broke in upon me by degrees. I went one day down on the wharf of Mr. Waters; and seeing two Irishmen unloading a scow of stone, I went, unasked, and helped them. When we had finished, one of them came to me and asked me if I were a slave. I told him I was. He asked, "Are ye a slave for life?" I told him that I was. The good Irishman seemed to be deeply affected by the statement. He said to the other that it was a pity so fine a little fellow as myself should be a slave for life. He said it was a shame to hold me. They both advised me to run away to the north; that I should find friends there, and that I should be free. I pretended not to be interested in what they said, and treated them as if I did not understand them; for I feared they might be treacherous. White men have been known to encourage slaves to escape, and then, to get the reward, catch them and return them to their masters. I was afraid that these seemingly good men might use me so; but I nevertheless remembered their advice, and from that time I resolved to run away. I looked forward to a time at which it would be safe for me to escape. I was too young to think of doing so immediately; besides, I wished to learn how to write, as I might have occasion to write my own pass. I consoled myself with the hope that I should one day find a good chance. Meanwhile, I would learn to write.

9   The idea as to how I might learn to write was suggested to me by being in Durgin and Bailey's ship-yard, and frequently seeing the ship carpenters, after hewing, and getting a piece of timber ready for use, write on the timber the name of that part of the ship for which it was intended. When a piece of timber was intended for the larboard side, it would be marked thus—"L."

🖳 TEXT TALK

How did Douglass learn to write his first letters?

See paragraph 9: Douglass copied letters he saw on timber that was labeled to show what part of a ship it would form.

B Ask each Beyond grade-level student to write one additional discussion question. Then have one or two students facilitate a discussion, using their questions to guide the conversation.

NOTES

When a piece was for the starboard side, it would be marked thus—"S." A piece for the larboard side forward, would be marked thus—"L. F." When a piece was for starboard side forward, it would be marked thus—"S. F." For larboard aft, it would be marked thus—"L. A." For starboard aft, it would be marked thus—"S. A." I soon learned the names of these letters, and for what they were intended when placed upon a piece of timber in the ship-yard. I immediately commenced copying them, and in a short time was able to make the four letters named. After that, when I met with any boy who I knew could write, I would tell him I could write as well as he. The next word would be, "I don't believe you. Let me see you try it." I would then make the letters which I had been so fortunate as to learn, and ask him to beat that. In this way I got a good many lessons in writing, which it is quite possible I should never have gotten in any other way. During this time, my copy-book was the board fence, brick wall, and pavement; my pen and ink was a lump of chalk. With these, I learned mainly how to write. I then commenced and continued copying the Italics in Webster's Spelling Book, until I could make them all without looking on the book. By this time, my little Master Thomas had gone to school, and learned how to write, and had written over a number of copy-books. These had been brought home, and shown to some of our near neighbors, and then laid aside. My mistress used to go to class meeting at the Wilk Street meetinghouse every Monday afternoon, and leave me to take care of the house. When left thus, I used to spend the time in writing in the spaces left in Master Thomas's copy-book, copying what he had written. I continued to do this until I could write a hand very similar to that of Master Thomas. Thus, after a long, tedious effort for years, I finally succeeded in learning how to write.

TEXT TALK

How does Douglass's journey to learning how to read and write reflect the abolition movement and purpose?

Answers will vary.

Think Questions

Circulate as students answer Think Questions independently. Scaffolds for these questions are shown on the opposite page.

QUESTION 1: Textual Evidence

Douglass believed that learning to read would be a valuable skill. He calls reading "that more valuable bread of knowledge." Reading helped Douglass convey his own ideas and argue against slavery.

QUESTION 2: Textual Evidence

Douglass was briefly instructed by his mistress, who was the wife of a slave owner. Later, when she stopped helping him, he traded bread with little white boys in exchange for knowledge. In *The Columbian Orator*, Douglass read a dialogue between a master and an enslaved person and a speech by Sheridan in favor of Catholic emancipation. These related to Douglass's own life because he was enslaved and wanted freedom. He found both texts to be inspirational because they reflected thoughts he'd already had about his condition. He says, "They gave tongue to interesting thoughts of my own soul, which had frequently flashed through my mind, and died away for want of utterance."

QUESTION 3: Textual Evidence

As he read more about slavery, Douglass thought more about his terrible condition and felt tortured by not having a way to change it. He says, "It had given me a view of my wretched condition, without the remedy. It opened my eyes to the horrible pit, but to no ladder upon which to get out."

QUESTION 4: Context Clues

I think *console* must mean "to comfort." The word is used to describe the ideas that would make Douglass feel hopeful that he might gain his freedom someday.

QUESTION 5: Word Meaning

Definition d most closely matches the meaning of the word *bear* in paragraph 5. Douglass describes a heavy feeling on his heart, so *bear* must mean "to weigh on or burden."

First Read

Read *Narrative of the Life of Frederick Douglass, An American Slave.* After you read, complete the Think Questions below.

☁ THINK QUESTIONS

1. Identify evidence from the excerpt that reveals why learning to read was so important to Frederick Douglass when he was a boy.

2. How did Douglass learn to read? Describe how he was affected by the texts he read.

3. Over time, Douglass begins to think that "learning to read had been a curse rather than a blessing." Why does he come to feel this way? Explain, citing evidence from the excerpt.

4. Based on context clues, what is the meaning of the word **console** as it is used in paragraph 4? Write your best definition of *console* here, explaining how you figured it out.

5. Read the following dictionary entry:

   bear
   bear \ber\ *verb*

   a. to carry
   b. to bring forth or produce
   c. to endure
   d. to weigh on or burden

   Which definition most closely matches the meaning of **bear** as it is used in paragraph 5? Write the correct definition of *bear* here and explain how you figured out the correct meaning.

SCAFFOLDS

Think Questions

Use the scaffolds below to differentiate instruction for your **ELL** English Language Learners and **A** Approaching grade-level learners.

ELL **BEGINNING** Write a response using the <u>word bank</u> and <u>sentence frames</u>.

INTERMEDIATE Write a response using the <u>sentence frames</u>.

ADVANCED, ADVANCED HIGH Write a response using the <u>Text-Dependent Question Guide</u>.

A **APPROACHING** Write a response using the <u>Text-Dependent Question Guide</u>.

| | INTERMEDIATE | APPROACHING |
| BEGINNING | | ADVANCED, ADVANCED HIGH |

Word Bank	Sentence Frames	Text-Dependent Question Guide
terrible freedom valuable comfort slavery escape hopeful upset thoughts trades	Douglass thought that learning how to read would be a ____ skill. Reading helped Douglass express his own ideas and make an argument against ____.	1. • What descriptive words and phrases does Douglass use to describe reading? • How did reading help Douglass?
	Douglass ____ bread with white boys. The dialogue and the speech in *The Columbian Orator* are both about the value of ____. Reading these texts made Douglass feel inspired because they reflected his own ____ about his condition as an enslaved person.	2. • Who does Douglass trade bread with? What does he get in return? • What ideas are in the dialogue and speech Douglass reads? • How do those ideas relate to Douglass?
	As he learned more, Douglass thought more about how ____ his condition was. It made him feel ____ because he doubted that he would ever be able to ____.	3. • How does reading expand Douglass's perspective on slavery? • How do Douglass's feelings change as his perspective changes? • Why does he feel this way?
	The words made Douglass feel ____. This gives me a clue that *console* means "to ____."	4. • Read: "'You will be free as soon as you are twenty-one, but I am a slave for life! Have not I as good a right to be free as you have?' These words used to trouble them; they would express for me the liveliest sympathy, and **console** me with the hope that something would occur by which I might be free." • What feelings are being described in this paragraph? • What does that tell me about the meaning of the word *console*?
	Bear as used in the text matches definition ____.	5. • Read: "I was now about twelve years old, and the thought of being a slave for life began to **bear** heavily upon my heart." • Does *bear* refer to carrying something? (#1) • Does *bear* refer to producing something? (#2) • Does *bear* refer to enduring? (#3) • Does *bear* refer to weighing on something? (#4)

Reading Comprehension OPTIONAL

Have students complete the digital reading comprehension questions ✅ when they finish reading.

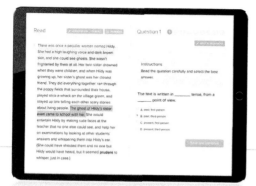

ANSWER KEY

QUESTION 1: B   QUESTION 5: C   QUESTION 9:
QUESTION 2: C   QUESTION 6: A   *See first chart.*
QUESTION 3: D   QUESTION 7: B   QUESTION 10:
QUESTION 4: A   QUESTION 8: C   *See second chart.*

Effect Reading Had on Him	Not an Effect from Reading
Obsessed with the idea of freedom	Developed a deeper affection for his owner
Felt tortured by the idea of being stuck as an enslaved person	Got whipped for taking bread in exchange for his lessons
Took a book with him whenever he went out on an errand	Refused to share his feelings on slavery with the white children who lived near him

Definition	Word
to give or confer something formally	bestow
to weigh or impact	bear
intense suffering or pain	anguish
to comfort at a difficult time	console
good judgment	prudence

Connect and Extend OPTIONAL

CONNECT TO EXTENDED WRITING PROJECT

Students can use *Narrative of the Life of Frederick Douglass, An American Slave* as a resource when writing their informational essays. Have students analyze the impact of Douglass's personal risk.

BEYOND THE BOOK

Writing: Changing the Face of American Currency

Imagine that the United States Treasury is planning to change the face on the $20 bill. Students will need to write an argumentative paragraph making a strong case for putting Frederick Douglass on the American bill.

Ask students to:

- Research Frederick Douglass's life and achievements to gather relevant information to use in their argumentative paragraph.

- Write a clear claim stating why they believe Frederick Douglass should appear on the $20 bill, and support that claim with credible evidence collected during their research and thoughtful analysis.

- Include citations for all of the resources they included in their paragraph.

Pair up students so they can provide one another with peer edits on their paragraphs.

To reflect, ask students:

- How would changing the faces that appear on our currency impact our national identity?

- What do the images on our currency reveal about our country and its history?

Skill:
Informational Text Elements

sync•skills

Use the Checklist to analyze Informational Text Elements in *Narrative of the Life of Frederick Douglass, An American Slave*. Refer to the sample student annotations about Informational Text Elements in the text.

••• CHECKLIST FOR INFORMATIONAL TEXT ELEMENTS

In order to determine how a text makes connections among and distinctions between individuals, ideas, or events, note the following:

- ✓ key details in the text that describe or explain important ideas, events, or individuals

- ✓ connections as well as distinctions between different individuals, ideas, and events, such as:

  - • particular characteristics
  - • shared experiences
  - • similar or different ideas
  - • important conversations

- ✓ analogies the author uses to determine the similarities between two pieces of information (e.g., a heart and a pump)

- ✓ comparisons the author makes between individuals, ideas, or events

To analyze how a text makes connections among and distinctions between individuals, ideas, or events, consider the following questions:

- ✓ What kinds of connections and distinctions does the author make in the text?

- ✓ Does the author include any analogies or comparisons? What do they add to the text?

- ✓ What other features, if any, help readers to analyze the events, ideas, or individuals in the text?

Reading & Writing Companion 61

Skill: Informational Text Elements

Introduce the Skill

Watch the Concept Definition video and read the following definition with your students.

An **informational text** presents readers with information or ideas about real people, places, things, and events. To present information clearly, writers use a common set of **informational text elements**, or features, that link key individuals, events, and ideas. Some examples of informational text include biographies, diaries, interviews, articles, letters, editorials, essays, and speeches. Many of these texts will include **supporting evidence**, or any relevant fact that an author includes to support his or her ideas, as well as **pertinent examples**. These examples have a logical connection to a subject, such as discussing the Gettysburg Address in an article on Civil War battles. To identify informational text elements, readers should look for key details in the text, as well as any photographs, charts, or maps the author includes, and analyze the connections and relationships among them. Analyzing the elements of an informational text helps the reader understand how they work together to support a central idea.

TURN AND TALK

1. What is the last nonfiction text you read?

2. How did the author make connections between the events or individuals?

ELL **SPEAKING FRAMES**
- The last nonfiction text I read was ___. It was about ___.
- The author made connections between the events and the individuals by ___.

V **SKILL VOCABULARY**

informational text / el texto informativo *noun* nonfiction writing that presents information about real people, places, things, and events COGNATE

informational text elements / los elementos del texto informativo *noun* characteristics of informational texts COGNATE

supporting evidence / la evidencia de apoyo *noun* textual evidence, descriptions, examples, reasons, expert opinions, facts, and statistics that further explain key aspects of the controlling idea

Your Turn

Ask students to complete the Your Turn activity.

QUESTION 1

A. Incorrect. While Douglass did enjoy reading and often read this book, this is not the strongest answer.

B. Incorrect. While Douglass wanted to be free, nothing in this paragraph indicates that reading helped him feel free.

C. Correct. Douglass's position weighed "heavily upon [his] heart," and this text presented the story of an enslaved person whose master emancipated him.

D. Incorrect. The enslaved person in the text is made free.

QUESTION 2

A. Incorrect. This detail introduces the part of the book that affected Douglass.

B. Incorrect. This detail shows that Douglass enjoyed the book, but not why it was important.

C. Incorrect. This detail does show why the book was important, but it is not the strongest answer.

D. Correct. This detail explicitly states why the book was so important to Douglass.

QUESTION 3

A. Incorrect. This answer is true but does not address the realization Douglass presents in paragraph 6.

B. Correct. Douglass makes the connection between the way the enslaved person in the story uses dialogue to get his master to set him free and the ways that Douglass could gain his own freedom.

C. Incorrect. This answer is not supported by the details in the text.

D. Incorrect. This answer is true but does not address the realization Douglass presents in paragraph 5.

Narrative of the Life of Frederick Douglass, An American Slave

Skill:
Informational Text Elements

Reread paragraphs 5 and 6 of *Narrative of the Life of Frederick Douglass, An American Slave*. Then, using the Checklist on the previous page, answer the multiple-choice questions below.

↻ YOUR TURN

1. According to the information in paragraph 5, why was discovering the *The Columbian Orator* important to Douglass?

   ○ A. Douglass enjoyed reading and could read this book often.
   ○ B. Douglass wanted to be free, and reading helped him feel free.
   ○ C. Douglass felt that he would always be an enslaved person, but this text gave him hope.
   ○ D. Douglass felt that he would always be an enslaved person, and this text presented a similar fate for another enslaved person.

2. Which detail from paragraph 6 best supports the idea that discovering *The Columbian Orator* was a key event in Douglass's life?

   ○ A. "In the same book, I met with one of Sheridan's mighty speeches on and in behalf of Catholic emancipation."
   ○ B. "These were choice documents to me. I read them over and over again with unabated interest."
   ○ C. "They gave tongue to interesting thoughts of my own soul, which had frequently flashed through my mind, and died away for want of utterance."
   ○ D. "What I got from Sheridan was a bold denunciation of slavery, and a powerful vindication of human rights."

3. What connection does Douglass make between the ideas in the *The Columbian Orator* and his own situation?

   ○ A. Douglass realizes that he is just like the enslaved person in the book.
   ○ B. Douglass realizes that like the enslaved person in the book, he could use the power of the truth to gain his own freedom.
   ○ C. Douglass realizes that he is like the enslaved person in the book, but he will never be free.
   ○ D. Douglass realizes that human rights are important.

Skill:
Figurative Language

sync•skills

Use the Checklist to analyze Figurative Language in *Narrative of the Life of Frederick Douglass, An American Slave*. Refer to the sample student annotations about Figurative Language in the text.

••• CHECKLIST FOR FIGURATIVE LANGUAGE

To determine the meanings of figures of speech in a text, note the following:

✓ words that mean one thing literally and suggest something else

✓ similes, such as "strong as an ox"

✓ metaphors, such as "her eyes were stars"

✓ allusions, or indirect references to people, texts, events, or ideas, such as

- saying of a setting, "the place was a Garden of Eden" (biblical allusion)
- saying of a character whose snooping caused problems, "he opened a Pandora's box" (allusion to mythology)
- calling someone who likes romance "a real Romeo" (allusion to Shakespeare)

✓ verbal irony, or people saying one thing and meaning another, such as

- referring to a stormy day as "beautiful weather"
- a character saying how happy he is to be somewhere when he is not

✓ analogies, or comparisons of two unlike things based on a specific similarity and used for clarification, such as

- remarking, "Life is like a ball game; anybody can have a losing day."
- in Shakespeare's Sonnet 18, "Shall I compare thee to a summer's day? / Thou art more lovely and more temperate."

✓ other language in the text used in a nonliteral way

Reading & Writing Companion **63**

 ## Skill: Figurative Language

Introduce the Skill

Watch the Concept Definition video and read the following definition with your students.

Figurative language is language used for descriptive effect, often to illustrate or imply ideas indirectly. Types of figurative language include simile, metaphor, and personification. A **simile** uses the words *like* or *as* to compare two seemingly unlike things. A **metaphor** directly compares two seemingly unlike things without using *like* or *as*. **Personification** is a **figure of speech** in which an animal, object, force of nature, or an idea is given human qualities.

When reading prose, and especially poetry, readers use **context**—including when and where a text was written, for example—to analyze the impact of word choice and to help determine or interpret the meaning of figurative words and phrases.

 ### TURN AND TALK

1. What are some examples of figurative language that you use or hear often?

2. Why do people and writers use figurative language?

ELL SPEAKING FRAMES

- One example of figurative language that I often hear is ____.
- When people use that figure of speech, what they mean is ____.
- Writers use figurative language because ____.

V SKILL VOCABULARY

figurative language / el lenguaje figurativo **noun** expressions used for descriptive or rhetorical effect that are not literally true but express some truth beyond the literal level COGNATE

simile / el símil **noun** a figure of speech that uses the words *like* or *as* to compare two seemingly unlike things COGNATE

metaphor / la metáfora **noun** a figure of speech that compares two seemingly unlike things but implies a comparison instead of stating it directly with the words *like* or *as* COGNATE

Narrative of the Life of Frederick Douglass, An American Slave

In order to interpret the meaning of a figure of speech in context, ask the following questions:

✓ Does any of the descriptive language in the text compare two seemingly unlike things?

✓ Do any descriptions include *like* or *as,* indicating a simile?

✓ Is there a direct comparison that suggests a metaphor?

✓ What literary, biblical, or mythological allusions do you recognize?

✓ Can you detect humor or sarcasm in the tone of the word or phrase, or a character saying one thing and clearly meaning the opposite?

✓ How does the use of this figure of speech change your understanding of the thing or person being described?

In order to analyze the impact of figurative language on the meaning of a text, use the following questions as a guide:

✓ Where does figurative language appear in the text? What does it mean?

✓ Why does the author use figurative language rather than literal language?

V SKILL VOCABULARY

personification / la personificación *noun* a figure of speech in which an animal, object, force of nature, or idea is given human form or qualities COGNATE

figure of speech / la figura literaria *noun* a word or phrase not meant to be taken literally, but rather used for effect

context / el contexto *noun* the set of facts or circumstances that surround a situation or event COGNATE

Narrative of the Life of Frederick Douglass, An American Slave

Skill:
Figurative Language

Reread paragraph 4 of *Narrative of the Life of Frederick Douglass, An American Slave*. Then, using the Checklist on the previous page, answer the multiple-choice questions below.

⟳ YOUR TURN

1. In paragraph 4, how does Douglass show his feelings for America?

   ○ A. He literally calls it a "Christian country," which means he likes it and thinks enslaved people shouldn't be taught to read.

   ○ B. He seems to sarcastically refer to it as a "Christian country," which shows that he doesn't think he should be taught to read.

   ○ C. He literally calls it a "Christian country," which shows that he doesn't like it very much.

   ○ D. He seems to sarcastically refer to it as a "Christian country," which shows that he doesn't like it because slavery exists and teaching enslaved people to read is not allowed.

2. This question has two parts. First, answer Part A. Then, answer Part B.

   Part A: What kind of figurative language is Douglass using when he writes, "This bread I used to **bestow** upon the hungry little urchins, who, in return, would give me that more valuable bread of knowledge"?

   ○ A. simile
   ○ B. metaphor
   ○ C. personification
   ○ D. verbal Irony

   Part B: What does the figurative language identified in Part A tell us about how Douglass feels about knowledge?

   ○ A. Douglass knows that the boys should value knowledge as much as he does, but they prefer bread.

   ○ B. Douglass knows that he needs to share knowledge, just like he shared bread with the boys from his neighborhood.

   ○ C. Douglass sees knowledge as a form of nourishment. Bread can nourish people who are hungry, and knowledge can nourish people who want to learn.

   ○ D. Douglass sees knowledge as something that can go stale if you do not use it, so he shares bread and knowledge with the boys in his neighborhood.

SkillsTV

Project the SkillsTV episode ▶ and pause at the following times to prompt discussion:

1:15 One student reads aloud some text from the selection. What do the students take away from the content of this passage?

2:14 When the second passage is read aloud, what is revealed about Douglass's skills as a writer?

3:43 What do the metaphors Douglass uses say about who he has become through reading?

Your Turn

Ask students to complete the Your Turn activity.

QUESTION 1

A. Incorrect. His tone is sarcastic in this phrase, and we know this because Douglass believes enslaved people should be able to read.

B. Incorrect. His tone is sarcastic in this phrase, and we know this because Douglass believes enslaved people should be able to read.

C. Incorrect. His tone is sarcastic in this phrase, and we know this because Douglass believes enslaved people should be able to read.

D. Correct. Douglass believes enslaved people should be able to read, and so by calling America a "Christian country," he uses a sarcastic phrase.

QUESTION 2

Part A

A. Incorrect. Douglass compares bread to knowledge, but he does not use *like* or *as*.

B. Correct. Douglass compares bread and knowledge without using *like* or *as*.

C. Incorrect. Douglass does not give human qualities to an object in this description.

D. Incorrect. Douglass uses a metaphor to compare bread and knowledge without using *like* or *as*.

Part B

A. Incorrect. The boys have access to an education, but they are hungry.

B. Incorrect. Douglass gives bread to the boys so they will teach him how to read and write in return. As a result, he is sharing bread, but not sharing knowledge yet.

C. Correct. Douglass sees knowledge as something that is as necessary for him as food is necessary for people who are hungry.

D. Incorrect. There is no textual evidence that relates to knowledge becoming stale in this passage.

Close Read

Skills Focus

QUESTION 1: Author's Purpose and Point of View

See paragraph 1: Douglass chooses words that convey a strong opinion about not being allowed to read. He calls it "mental darkness" and compares it to being treated like an animal. His point of view, or opinion, helps reveal that his purpose in writing is to critique his enslavement.

QUESTION 2: Central or Main Idea

See paragraph 4.

QUESTION 3: Informational Text Elements

See paragraph 8.

QUESTION 4: Figurative Language

See paragraph 7.

QUESTION 5: Connect to Essential Question

See paragraph 7: Douglass uses personification to explain how often he thought about gaining his freedom. This use of figurative language helps show how tortured he feels by the desire for freedom and why he would feel driven to find a way to attain it. This also helps me understand why he is so committed to learning. He is desperate to gain his freedom.

Narrative of the Life of Frederick Douglass, An American Slave

Close Read

Reread *Narrative of the Life of Frederick Douglass, An American Slave*. As you reread, complete the Skills Focus questions below. Then use your answers and annotations from the questions to help you complete the Write activity.

SKILLS FOCUS

1. Autobiographical texts such as *Narrative of the Life of Frederick Douglass, An American Slave* utilize key details from the author's perspective. Identify a strong opinion that Douglass shares, and explain how it helps to reveal his purpose.

2. Identify details that reveal Douglass's central or main idea in this excerpt from *Narrative of the Life of Frederick Douglass, An American Slave*. Explain how the textual evidence supports that central or main idea.

3. Reread the final two paragraphs in the excerpt. Identify the informational elements within these two paragraphs. Use and cite at least two specific examples in your response.

4. Identify specific instances of figurative language Douglass uses to describe slavery and freedom, and explain what the language helps you understand about Douglass's message.

5. In "Mother to Son," "Learning to Read," and *Narrative of the Life of Frederick Douglass, An American Slave*, the authors use figurative language to develop ideas about hardship and perseverance. In "Mother to Son," Hughes uses an extended metaphor to describe the hardship the speaker experiences as she pursues a better life. In "Learning to Read," Watkins uses a simile to describe the positive outcome of the speaker's persistence in learning to read. Identify figurative language Douglass uses to describe slavery and freedom, and explain what the language helps you understand about why he took chances to learn how to read and write.

WRITE

COMPARATIVE: The speakers of the poems "Mother to Son" and "Learning to Read," and Frederick Douglass in his autobiography, describe the risks involved to make successes of their lives. While Douglass's autobiography uses informational text elements to convey his experience, all three texts send a message about the importance of education. Think about the use of language, descriptions, and events, and explain how they contribute to this message.

Writer's Notebook

Connect to Essential Question: Give students time to reflect on how *Narrative of the Life of Frederick Douglass, An American Slave* connects to the unit's essential question "Why do we take chances?" by freewriting in their Writer's Notebooks.

ELL Beginning & Intermediate

Read aloud the unit's essential question: "Why do we take chances?" Encourage students to draw their connections or allow students to write in their native language. Circulate the room, prompting students for their thoughts as they respond orally or through pantomime.

ELL Advanced & Advanced High

Allow students to share their connections orally in pairs or small groups before freewriting.

StudySyncTV   Project the StudySyncTV episode ▶ and pause at the following times to prompt discussion:

0:50   How do the students use textual evidence to determine that the children are taking a risk by teaching Douglass how to read?

2:08   Pattelynn says that "sometimes the road to good things can be painful." How does the group use textual evidence and make inferences to develop her idea?

4:17   How do the students use details from the text to draw connections to their own experiences? What evidence do they use to support their ideas?

Collaborative Conversation

SCAFFOLDS

Break students into collaborative conversation groups to discuss the Close Read prompt. Ask students to use the StudySyncTV episode as a model for their discussion. Remind them to reference their Skills Focus annotations in their discussion.

The speakers of the poems "Mother to Son" and "Learning to Read," and Frederick Douglass in his autobiography, describe the risks involved to make successes of their lives. While Douglass's autobiography uses informational text elements to convey his experience, all three texts send a message about the importance of education. Think about the use of language, descriptions, and events, and explain how they contribute to this message.

Use the scaffolds below to differentiate instruction for your **ELL** English Language Learners and **A** Approaching grade-level learners.

ELL BEGINNING, INTERMEDIATE Use the discussion guide and speaking frames to facilitate the discussion with support from the teacher.

ADVANCED, ADVANCED HIGH Use the discussion guide and speaking frames to facilitate the discussion in mixed-level groups.

A APPROACHING Use the discussion guide to facilitate the discussion in mixed-level groups.

APPROACHING
ADVANCED, ADVANCED HIGH
BEGINNING, INTERMEDIATE

Discussion Guide	Speaking Frames
1. How does "Mother to Son" use language and descriptions? How does it contribute to the text's message about the importance of education?	• The text describes ____. • It reveals the message of ____ because ____.
2. How does "Learning to Read" use language and descriptions? How does it contribute to the text's message about the importance of education?	• The text describes ____. • It reveals the message of _____ because ____.
3. What informational text elements are used in *Narrative of the Life of Frederick Douglass, An American Slave*? How do they contribute to the text's message about the importance of education?	• The informational text elements used are ____. • It reveals the message of ____ because ____.

Review Prompt and Rubric

Before students begin writing, review the writing prompt and rubric with the class.

COMPARATIVE: The speakers of the poems "Mother to Son" and "Learning to Read," and Frederick Douglass in his autobiography, describe the risks involved to make successes of their lives. While Douglass's autobiography uses informational text elements to convey his experience, all three texts send a message about the importance of education. Think about the use of language, descriptions, and events, and explain how they contribute to this message.

 PROMPT GUIDE

- What language and descriptions does each author use?
- What informational text elements are used by Douglass?

- How do these elements contribute to the message of the text?
- How are the texts' messages revealed through the language?

An additional rubric item for Language and Conventions appears in your digital teacher and student accounts.

Score	Informational Text Elements	Figurative Language
4	The writer clearly analyzes and explains how the texts make connections among and distinctions between individuals, ideas, or events. The writer provides exemplary analysis, using relevant evidence from the text.	The writer clearly determines the meanings of words and phrases as they are used in the texts, including figurative and connotative meanings. The writer provides an exemplary analysis of the impact of specific word choices on meaning and tone, using relevant evidence from the text.
3	The writer analyzes and explains how the texts make connections among and distinctions between individuals, ideas, or events. The writer provides sufficient analysis, using relevant evidence from the text most of the time.	The writer determines the meanings of words and phrases as they are used in the texts, including figurative and connotative meanings. The writer sufficiently analyzes the impact of specific word choices on meaning and tone and the writer mostly uses relevant evidence from the text.
2	The writer begins to analyze or explain how the texts make connections among and distinctions between individuals, ideas, or events, but the analysis is incomplete. The writer uses relevant evidence from the text only some of the time.	The writer begins to determine the meanings of words and phrases as they are used in the texts, including figurative and connotative meanings. The writer provides an incomplete analysis of the impact of specific word choices on meaning and tone and occasionally uses relevant evidence from the text.
1	The writer attempts to analyze or explain, but the analysis is not successful. The writer uses little or no relevant evidence from the text.	The writer attempts to determine the meanings of words and phrases as they are used in the texts, including figurative and connotative meanings. The writer's analysis of the impact of specific word choices on meaning and tone is not successful and uses little or no relevant evidence from the text.
0	The writer does not provide a relevant response to the prompt or does not provide a response at all.	The writer does not provide a relevant response to the prompt or does not provide a response at all.

SCAFFOLDS

Write

Ask students to complete the writing assignment using textual evidence to support their answers.

Use the scaffolds below to differentiate instruction for your **ELL** English Language Learners and **A** Approaching grade-level learners.

ELL **BEGINNING** With the help of the <u>word bank</u>, write a response using <u>paragraph frame 1</u>.

INTERMEDIATE With the help of the <u>word bank</u>, write a response using <u>paragraph frames 1 and 2</u>.

ADVANCED, ADVANCED HIGH Write a response of differentiated length using the <u>sentence starters</u>.

A **APPROACHING** Write a response of differentiated length using the <u>sentence starters</u>.

BEGINNING INTERMEDIATE			ADVANCED, ADVANCED HIGH / APPROACHING
Word Bank	**Paragraph Frame 1**	**Paragraph Frame 2**	**Sentence Starters**
desire communicate images importance metaphor	All three texts use descriptive language to ____ the importance of education. "Mother to Son" creates ____ of two sets of stairs: the crystal stairs and the splintered torn up stairs. These descriptions reveal the possible benefits of education through a ____. In "Learning to Read," Harper describes learning to read by "hook or crook." This language reveals the ____ of education. The informational text elements in *Narrative of the Life of Frederick Douglass, An American Slave* help the author reveal his strong ____ to be able to read. He describes in detail the lengths he went to in order to learn.	All of these texts use descriptive language and metaphor to express ____. The importance of a good education is also revealed through the ____ in each text. Reading each text provides the reader with ____ that reveal the importance of education. Though each text presents its message in a different manner, they all convey ____.	• All three texts use descriptive language to . . . • "Mother to Son" creates . . . of . . . • These descriptions reveal . . . • In "Learning to Read," Harper describes . . . • This language reveals . . . • The . . . in *Narrative of the Life of Frederick Douglass, An American Slave* helps the author reveal . . . • He describes in detail . . .

Peer Review

Students should submit substantive feedback to two peers using the review instructions below.

- How well does this response answer the prompt?
- How well does the writer support his or her ideas with details from the text?
- What did the writer do well in this response? What does the writer need to work on?

Rate

Respond to the following with a point rating that reflects your opinion.

	1 2 3 4
Ideas	▪▪▪☐
Evidence	▪▪▪▪
Language and Conventions	▪▪☐☐

Submit

ELL **A** **SENTENCE FRAMES**

- You were able to (completely / partly / almost) answer the prompt.
- You supported the idea of ____ with the detail of ____.
- One idea that needs more support is ____.
- My favorite part of your response is ____.

The Day I Saved a Life

INFORMATIONAL TEXT
Thomas Ponce
2018

Introduction

Thomas Ponce (b. 2000) is a Florida native, animal rights activist, and citizen lobbyist. He has been a vegetarian since age four, and at age five began writing about animal rights. He is the creator of the group Lobby for Animals, and he has received awards from major organizations such as PETA and the Farm Animal Rights Movement. In "The Day I Saved a Life," Ponce describes a key day in his life, which would lead directly to a greater awareness about the plight of sharks and his decision to actively work to improve their conditions.

For his 11th birthday, Thomas Ponce's family took him to Venice Beach. For Thomas, this trip wasn't about swimming. Thomas knew that Venice is also known as "Shark Tooth Beach," and he was excited to comb the sands in search of ancient shark teeth. With his sifter in hand, he began searching and quickly found teeth from bull sharks and great whites, but then he hit the jackpot: a black four-inch tooth which belonged to a Megalodon. Later, he and his family went to the pier to watch the sun set on a perfect day. Nearby, Thomas saw a fisherman pull a baby shark out of the water and proclaim that he was going to eat well tonight. Thomas ran over and talked to the man about how important sharks are for the ocean's ecosystem, and how their slow reproductive rate makes every shark important. Thomas succeeded in convincing the fisherman to release the shark, and ever since then, he's been working to advocate for shark's rights.

 Proficiency-leveled summaries and summaries in multiple languages are available digitally.

 Audio and audio text highlighting are available with this text.

CONNECT TO ESSENTIAL QUESTION

Why do we take chances?

Standing up for what you believe sometimes involves risk. In this personal narrative, a young man stands up for animal rights when a fisherman intends to kill a shark.

Access Complex Text

LEXILE: 970L   **WORD COUNT:** 1,084

The following areas may be challenging for students, particularly English Language Learners and Approaching grade-level learners.

Prior Knowledge

- The text refers to biological concepts such as the ocean ecosystem and the shark's role in it as a predator.

- Explain that sharks are generally at the top of a food chain, although killer whales have been known to prey on them. Because sharks are major predators, they keep the populations of the species they prey on in check.

Specific Vocabulary

- Higher-level vocabulary, such as *inhumane* (without humanity, compassion, or kindness), and technical language, such as *vivisection* (operating on a live animal for scientific research), may need defining.

- Students will have focused skill lessons on using context clues and determining the meaning of technical language after the First Read.

 **SCAFFOLDS**   **ENGLISH LANGUAGE LEARNERS**   **APPROACHING GRADE LEVEL**   **B BEYOND GRADE LEVEL**

These icons identify differentiation strategies and scaffolded support for a variety of students. See the digital lesson plan for additional differentiation strategies and scaffolds.

Instructional Path

First Read: The Day I Saved a Life

Objectives: After an initial reading and discussion of the informational text, students will be able to identify and restate the text's key ideas and details.

Skill: Context Clues

Objectives: After rereading and discussing a model of close reading, students will be able to use context clues, such as definition, comparison, contrast, and examples, to clarify the meanings of words.

Skill: Technical Language

Objectives: After rereading and discussing a model of close reading, students will be able to identify and determine the meaning of technical language in a text.

Close Read: The Day I Saved a Life

Objectives: After engaging in a close reading and discussion of the text, students will be able to tell of an experience with a subject and use technical language from the subject in a short, written response.

Progress Monitoring

Opportunities to Learn	Opportunities to Demonstrate Learning	Opportunities to Reteach

Context Clues

Opportunities to Learn	Opportunities to Demonstrate Learning	Opportunities to Reteach
⚙ Skill: Context Clues	⚙ Skill: Context Clues • Your Turn ▭ Close Read • Complete Vocabulary Chart • Skills Focus • Write	⚙ Spotlight Skill: Context Clues

Technical Language

Opportunities to Learn	Opportunities to Demonstrate Learning	Opportunities to Reteach
⚙ Skill: Technical Language	⚙ Skill: Technical Language • Your Turn ▭ Close Read • Complete Vocabulary Chart • Skills Focus • Write	⚙ Unit 4 Skill: Technical Language - Cover Letter to LucasArts ⚙ Unit 6 Skill: Technical Language - Everybody Out (from 'What If?') ⚙ Spotlight Skill: Technical Language

First Read

Thomas Ponce

The Day I Saved a Life

Entry Point

Introduce the Text

As a class, watch the video preview ▶ and have students read the introduction in pairs to make connections to the video preview.

To activate prior knowledge and experiences, ask students:

- What key words or images from the video do you think will be most important to the text you are about to read?

ELL SPEAKING FRAMES

- The ____ in the video makes me think ____.
- The video shows ____. This makes me wonder ____.
- I think the text will ____. I think this because ____.
- I predict that there will be ____. I believe this because ____.

As students prepare to read "The Day I Saved a Life," share the following information with them to provide context.

✓ There are more than 500 species of sharks, ranging in size from hand length to 39 feet long. Half of all shark species are less than one yard long. A person is more likely to be killed by lightning than by a shark. It is estimated fishing practices kill 100 million sharks each year.

✓ A green flash is an optical phenomenon that sometimes occurs at sunset or sunrise, especially over ocean waters. As the upper edge of the sun touches the horizon, a green spot of light flashes, caused by refraction in Earth's atmosphere.

✓ *Vivisection*, while literally meaning "live cutting," is sometimes applied to all experimentation on live animals. Some people believe such experimentation is necessary to advance medical knowledge; others oppose it entirely as cruel. Those in the middle advocate restricting animal experimentation to essential medical research, using alternative methods when possible, and eliminating unnecessarily cruel practices.

"I swear the shark looked at me with gratitude. He was alive because I spoke up for him and he knew it."

Skill: Technical Language

Fossilized is technical language. The context tells me fossilized teeth are really old. The dictionary definition of fossilized supports this: "to change into a fossil," which is "the remains or trace of an ancient life form." Now I know both fossil and fossilized.

Skill: Context Clues

I'm not sure what a scooper is, but it's a noun because my comes before it. He uses it to dig into the sand. I see scoop in scooper, and later he uses scoop to mean the same thing. It must be a tool used to scoop up sand.

1 We've all seen Hollywood's depiction of sharks, the media's over-dramatization of shark attacks and felt that pit in our stomach at the sight of a shark. Movies like *Jaws, Day of the Shark, Shark Night, Deep Blue Sea*, etc., give us the impression of a mindless killing machine out to kill all human beings. Well, I've seen another side of the shark and I've seen it up close and personal.

2 It all started on December 16, 2011, my birthday. My family took me to Venice Beach, which is also known as Shark Tooth Beach. This was the trip I had been waiting for. I had seen this location on the Discovery Channel over a year ago and had wanted to go ever since. Having the opportunity to find fossilized shark teeth that have been in the waters for over millions of years was something I was **ecstatic** about! When we arrived at our destination, I was amazed at all the sights, sounds and smells. The water was crystal clear and blue and the sand was so warm between my toes. The occasional breeze whisked my mind away to a beautiful tropical paradise. It was a perfect day to go sifting for shark teeth. I walked into the water up to my knees, sifter in hand, and began sifting. I dug my scooper into the sand, beneath the water, and pulled up many small teeth. I found great white teeth, bull shark teeth, tiger shark teeth and a few I was unsure about, it was amazing. Then it happened. I hit the jackpot! I discovered in my scoop the largest tooth I had ever seen. It was four inches long and black in color. Its edges were serrated and you could still see the gum line. The great white teeth I found paled in comparison to this massive tooth. It was a Megalodon tooth! My dream had come true, I had found one! This was the best birthday present I could have ever gotten, or so I thought.

3 As we were leaving the beach, a friendly local told us about a pier close by that was a perfect place to watch the sunset. I was determined to see the green flash that everyone talks about when the sun sets. We headed back to our hotel to change and then went straight to the pier. The view from the pier was miraculous. The skies were clear and the weather was perfect for being outside, not too hot and there was a cool breeze coming off the water. As we watched the sunset, the sky turned orange and pink as the sun went down. It was absolutely breathtaking! In the water we saw dolphins swimming and a man painting sea turtles at the edge of the pier. It was a night right out of a novel.

Copyright © BookheadEd Learning, LLC

Analyze Vocabulary Using Context Clues

In paragraph 4, focus on the sentence that uses the word *keystone*. Point out these context clues:

1. I know that predators prey on, or eat, other animals, and *keystone* is an adjective describing *predator*. I think *keystone* means something like "important," maybe even "essential"—something the environment depends on

2. When I read the sentence again, using *essential* in place of *keystone*, the sentence makes sense: "I told him how sharks are *essential* predators."

Technical Language

What technical term did the reader notice, and how did she first determine its meaning?

The reader noticed *fossilized* and first used context to determine its meaning.

Context Clues

How does the reader determine the part of speech of the word *scooper*?

The reader notices that the word *my* comes before *scooper*, which suggests the scooper is a thing. A word that is a thing must be a noun.

TEXT TALK

What is the author doing at the beginning of the day he writes about?

See paragraph 2: It's his birthday, and he goes to the beach with his family to look for shark teeth.

SELECTION VOCABULARY

ecstatic / eufórico/a **adjective** feeling overwhelming joy or excitement

 • What is the author talking about when he uses the word *ecstatic*?

keystone / la especie clave **adjective** a group of organisms essential to an ecosystem

Skills Focus

QUESTION 5: Connect to Essential Question

Ponce steps in and tries everything he can do to persuade the fisherman not to kill the shark. That was taking a chance because who knows how the fisherman would react, and he still might go ahead and kill the shark anyway. I'd like to think I would have done the same thing, but I'm not sure. Ponce begins to fight for sharks' rights after this experience.

Skills Focus

QUESTION 1: Technical Language

Finning must refer to cutting off the fins of sharks. I don't know why people just want the fins, but it's cruel. It helps prove Ponce's point that sharks need protecting.

Skills Focus

QUESTION 3: Context Clues

If killing sharks in huge numbers brings them close to extinction, then extinction must mean the removal of all sharks from the planet. There would be no more sharks left. That's obviously a negative because, at the very least, it would upset the balance of life in the ocean.

Skills Focus

QUESTION 4: Technical Language

I know vegetarians don't eat meat, but he says now he's a vegan. Maybe that's taking it one step further and not eating anything from an animal. I'll check this in a dictionary. Using this term supports his argument for protecting animals.

4   As we were leaving the pier I saw a fisherman pull a baby bonnethead shark up on his line. He pulled him onto the pier, hooting and hollering about his catch and how he was "going to eat tonight." The fisherman then started sharpening his very large knife, readying himself to gut the shark right then and there. The shark flapped and shook, grasping to hold onto life. It was horrible to see. I knew I had to do something,

One of a pair of new Bonnethead sharks at Chessington World of Adventures, Surrey, England

so I approached the fisherman and asked him to set the shark free. I explained how it was a living creature, a baby with a family and that it deserved to live. I explained to him the important role sharks play in our ecosystem. I pleaded with him to free him and not eat him. I even offered to buy him dinner. I told him how sharks are **keystone** species and how they keep the ocean ecosystem in balance; I explained about their slow reproductive rate and how we needed every shark in the ocean to keep it healthy. I explained how the effects of removing sharks would be felt throughout the ecosystem like a domino effect. I was not letting up, I knew I had to keep fighting for that shark. After what seemed like an eternity, the fisherman finally **conceded** and told me that I could set him free. I couldn't believe it, I did it! I immediately walked over, picked up the shark and placed him back into the water and told him to live free. I swear the shark looked at me with gratitude. He was alive because I spoke up for him and he knew it. I saw the understanding in his eyes and knew there was much more to sharks than what I had been led to believe.

5   That day changed me forever and now I fight for sharks' rights. I have always been an active animal and environmental advocate and a vegetarian and now vegan. I had run many fundraisers for farm animals and for spaying and neutering your pets. I had leafletted about animals in captivity and in **vivisection** labs; I had signed petitions against animal cruelty and protested at various sites where cruelty had been taking place, but until that day I hadn't really concentrated my efforts on sharks. I started doing some research and I watched a documentary called *Sharkwater* and it gave me insight into the plight of the shark. It showed me the horrors they faced due to finning. They were being killed in huge quantities for their fins and were becoming extremely close to extinction. The sharks are stripped of their fins then discarded, while still alive, back into the ocean. It was a horrible discovery and one that moved me to act and speak up for the sharks. From that moment on, I have dedicated myself to making as many people aware of what's going on with sharks as I can. My hope is that through educating people on the cruel and inhumane acts being done to sharks and by explaining the importance of sharks to the ocean ecosystem, as well as our own environment,

TEXT TALK

What happens in the evening at the pier?

See paragraph 4: A fisherman catches a shark and is going to kill it, but the author persuades him not to.

What does the author do now as a result of that incident?

See paragraph 5: He is an advocate for sharks' rights.

V SELECTION VOCABULARY

conceded / admitir **verb** to surrender or give up

 • What does the fisherman do after he concedes?

vivisection / la vivisección **noun** dissecting a living body for scientific research COGNATE

 • What has the writer leafletted and signed petitions about?

that I can make a difference in helping to preserve this beautiful species. I hope to one day soon be speaking at Congress on behalf of sharks and **lobbying** to bring change to the finning laws in our country.

6 December 16, 2011 the ocean gave me two gifts, a Megalodon tooth and an appreciation and love of sharks. In return, I gave it back one of its own and a voice that could be heard and would never be silenced.

By Thomas Ponce, President and Founder of Lobby For Animals. Used by permission of Thomas Ponce.

SELECTION VOCABULARY

lobby / cabildear **verb** to try to influence a politician on behalf of a cause

 • Why will the speaker be lobbying?

TEXT TALK

What did Thomas Ponce see in sharks that other people overlooked? What does this teach you about being misunderstood?

Answers will vary.

Think Questions

Circulate as students answer Think Questions independently. Scaffolds for these questions are shown on the opposite page.

QUESTION 1: Textual Evidence

The author gets ecstatic just at the thought of finding fossilized shark teeth. More important, he saves the life of a shark. He persuades a fisherman not to kill the shark by explaining how important sharks are to the ocean ecosystem. He also speaks up for sharks by educating people about them and intending to lobby Congress to pass laws protecting them from finning.

QUESTION 2: Textual Evidence

The description of the evening at the pier creates a peaceful and beautiful scene with words and phrases like "miraculous," "skies were clear," "the sky turned pink and orange," and "breathtaking." The images of dolphins swimming and a man painting add to the quiet nature of the scene. This peace is broken and in sharp contrast to what follows: a fisherman catching a shark, "hollering" about eating it, and getting ready to kill it with a knife.

QUESTION 3: Textual Evidence

On December 16, 2011, the author became an advocate for shark's rights. He had always worked to protect animals; from that day on, he concentrated his efforts on doing research about sharks and then educating people on the need to protect sharks— particularly from the finning industry.

QUESTION 4: Context Clues

The author says that going to Shark Tooth Beach "was the trip I had been waiting for." He calls it an "opportunity" and ends the sentence with an exclamation point, so *ecstatic* must mean "very happy."

QUESTION 5: Context Clues

The fisherman was going to kill the shark, but after the author keep trying to persuade him not to, he "conceded" and let the shark go free. So *conceded* probably means something like "agreed." An online dictionary says *concede* means "admit to be true" but also includes "agree," so my meaning was close.

First Read

Read "The Day I Saved a Life." After you read, complete the Think Questions below.

THINK QUESTIONS

1. How does the author show his love of sharks? Provide specific examples from the text.

2. What effect does the author's sensory description of the beautiful evening at the pier have on the story? What is its function in the text? Use specific evidence from the text to support your answer.

3. What changed specifically for the author on this particular day? How was his life different afterward? Provide specific examples from the text.

4. Based on the context, what do you think the word **ecstatic** means? Write your definition here, and indicate which context clues informed your thinking.

5. Use context clues to determine the meaning of the word **concede** as it used in the text. Write your definition of *concede* here, and state which clues from the text helped you determine the answer. Confirm your definition using a print or online dictionary.

Think Questions

Use the scaffolds below to differentiate instruction for your **ELL** English Language Learners and **A** Approaching grade-level learners.

SCAFFOLDS

ELL **BEGINNING** Write a response using the <u>word bank</u> and <u>sentence frames</u>.

INTERMEDIATE Write a response using the <u>sentence frames</u>.

ADVANCED, ADVANCED HIGH Write a response using the <u>Text-Dependent Question Guide</u>.

A **APPROACHING** Write a response using the <u>Text-Dependent Question Guide</u>.

BEGINNING	INTERMEDIATE	APPROACHING / ADVANCED, ADVANCED HIGH
Word Bank	**Sentence Frames**	**Text-Dependent Question Guide**
life contrast rights happy admit ecstatic important peaceful lobby waiting protecting ends	The author gets _____ about finding shark teeth. He saves the _____ of a shark. He talks to people about _____ sharks.	1. • What event does the title refer to? • How does the author react to going to Shark Tooth Beach? • What does the author do now concerning sharks?
	The description of the evening creates a _____ scene. The quiet _____ when the fisherman catches a shark. This event is a _____ to the peace.	2. • What are some words and phrases that describe the evening on the pier? • What feeling do these images create? • What happens as the author is leaving the pier? • What effect does this event have?
	On December 16, 2011, the author began to work for sharks' _____. He wants to _____ for laws to stop finning.	3. • What did the author do before December 16, 2011? • What has he done since then? • What specifically changed?
	The author says that he had been _____ for the trip. He really wants to find shark teeth. This is a clue that *ecstatic* means "very _____."	4. • Read: "This was the trip I had been waiting for," "had wanted to go ever since," and "opportunity." • How does the author feel about going to the beach? • What does *ecstatic* likely mean?
	The author told the fisherman that sharks were _____. The fisherman conceded and set the shark free. This is a clue that *concede* means "_____ to be true," or "agree."	5. • Read: "I explained how the effects of removing sharks would be felt throughout the ecosystem like a domino effect. I was not letting up, I knew I had to keep fighting for that shark. After what seemed like an eternity, the fisherman finally **conceded** and told me that I could set him free." • What was the fisherman going to do with the shark? • What did he do after he conceded? • What does *conceded* likely mean?

Reading Comprehension OPTIONAL

Have students complete the digital reading comprehension questions ✓ when they finish reading.

ANSWER KEY

QUESTION 1: C   **QUESTION 5:** C   **QUESTION 9:**

QUESTION 2: A   **QUESTION 6:** A   *See first chart.*

QUESTION 3: D   **QUESTION 7:** C   **QUESTION 10:**

QUESTION 4: A   **QUESTION 8:** D   *See second chart.*

Definition	Word
feeling overwhelming happiness or excitement	ecstatic
something on which associated things depend	keystone
to surrender, yield	concede
the practice of performing operations of live animals for scientific research	vivisection
to seek to influence a politician about an issue	lobby

First	Second	Third	Fourth	Fifth
The narrator enjoys the sights, sounds, and smells of Shark Tooth Beach.	The narrator finds a Megalodon tooth.	A fisherman pulls a baby Bonnethead shark up on his line.	As it is set free, the shark looks back gratefully at the narrator.	The narrator learns more about the plight of sharks from a documentary.

Connect and Extend OPTIONAL

CONNECT TO EXTENDED WRITING PROJECT

Students can find inspiration from "The Day I Saved a Life" when writing their informational essays. Have them reflect on Thomas Ponce's decision to take action about sharks.

BEYOND THE BOOK

Research: Going Vegan

In his essay, Thomas Ponce says that he is vegan. Have your students conduct research about what it means to be vegan. Veganism can be a broad subject, so consider having students choose one of the following as a basis for their research:

- Following a vegan, or plant-based, diet that abstains from all animal products (meat, fish, dairy, honey, etc.) because of animal rights.
- Being vegan because you're an environmental advocate.
- Eating a vegan diet for health reasons.
- Promoting veganism in different aspects of life (vegan cosmetics, accessories, clothes, etc.) as a stand against animal cruelty.

Have students present their research. In addition, you may also choose to have your students give their opinions about adopting a vegan lifestyle. Their opinions may accompany their research in order to have a classroom discussion or debate.

To reflect, ask students:

- Why do people choose to be vegan?
- What effects can veganism have on the world?
- Do you think veganism will continue to gain in popularity? Why or why not?

Skill:
Context Clues

Use the Checklist to analyze Context Clues in "The Day I Saved a Life." Refer to the sample student annotations about Context Clues in the text.

••• CHECKLIST FOR CONTEXT CLUES

In order to use context as a clue to infer the meaning of a word or phrase, note the following:

✓ clues about the word's part of speech

✓ clues about the word's meaning in the surrounding text

✓ signal words that cue a type of context clue, such as:

• *for example* or *for instance* to signal an example clue

• *like, similarly,* or *just as* to signal a comparison clue

• *but, however,* or *unlike* to signal a contrast clue

To determine the meaning of a word or phrase as it is used in a text, consider the following questions:

✓ What is the overall sentence, paragraph, or text about?

✓ How does the word function in the sentence?

✓ What clues can help me determine the word's part of speech?

✓ What text clues can help me figure out the word's definition?

✓ Are there any examples that show what the word means?

✓ What do I think the word means?

To verify the preliminary determination of the meaning of the word or phrase based on context, consider the following questions:

✓ Does the definition I inferred make sense within the context of the sentence?

✓ Which of the dictionary's definitions makes sense within the context of the sentence?

Copyright © BookheadEd Learning, LLC

V SKILL VOCABULARY

context clue / la clave del contexto **noun** a hint in the surrounding text that can help a reader infer the meaning of an unfamiliar word, phrase, or description

infer / inferir **verb** to determine something by using reasoning and evidence from the text COGNATE

definition context clue / la clave del contexto de definición **noun** text that provides a definition of a word

---

Skill: Context Clues

Introduce the Skill

Watch the Concept Definition video ▶ and read the following definition with your students.

When readers come across words they don't know, they often use context to determine the meanings of the unfamiliar words. **Context clues** are hints in the surrounding text that a reader can use to **infer** the meaning of an unfamiliar word. Some common types of context clues include the following:

• **Definition:** an explanation of the word's meaning before or after the word appears, usually set off by a comma

• **Example:** one or more examples in a text that may demonstrate the meaning of a word

• **Comparison**: determining a word's meaning based on how it is like something else in the text

• **Contrast**: determining a word's meaning based on how it is unlike something else in the text

In addition, the genre of a text and what it is about also provide context clues for a word's meaning. Readers can verify their preliminary definitions of words or phrases by using a print or digital resource.

TURN AND TALK

1. What are context clues?

2. What are four different types of context clues?

ELL SPEAKING FRAMES

• Context clues are ____.
• A reader uses context clues to ____.
• One type of context clue is ____.
• It provides a clue to the meaning of a word through ____.

⚙ Your Turn

Ask students to complete the Your Turn activity.

QUESTION 1

A. Incorrect. This is not the meaning of the phrase "domino effect."

B. Correct. With a "domino effect," one thing causes another to happen, which in turn causes another, and so on, like lined-up dominoes falling one after the other once you push over the first one.

C. Incorrect. This is not the meaning of the phrase "domino effect."

D. Incorrect. This is not the meaning of the phrase "domino effect."

QUESTION 2

A. Incorrect. This quote does not contain context suggesting the meaning of "domino effect."

B. Incorrect. This quote does not contain context suggesting the meaning of "domino effect."

C. Correct. This quote is a context clue that removing sharks affects other parts of the ecosystem.

D. Incorrect. This quote does not contain context suggesting the meaning of "domino effect."

QUESTION 3

A. Incorrect. The context after *conceded* does not suggest that the fisherman refused.

B. Incorrect. The context after *conceded* does not suggest that the fisherman argued.

C. Correct. The context clue "the fisherman finally . . . told me that I could set him free" helps you infer that *conceded* means the fisherman gave up on wanting to kill the shark and let the author free it.

D. Incorrect. The context after *conceded* does not suggest that the fisherman refused.

The Day I Saved a Li

Skill:
Context Clues

Reread paragraph 4 of "The Day I Saved a Life." Then, using the Checklist on the previous page, answer the multiple-choice questions below.

↻ YOUR TURN

1. What is the meaning of "domino effect"? Use context clues to figure out what the phrase means.

   ○ A. Killing is a serious thing and not to be taken lightly, like a game.
   ○ B. If one thing happens, it will cause another, and so on.
   ○ C. One good turn deserves another.
   ○ D. The world is a complex place, intricately structured.

2. Which quote from the text best supports the reasoning you used in question 1?

   ○ A. "The shark flapped and shook, grasping to hold onto life. It was horrible to see."
   ○ B. "I was not letting up, I knew I had to keep fighting for that shark."
   ○ C. "I explained to him the important role sharks play in our ecosystem. . . . I explained how the effects of removing sharks would be felt throughout the ecosystem."
   ○ D. "I swear the shark looked at me with gratitude. He was alive because I spoke up for him and he knew it."

3. What is the meaning of *conceded* as it used in the paragraph? Use context clues to figure out what the word means.

   ○ A. refused
   ○ B. argued
   ○ C. gave up
   ○ D. insisted

Reading & Writing Companion   73

V SKILL VOCABULARY

example context clue / la clave del contexto de ejemplo *noun* text that provides a clue to the meaning of a word through one or more examples

comparison context clue / la clave del contexto de comparación *noun* text that provides a clue to the meaning of a word through a comparison

contrast context clue / la clave del contexto de contraste *noun* text that provides a clue to the meaning of a word through a contrast

Skill:
Technical Language

Use the Checklist to analyze Technical Language in "The Day I Saved a Life." Refer to the sample student annotations about Technical Language in the text.

••• CHECKLIST FOR TECHNICAL LANGUAGE

In order to determine the meaning of words and phrases as they are used in a text, note the following:

- ✓ the subject of the book or article
- ✓ any unfamiliar words that you think might be technical terms
- ✓ words that have multiple meanings that change when used with a specific subject
- ✓ the possible contextual meaning of a word, or the definition from a dictionary

To determine the meaning of words and phrases as they are used in a text, including technical meanings, consider the following questions:

- ✓ What is the subject of the informational text?
- ✓ How does the use of technical language help establish the author as an authority on the subject?
- ✓ Are there any technical words that have an impact on the meaning and tone, or quality, of the book or article?
- ✓ Does the writer use analogies, or a comparison between two things for the purpose of explanation or clarification? What impact do they have on your understanding of the subject?
- ✓ Does the writer use any allusions to another topic or subject as a way to explain something? What impact do they have on the author's treatment of the main subject?

Reading & Writing Companion

▼ SKILL VOCABULARY

technical language / el lenguaje técnico *noun* words that are used in certain fields of knowledge, such as astronomy or computer science COGNATE

subject / la materia *noun* an area of knowledge to study

precise / preciso/a *adjective* clearly defined and accurate COGNATE

authority / la autoridad *noun* the power or right to give orders or make decisions; the power to be in charge COGNATE

⚙ Skill: Technical Language

Introduce the Skill

Watch the Concept Definition video ▶ and read the following definition with your students.

Technical language refers to words that are used in certain fields of knowledge. The **subject** is the field of knowledge the author writes about, such as astronomy or computer science, and it is an important part of determining the meaning of technical language. For example, if you know that archaeologists study human history based on things found in ancient ruins, and you read that an archaeologist has discovered an important artifact, you can guess that in this context the word *artifact* refers to an object made by a human being, usually an item of cultural or historical interest. Writers include technical language to educate readers, to make their explanation more **precise** and accurate, or to establish their **authority** on a subject. When a writer is being precise, they must be detailed but straightforward in their explanations of complex ideas and concepts. Being an authority, or expert, on a subject gives the writer credibility with readers.

⚙ TURN AND TALK

1. What is a particular subject you are interested in?

2. What are some terms that only people who know about that subject area will likely be familiar with?

ELL SPEAKING FRAMES
- I am interested in the subject of ____.
- A word in that subject area is ____.
- Another word from that subject is ____.

⚙ Your Turn

Ask students to complete the Your Turn activity.

QUESTION 1

A. Incorrect. This is not the meaning of the technical term *ecosystem*.

B. Correct. An ecosystem consists of all the living organisms in a particular environment and their interactions with one another.

C. Incorrect. This is not the meaning of the technical term *ecosystem*.

D. Incorrect. This is not the meaning of the technical term *ecosystem*.

QUESTION 2

A. Incorrect. A keystone species is not an animal that eats both plants and animals.

B. Incorrect. A keystone species is not an animal that can survive in only one place.

C. Incorrect. A keystone species is not an animal that preys constantly and never stops hunting.

D. Correct. If a keystone species is removed from its environment, the environment changes drastically.

QUESTION 3

A. Incorrect. The fact that the shark tried to hold on to its life does not relate to its being a keystone species.

B. Incorrect. The fact that the shark is alive does not relate to its being a keystone species.

C. Incorrect. The fact that the shark has a slow reproductive rate does not relate to its being a keystone species.

D. Correct. This information helps explain what a keystone species is.

Skill: Technical Language

Reread paragraph 4 of "The Day I Saved a Life." Then, using the Checklist on the previous page, answer the multiple-choice questions below.

⟳ YOUR TURN

1. What is the meaning of the technical term *ecosystem*?

  ○ A. the world's oceans and the flow of water between them
  ○ B. the network of animals and plants that interact in an environment
  ○ C. a species of animal that lives in one place
  ○ D. planet Earth and all the living things on it

2. What is the meaning of the technical term *keystone species*?

  ○ A. an animal that eats both plants and animals
  ○ B. an animal that can survive in only one place
  ○ C. an animal that preys constantly and never stops hunting
  ○ D. an animal that plays a crucial role in its environment

3. Which quote from the text best supports the reasoning you used in question 2?

  ○ A. "The shark flapped and shook, grasping to hold onto life."
  ○ B. "I explained how it was a living creature, a baby with a family"
  ○ C. "I explained about their slow reproductive rate"
  ○ D. "I explained how the effects of removing sharks would be felt throughout the ecosystem"

Reading & Writing Companion   75

Close Read

eread "The Day I Saved a Life." As you reread, complete the Skills Focus questions below. Then use your nswers and annotations from the questions to help you complete the Write activity.

SKILLS FOCUS

Explain the meaning of *finning* in paragraph 5, and discuss how and why this technical term helps make Ponce's argument more meaningful and gives it more of an impact.

2. Use context clues to determine the meaning of *jackpot*. How does this help to describe Ponce's discoveries? Does it make everything else he describes seem more important or less so? Use specific evidence from the text to support your answer.

3. Use context clues to determine the meaning of *extinction*. Is this word positive or negative? Is it

contrasted with any other word in the text? How does it compare to the rest of the text that surrounds it? Use specific evidence from the text to support your response.

4. What is the meaning of the technical term *vegan*? Does it help Ponce's argument to use this term? Why or why not? Cite specific evidence from the text to support your answer.

5. What was risky about Thomas Ponce's actions? Would you have made the same decision that he did? Why or why not? What does Ponce seem to have learned from his experience?

WRITE

NARRATIVE: Using Ponce's essay as a point of reference, write a persuasive narrative essay where you defend a subject about which you are passionate. Be sure to include technical language where applicable, as this can lend authority to your opinions and ideas.

Copyright © BookheadEd Learning, LLC

Reading & Writing Companion

Close Read

Skills Focus

QUESTION 1: Technical Language

See paragraph 5.

QUESTION 2: Context Clues

See paragraph 2: Hitting the jackpot is obviously a good thing because he equates it with finding a huge tooth, which is important to him. It must be like the biggest prize.

QUESTION 3: Context Clues

See paragraph 5.

QUESTION 4: Technical Language

See paragraph 5.

QUESTION 5: Connect to Essential Question

See paragraph 4.

 CHECK FOR SUCCESS

If students struggle to respond to Skills Focus question 1, ask them the following questions:

1. Which sentence in paragraph 5 helps explain what finning is?

2. How do you feel when you read about finning?

 ## Writer's Notebook

Connect to Essential Question: Give students time to reflect on how "The Day I Saved a Life" connects to the unit's essential question "Why do we take chances?" by freewriting in their Writer's Notebooks.

 Beginning & Intermediate

Read aloud the unit's essential question: "Why do we take chances?" Encourage students to draw their connections or allow students to write in their native language. Circulate the room, prompting students for their thoughts as they respond orally or through pantomime.

Advanced & Advanced High

Allow students to share their connections orally in pairs or small groups before freewriting.

Collaborative Conversation

 SCAFFOLDS

Break students into collaborative conversation groups to discuss the Close Read prompt. Ask students to use the StudySyncTV episode as a model for their discussion. Remind them to reference their Skills Focus annotations in their discussion.

Using Ponce's essay as a point of reference, write a persuasive narrative essay where you defend a subject about which you are passionate. Be sure to include technical language where applicable, as this can lend authority to your opinions and ideas.

Use the scaffolds below to differentiate instruction for your **ELL** English Language Learners and **A** Approaching grade-level learners.

ELL **BEGINNING, INTERMEDIATE** Use the <u>discussion guide</u> and <u>speaking frames</u> to facilitate the discussion with support from the teacher.

ADVANCED, ADVANCED HIGH Use the <u>discussion guide</u> and <u>speaking frames</u> to facilitate the discussion in mixed-level groups.

A **APPROACHING** Use the <u>discussion guide</u> to facilitate the discussion in mixed-level groups.

APPROACHING

ADVANCED, ADVANCED HIGH

BEGINNING, INTERMEDIATE

Discussion Guide	Speaking Frames
1. What subject area does Ponce talk about?	• The subject area is ____.
2. What happened to Ponce that led him to learn about this subject?	• Ponce met a fisherman who ____. • Ponce tried to persuade the fisherman to ____.
3. What role does technical language have in Ponce's essay?	• Technical language in the essay includes ____. • This language helps Ponce ____.

Review Prompt and Rubric

Before students begin writing, review the writing prompt and rubric with the class.

NARRATIVE: Using Ponce's essay as a point of reference, write a persuasive narrative essay where you defend a subject about which you are passionate. Be sure to include technical language where applicable, as this can lend authority to your opinions and ideas.

 PROMPT GUIDE

- What subject area does Ponce talk about?
- What happened to Ponce that led him to learn about this subject?
- What role does technical language have in Ponce's essay?

- Like Ponce's essay, what can you write your essay about?
- What technical language can you use?

Score	Technical Language	Language and Conventions
4	The writer effectively defends a subject about which he or she is passionate. The writer skillfully includes technical language that lends authority to his or her words.	The writer demonstrates a consistent command of grammar, punctuation, and usage conventions. Although minor errors may be evident, they do not detract from the fluency or the clarity of the writing.
3	The writer defends a subject about which he or she is passionate. The writer includes some technical language that lends authority to his or her words.	The writer demonstrates an adequate command of grammar, punctuation, and usage conventions. Although some errors may be evident, they create few (if any) disruptions in the fluency or clarity of the writing.
2	The writer attempts to defend a subject about which he or she is passionate but is not entirely successful. The writer includes one or two examples of technical language.	The writer demonstrates a partial command of grammar, punctuation, and usage conventions. Some distracting errors may be evident, at times creating minor disruptions in the fluency or clarity of the writing.
1	The writer does not successfully defend a subject about which he or she is passionate. The writer includes no technical language.	The writer demonstrates little or no command of grammar, punctuation, and usage conventions. Serious and persistent errors create disruptions in the fluency of the writing and sometimes interfere with meaning.
0	The writer does not provide a relevant response to the prompt or does not provide a response at all.	Serious and persistent errors overwhelm the writing and interfere with the meaning of the response as a whole, making the writer's meaning impossible to understand.

Write

Ask students to complete the writing assignment using textual evidence to support their answers.

Use the scaffolds below to differentiate instruction for your **ELL** English Language Learners and **A** Approaching grade-level learners.

ELL **BEGINNING** With the help of the word bank, write a response using paragraph frame 1.

INTERMEDIATE With the help of the word bank, write a response using paragraph frames 1 and 2.

ADVANCED, ADVANCED HIGH Write a response of differentiated length using the sentence starters.

A **APPROACHING** Write a response of differentiated length using the sentence starters.

| BEGINNING | | ADVANCED, ADVANCED HIGH | |
| INTERMEDIATE | | APPROACHING | |
Word Bank	Paragraph Frame 1	Paragraph Frame 2	Sentence Starters
plastic effect reused ecosystems ecstatic	One time I went to the store with my mother. We ____ our own bags. Many people did not. They got ____ bags. I saw plastic bags blowing around the parking lot. Some were stuck in trees. Plastic bags have a negative ____. I learned they can harm ____. Now I work hard to ban plastic bags. I will be ____ when plastic bags are banned.	I am passionate about this subject because ____. Now I understand that ____. I hope ____.	• One time I . . . • What happened next was . . . • I learned that . . . • Now I am passionate about . . .

Peer Review

Students should submit substantive feedback to two peers using the review instructions below.

- How well does this response answer the prompt?
- How well does the writer defend a subject with a personal narrative?
- Does the essay use technical language that lends authority to the writer?
- What did the writer do well in this response? What does the writer need to work on?

Rate

Respond to the following with a point rating that reflects your opinion.

	1 2 3 4
Ideas	▪ ▪ ▪ ☐
Evidence	▪ ▪ ▪ ▪
Language and Conventions	▪ ▪ ☐ ☐

Submit

ELL A

SENTENCE FRAMES

- You were able to (completely / partly / almost) answer the prompt because ____.
- You could answer the prompt better by ____.

- You could make the essay sound more persuasive by ____.
- You might also include the technical term ____.
- My favorite part of your essay is ____.

The Call of the Wild

FICTION
Jack London
1903

Introduction

studysync

Author Jack London (1876–1916) was a writer and adventurer, beginning his life in the San Francisco Bay area, and then traveling the world—seal hunting in the Far East, mucking for gold in the Yukon Territory, sailing the South Pacific, and more. While participating in the Klondike Gold Rush, he reportedly encountered a mythical wolf that served as the inspiration for *The Call of the Wild*, his most popular novel. The book details the adventures of Buck, a large and powerful St. Bernard mix, as he experiences both love and abuse from a succession of owners. In this excerpt, Buck, by now a sled dog, stirs up rebellion among the team when he stands up to the aggressive alpha dog, Spitz.

In this excerpt, Buck, a sled dog, stirs up rebellion among the team after he stands up to the aggressive alpha dog, Spitz. Traveling across the Yukon, the team is making great progress, but their driver Francois has trouble keeping the dogs in line. Due to Buck's rebelliousness, the rest of the team has begun to challenge Spitz, stealing his fish and starting fights. Francois knows that Buck is the instigator, but Buck is too clever to be caught causing trouble. When he is in the harness, he runs tirelessly. One night after supper, the dogs catch sight of a rabbit and proceed to chase it. Even though the rabbit continues to stay one step ahead, Buck is ecstatic living in the moment. Driven only by his instincts, Buck is aglow with happiness.

 Proficiency-leveled summaries and summaries in multiple languages are available digitally.

 Audio and audio text highlighting are available with this text.

CONNECT TO ESSENTIAL QUESTION

Why do we take chances?

In Jack London's classic novel *The Call of the Wild*, the sled dog Buck stirs up a rebellion when he risks standing up to the aggressive alpha dog, Spitz.

Access Complex Text

LEXILE: 1160L   WORD COUNT: 759

The following areas may be challenging for students, particularly English Language Learners and Ⓐ Approaching grade-level learners.

Prior Knowledge	Sentence Structure	Organization
• Students unfamiliar with Alaska and snowy climates may struggle to visualize the setting. • Students who have never seen a dogsled may not understand the significance of the dogs not getting along with one another.	• The combination of compound sentences and complex sentences in some paragraphs will challenge students. • Visualizing the actions may help students understand what is being described in compound sentences and complex sentences.	• Students may find it confusing that the viewpoints of the dogs are included in places. • The description of various incidents among the dogs may cause students to struggle with tracking the chronology of events.

 SCAFFOLDS   **ENGLISH LANGUAGE LEARNERS**   **APPROACHING GRADE LEVEL**   **BEYOND GRADE LEVEL**

These icons identify differentiation strategies and scaffolded support for a variety of students. See the digital lesson plan for additional differentiation strategies and scaffolds.

Instructional Path

The print teacher's edition includes essential point-of-use instruction and planning tools.
Complete lesson plans and program documents appear in your digital teacher account.

First Read: The Call of the Wild

Objectives: After an initial reading and discussion of the excerpt, students will be able to identify and describe character traits and setting details, as well as articulate the conflict that is integral to the story's plot.

Skill: Language, Style, and Audience

Objectives: After rereading and discussing a model of close reading, students will be able to analyze the impact of specific word choice on meaning and tone in the text.

Skill: Media

Objectives: After rereading and discussing a model of close reading, students will be able to analyze the extent to which a filmed production of a story stays faithful to or departs from the text, and will be able to evaluate the choices made by the director or actors.

Close Read: The Call of the Wild

Objectives: After engaging in a close reading and discussion of the text, students will be able to write a short response analyzing how word choice affects meaning and tone and how the text aligns with a video version of the same story.

Progress Monitoring

Opportunities to Learn	Opportunities to Demonstrate Learning	Opportunities to Reteach
Language, Style, and Audience		
⚙ Skill: Language, Style, and Audience	⚙ Skill: Language, Style, and Audience • Your Turn ▭ Close Read • Complete Vocabulary Chart • Skills Focus • Write	⚙ Unit 4 Skill: Language, Style, and Audience - Speech to the Ohio Women's Conference: Ain't I a Woman? ⚙ Unit 5 Skill: Language, Style, and Audience - Refugee ⚙ Spotlight Skill: Language, Style, and Audience
Media		
⚙ Skill: Media	⚙ Skill: Media • Your Turn ▭ Close Read • Skills Focus • Write	⚙ Unit 4 Skill: Media - Across Five Aprils ⚙ Spotlight Skill: Media

First Read

Jack London

The Call of the Wild

Introduce the Text

As a class, watch the video preview 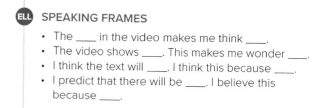 and have students read the introduction in pairs to make connections to the video preview.

To activate prior knowledge and experiences, ask students:

- What part of the video stood out to you the most?

- What questions do you have after reading the introduction?

- How does this information connect to something you already know?

ELL SPEAKING FRAMES

- The ____ in the video makes me think ____.
- The video shows ____. This makes me wonder ____.
- I think the text will ____. I think this because ____.
- I predict that there will be ____. I believe this because ____.

Entry Point

As students prepare to read *The Call of the Wild,* share the following information with them to provide context.

✓ Jack London (1876–1916) was a writer who often wrote about adventures in the wilderness. He was born in San Francisco, California, and he moved frequently as a child. He became an avid reader by going to public libraries.

✓ London left school at 14 to earn money and go on adventures. He then returned to California to complete his education when he was 19. After completing high school and briefly attending college, London continued to travel. He took part in the Klondike Gold Rush in Alaska and Canada.

✓ London did not strike gold, but he dedicated himself to writing once he returned home in 1898. By 1899, magazines began to publish London's short stories about adventures. London's first novel, *The Call of the Wild,* was then published in 1903. It quickly became popular and brought him international fame.

"He was ranging at the head of the pack, running the wild thing down"

NOTES

from Chapter III, The Dominant Primordial Beast

1 They made Sixty Mile, which is a fifty-mile run, on the first day; and the second day saw them booming up the Yukon well on their way to Pelly. But such splendid running was achieved not without great trouble and vexation on the part of Francois. The insidious revolt led by Buck had destroyed the **solidarity** of the team. It no longer was as one dog leaping in the

Dog sled in Alaska, circa 1890s

traces. The encouragement Buck gave the rebels led them into all kinds of petty misdemeanors. No more was Spitz a leader greatly to be feared. The old awe departed, and they grew equal to challenging his authority. Pike robbed him of half a fish one night, and gulped it down under the protection of Buck. Another night Dub and Joe fought Spitz and made him forego the punishment they deserved. And even Billee, the good-natured, was less good-natured, and whined not half so **placatingly** as in former days. Buck never came near Spitz without snarling and bristling menacingly. In fact, his conduct approached that of a bully, and he was given to swaggering up and down before Spitz's very nose.

2 The breaking down of discipline likewise affected the dogs in their relations with one another. They quarrelled and bickered more than ever among themselves, till at times the camp was a howling bedlam. Dave and Sol-leks alone were unaltered, though they were made irritable by the unending squabbling. Francois swore strange barbarous oaths, and stamped the snow in futile rage, and tore his hair. His lash was always singing among the dogs, but it was of small avail. Directly his back was turned they were at it again. He backed up Spitz with his whip, while Buck backed up the remainder of the team. Francois knew he was behind all the trouble, and Buck knew he knew; but Buck was too clever ever again to be caught red-handed. He worked faithfully in the harness, for the toil had become a delight to him; yet it was a

Skill:
Media

In both types of media, Buck's attitude about work changed. In the video, Buck wants to please his master, and so he happily changes his mind. The text is different. Buck seems to enjoy working but also enjoys causing trouble.

78 Reading & Writing Companion

SELECTION VOCABULARY

solidarity / la solidaridad **noun** a feeling of being united COGNATE

placatingly / pacíficamente **adverb** to act in a way that causes others to feel less angry

ELL
• How does a dog with a good nature behave toward other dogs?
• How does this behavior change if other dogs misbehave?

Analyze Vocabulary Using Context Clues

In paragraph 1, focus on the sentence that uses the word *solidarity*. Point out these context clues:

1. I know that solidarity is something the team had, and Buck's revolt destroyed it. I think solidarity is like team work or unity, because it makes sense that a revolt would destroy those things.

2. When I read the sentence again, using *unity* in place of *solidarity*, the sentence makes sense: "The insidious revolt led by Buck had destroyed the *unity* of the team."

Media

What similarity and difference does the reader notice between paragraph 2 of the text and the video?

The reader notices that in both media, Buck has changed. However, the degree to which he has changed varies between the written text and the video.

TEXT TALK

What is the main problem that Francois faces?

See paragraph 1: The dogs pulling his sled do not get along.

Which dog is making the strongest challenge to Spitz's leadership?

See paragraph 1: Buck is strongly challenging Spitz's leadership.

What type of discipline does Francois use unsuccessfully on the dogs? What can you infer about this?

See paragraph 2: He tries to use a whip on the dogs. Force is not what makes the dogs work.

Language, Style, and Audience

What analogy and word choices did the reader notice in the paragraph 3, and how did they affect her understanding of the text?

The reader highlighted the repeated use of "leap by leap" and the analogy referring to "flashed." She said the word choices draw her in and make the story more real and more active.

Skills Focus

QUESTION 2: Language, Style, and Audience

The analogy here compares Buck to both an artist and a soldier. London phrased the comparison this way to help the reader understand what he means by the "ecstasy, this forgetfulness of living." The analogy compares Buck's ecstasy to the passion and intense concentration of an artist caught up in her art, or a soldier in war.

TEXT TALK

Buck is compared to two types of people during the chase. What are they?

See paragraph 5: Buck is compared to an artist and a soldier.

---

greater delight slyly to **precipitate** a fight amongst his mates and tangle the traces.

3 At the mouth of the Tahkeena, one night after supper, Dub turned up a snowshoe rabbit, blundered it, and missed. In a second the whole team was in full cry. A hundred yards away was a camp of the Northwest Police, with fifty dogs, huskies all, who joined the chase. The rabbit sped down the river, turned off into a small creek, up the frozen bed of which it held steadily. It ran lightly on the surface of the snow, while the dogs ploughed through by main strength. Buck led the pack, sixty strong, around bend after bend, but he could not gain. He lay down low to the race, whining eagerly, his splendid body flashing forward, leap by leap, in the wan white moonlight. And leap by leap, like some pale frost wraith, the snowshoe rabbit flashed on ahead.

4 All that stirring of old instincts which at stated periods drives men out from the sounding cities to forest and plain to kill things by chemically **propelled** leaden pellets, the blood lust, the joy to kill—all this was Buck's, only it was infinitely more intimate. He was ranging at the head of the pack, running the wild thing down, the living meat, to kill with his own teeth and wash his muzzle to the eyes in warm blood.

5 There is an ecstasy that marks the summit of life, and beyond which life cannot rise. And such is the **paradox** of living, this ecstasy comes when one is most alive, and it comes as a complete forgetfulness that one is alive. This ecstasy, this forgetfulness of living, comes to the artist, caught up and out of himself in a sheet of flame; it comes to the soldier, war-mad on a stricken field and refusing quarter; and it came to Buck, leading the pack, sounding the old wolf-cry, straining after the food that was alive and that fled swiftly before him through the moonlight. He was sounding the deeps of his nature, and of the parts of his nature that were deeper than he, going back into the womb of Time. He was mastered by the sheer surging of life, the tidal wave of being, the perfect joy of each separate muscle, joint, and sinew in that it was everything that was not death, that it was aglow and rampant, expressing itself in movement, flying exultantly under the stars and over the face of dead matter that did not move.

London, Jack. *The Call of the Wild*. 1903. Scholastic Paperbacks, 2001.

Skill:
Language, Style, and Audience

The author compares the speed of Buck and the rabbit using "leap by leap" and the word "flashed." Buck's chase of the rabbit comes alive through this analogy. It is written in an active way and draws me into the story.

SELECTION VOCABULARY

precipitate / precipitar **verb** to cause something to happen quickly and unexpectedly, usually something bad or undesirable COGNATE

 • What does Buck want to do?

propel / propulsar **verb** to cause something to move forward with force COGNATE

ELL • How do the "leaden pellets" travel?

paradox / la paradoja **noun** a statement that is seemingly contradictory or impossible and yet often reveals a larger truth COGNATE

ELL • What two feelings can one have about being alive, as described by London?
• What is unusual about having these feelings at the same time?

Reading Comprehension OPTIONAL

Have students complete the digital reading comprehension questions ✓ when they finish reading.

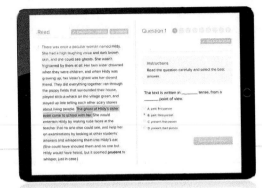

ANSWER KEY

QUESTION 1: A	QUESTION 5: B	QUESTION 9:
QUESTION 2: A	QUESTION 6: A	*See first chart.*
QUESTION 3: D	QUESTION 7: C	QUESTION 10:
QUESTION 4: D	QUESTION 8: C	*See second chart.*

Synonym	Word
unity	solidarity
pushed forward	propelled
please	placate
come before	precipitate
a seemingly absurd or contradictory statement	paradox

Character	Description
Buck	"He was ranging at the head of the pack, running the wild thing down"
Francois	"swore strange barbarous oaths, and stamped the snow in futile rage, and tore his hair"
Pike	"robbed him of half a fish one night, and gulped it down under the protection of Buck"
Billee	"the good-natured, was less good-natured, and whined not half so placatingly as in former days"

Connect and Extend OPTIONAL

CONNECT TO EXTENDED WRITING PROJECT

Students can find inspiration from *The Call of the Wild* when writing their informational essays. Have them reflect on Jack London's characterization of Buck as he takes chances.

BEYOND THE BOOK

Writing: Mimicking a Master

Students will mimic the writing of Jack London to write a descriptive paragraph about events in their own lives.

Ask students to:

- Reread paragraph 3 of the excerpt from *The Call of the Wild*.
- Change the characters, setting, and events to something from their own lives.
- As closely as possible, mimic London's writing style to write about their own experience.
- Read the finished piece aloud to a partner.

To reflect, ask students:

- How did this writing style affect your story? Why do you think that was?

Think Questions

Circulate as students answer Think Questions independently. Scaffolds for these questions are shown on the opposite page.

QUESTION 1: Textual Evidence

Buck "destroyed the solidarity of the team" by encouraging the rebels. The rebels stopped following the leadership of Spitz, they stole fish, and they fought and bullied Spitz. By challenging the leader, Buck also challenged the rules that had reinforced the solidarity of the team.

QUESTION 2: Textual Evidence

In paragraph 2, Buck's cleverness and ability to stir up trouble without getting caught shows that he took pleasure in causing trouble for Francois.

QUESTION 3: Textual Evidence

Buck led all the dogs to chase the snowshoe rabbit that Dub turned up, including the fifty dogs from a nearby camp. This shows that Buck is a leader of dogs, but he is not disciplined.

QUESTION 4: Context Clues

The word *paradox* is used to describe forgetting that one is alive while feeling the ecstasy that comes when one is most alive. I think *paradox* means "two things that seem contradictory but are both true."

QUESTION 5: Greek and Latin Affixes and Roots

I think *placatingly* means "calmly." I determined this meaning because the root placare means "to calm down," and *calmly* fits in the sentence if I use it to replace *placatingly*: "And even Billee, the good-natured, was less good-natured, and whined not half so *calmly* as in former days."

The Call of the Wild

First Read

Read *The Call of the Wild*. After you read, complete the Think Questions below.

 THINK QUESTIONS

1. Refer to several details in paragraph 1 to explain how Buck "destroyed the solidarity of the team." Cite evidence that is directly stated in the text, and make inferences to support your explanation.

2. What evidence is there in paragraph 2 that Buck took pleasure in causing trouble for Francois?

3. How did Buck react when Dub turned up a snowshoe rabbit? What inferences can you make about Buck from his behavior? Support your answer with specific evidence from the text.

4. Use context to determine the meaning of the word **paradox** as it is used in paragraph 5. Write your definition of *paradox* and tell how you determined the meaning of the word. Then check your definition in a print or digital dictionary to confirm the word's meaning.

5. By understanding that the Latin word *placare* means "to calm down" or "appease," use the context clues provided in paragraph 1 to determine the meaning of **placatingly**. Write your definition of *placatingly* and tell how you determined the meaning of the word.

Think Questions

Use the scaffolds below to differentiate instruction for your **ELL** English Language Learners and **A** Approaching grade-level learners.

ELL **BEGINNING** Write a response using the <u>word bank</u> and <u>sentence frames</u>.

INTERMEDIATE Write a response using the <u>sentence frames</u>.

ADVANCED, ADVANCED HIGH Write a response using the <u>Text-Dependent Question Guide</u>.

A **APPROACHING** Write a response using the <u>Text-Dependent Question Guide</u>.

| | INTERMEDIATE | APPROACHING |
| BEGINNING | | ADVANCED, ADVANCED HIGH |

Word Bank	Sentence Frames	Text-Dependent Question Guide
contradictory calmly led leadership	Buck "destroyed the solidarity of the team" by ____ the rebels. The rebels stopped following the ____ of Spitz, they stole fish, and they fought and bullied Spitz. By challenging the leader Buck, also challenged the ____ that had ____ the solidarity of the team.	1. • How does the team behave at the beginning of the paragraph? • What does it mean for a team to have solidarity? • What does Buck do? • What is the team like without solidarity?
reinforced disciplined rules	In paragraph 2, Buck's ____ and ability to stir up ____ without getting caught shows that he took pleasure in causing trouble for Francois.	2. • What things does Buck do that cause trouble? • What would it look like to take pleasure in causing trouble? • What is it about Buck that makes it seem like he enjoys causing trouble?
trouble forgetting encouraging sentence	Buck ____ all the dogs to chase the snowshoe rabbit that Dub turned up, including the fifty dogs from a nearby camp. This shows that Buck is a leader of dogs, but he is not ____.	3. • What happened when Dub turned up the snowshoe rabbit? • Who was chasing the rabbit? • Who was leading the chase?
cleverness	The word *paradox* is used to describe ____ that one is alive while feeling the ecstasy that comes when one is most alive. I think *paradox* means two things that seem ____ but are both true.	4. • Read: "There is an ecstasy that marks the summit of life, and beyond which life cannot rise. And such is the **paradox** of living, this ecstasy comes when one is most alive, and it comes as a complete forgetfulness that one is alive." • What two things is the word *paradox* describing? • How do those two things relate to each other?
	I think *placatingly* means ____. I determined this meaning because the root *placare* means "to calm down," and "calmly" fits in the ____if I use it to replace *placatingly*: "And even Billee, the good-natured, was less good-natured, and whined not half so *calmly* as in former days."	5. • Read: "And even Billee, the good-natured, was less good-natured, and whined not half so **placatingly** as in former days." • Is *placatingly* a noun, a verb, an adjective, or an adverb? • How does a dog with a good nature behave toward other dogs? • How does this behavior change if other dogs misbehave?

Skill: Language, Style, and Audience

Introduce the Skill

Watch the Concept Definition video and read the following definition with your students.

Authors use language to convey meaning or to affect the way their audience thinks and perceives. An **audience** is the intended reader or listener. Readers can analyze an author's style to better understand the tone and meaning of a text.

Style refers to the way an author uses language (words, sentences, paragraphs) to achieve a purpose. One element of style is word choice. **Word choice** is a technique in which writers choose specific words for precise meaning or to convey a certain tone. **Meaning** is a reader's interpretation of the text's deeper messages, themes, or ideas. **Tone** expresses a writer's **attitude** (or thoughts and feelings) toward his or her subject. Tone can be described, for example, as formal, casual, conversational, ironic, sad, bitter, humorous, or serious.

The Call of the Wil

LANGUAGE, STYLE, AND AUDIENCE
.skills

Skill:
Language, Style, and Audience

Use the Checklist to analyze Language, Style, and Audience in *The Call of the Wild*. Refer to the sample student annotations about Language, Style, and Audience in the text.

••• CHECKLIST FOR LANGUAGE, STYLE, AND AUDIENCE

In order to determine an author's style, do the following:

✓ identify and define any unfamiliar words or phrases

✓ use context, including the meaning of surrounding words and phrases

✓ note possible reactions to the author's word choice

✓ examine your reaction to the author's word choice

✓ identify any analogies, or comparisons in which one part of the comparison helps explain the other

To analyze the impact of specific word choice on meaning and tone, ask the following questions:

✓ How did your understanding of the language change during your analysis?

✓ How does the writer's word choice impact or create meaning in the text?

✓ How does the writer's word choice impact or create a specific tone in the text?

✓ How could various audiences interpret this language? What different possible emotional responses can you list?

✓ What analogies do I see here? Where might an analogy have clarified meaning or created a specific tone?

Reading & Writing Companion   81

TURN AND TALK

1. Think of your favorite story by a particular author. Would it be the same story if it were written by someone else?

2. Why is word choice so important? How do the choices that an author makes affect the reader?

ELL SPEAKING FRAMES

- My favorite story is by ____. If the story were written by another author it would ____.
- Word choice is important because ____.
- The word choices an author makes affect the reader by ____.

V SKILL VOCABULARY

style / el estilo *noun* a way of expressing something that is characteristic of the person or time period COGNATE

word choice / la elección de palabras *noun* specific words chosen for precise meaning or to generate an emotional response

tone / el tono *noun* the writer's or speaker's attitude toward his or her subject matter COGNATE

Copyright © BookheadEd Learning, LLC

he Call of the Wild

LANGUAGE, STYLE, AND AUDIENCE

●skills

Skill:
Language, Style, and Audience

Reread paragraph 5 of *The Call of the Wild*. Then, using the Checklist on the previous page, answer the multiple-choice questions below.

⟳ YOUR TURN

. By using the phrase "There is an ecstasy that marks the summit of life, and beyond which life cannot rise," what is Jack London trying to say about Buck?

- ○ A. That Buck is not fast enough to catch and kill the rabbit.
- ○ B. That Buck is about to kill the rabbit.
- ○ C. That Buck could not possibly feel more alive than he is right now.
- ○ D. That Buck is about to die.

2. Why does Jack London mention life and death throughout his analogies about Buck and the rabbit?

- ○ A. He wants to suggest that Buck will die once he kills the rabbit.
- ○ B. He is trying to say that Buck is dying.
- ○ C. He wants to draw a comparison between life and death and the act of Buck chasing the rabbit.
- ○ D. He is trying to make everyone who reads the story feel bad for the rabbit.

3. What is the meaning behind the author's phrase "it comes to the soldier, war-mad and refusing quarter"?

- ○ A. That a soldier driven crazy by battle will still fight on and refuse the safety of shelter.
- ○ B. That a soldier driven crazy by battle will not be paid.
- ○ C. That a soldier driven crazy by battle will refuse to get paid.
- ○ D. That soldiers always refuse safety in order to get paid.

Copyright © Bookheaded Learning, LLC

  Reading & Writing Companion

V SKILL VOCABULARY

attitude / la actitud **noun** a state involving beliefs and feelings that causes a person to think or act in a certain way COGNATE

audience / la audiencia **noun** the people who read a written text, listen to an oral response or presentation, or watch a performance COGNATE

meaning / el significado **noun** what is meant by a word; the general message of a text or idea

⚙ Your Turn

Ask students to complete the Your Turn activity.

QUESTION 1

A. Incorrect. The author is talking about Buck's experience of his life, not his speed.

B. Incorrect. The author is talking about Buck's experience of his life, not if he will be able to kill the rabbit.

C. Correct. The author is talking about Buck's experience of his life and how Buck is feeling very good in the chase.

D. Incorrect. There is nothing to indicate the author is saying this.

QUESTION 2

A. Incorrect. The text does not suggest that this might happen.

B. Incorrect. Although Buck may be hungry, the excerpt does not focus on whether Buck is dying.

C. Correct. He wants the reader to understand how alive Buck feels in this moment and that the rabbit may die.

D. Incorrect. There is no textual evidence to support this idea.

QUESTION 3

A. Correct. *Quarter* means "a place where soldiers take shelter," and when soldiers are feeling that ecstasy, they will keep fighting instead of seeking the safety of shelter.

B. Incorrect. *Quarter* does not refer to money here.

C. Incorrect. *Quarter* does not refer to money here.

D. Incorrect. *Quarter* does not refer to money here.

Skill: Media

Introduce the Skill

Watch the Concept Definition video and read the following definition with your students.

Media is the plural form of the word *medium*. A **medium** is a means of sending a communication to an intended audience. Throughout most of human history, people communicated through three main media: speech, writing, and visual arts such as drawing, painting, and sculpture. But in the 19th century, media options suddenly exploded. The invention of photography, and then the telegraph and the telephone, changed the world. Within a century radio, motion pictures, and television followed.

Stories and ideas change as they are translated from one medium to another. A dialogue between two characters in a novel, for example, becomes very different when it is delivered by actors in a film—with close-ups, sound effects such as music, and other elements unique to the medium of film itself.

Today, new media are being invented at a much faster pace than ever before, and each of these forms of online communication has its own "language" and creates its own experience.

 TURN AND TALK

1. Are there any books that you've read that have been turned into a television show or movie?

2. Do you like the book version better or the film? Why? What are the differences?

ELL SPEAKING FRAMES
- [Book title] was turned into a [movie / television show] called ____.
- The reason I like the [book / movie / television show] better is ____.
- The differences between the versions are ____.

Skill:
Media

Use the Checklist to analyze Media in *The Call of the Wild*. Refer to the sample student annotations about Media in the text.

••• CHECKLIST FOR MEDIA

In order to determine the extent to which a filmed or live production of a story or drama stays faithful to or departs from the text or script, do the following:

- ✓ note key elements from the text and how they changed or were removed in the film

- ✓ think about the advantages and disadvantages of using different media to present a particular topic, idea, or event

- ✓ consider the choices made by the director of a film, and how they may emphasize or minimize an event or even a line of dialogue from a written work

- ✓ weigh and understand the strengths and weaknesses of different media

To analyze the extent to which a filmed or live production of a story or drama stays faithful to or departs from the text or script, and to evaluate the choices made by the director or actors, ask the following questions:

- ✓ How does the filmed production of a story stay faithful to or depart from the text?

- ✓ What are the strengths of different media, such as novels or motion pictures, when telling a story? What are their weaknesses?

- ✓ How might the choices a director makes when making a film based on a novel completely change the point of view?

V SKILL VOCABULARY

medium / el medio **noun** a form of communication, such as television, the Internet, and radio   COGNATE

media / los medios **noun** the plural form of the word *medium*; a means of sending a communication to an intended audience

The Call of the Wild

Skill:
Media

Reread paragraph 4 of *The Call of the Wild,* and rewatch the video clip of *The Call of the Wild* from 03:57 to 05:20, available on the StudySync site. Then, using the Checklist on the previous page, answer the multiple-choice questions below.

YOUR TURN

1. What is Buck's reason for pursuing food in the text?

   ○ A. Francois didn't give him any food, and he was hungry.
   ○ B. He pulled 1,000 pounds, and that made him really hungry.
   ○ C. He was going to eat the snowshoe rabbit, but Dub stole it from him.
   ○ D. His instincts—in particular, the joy to kill—are what give him the desire to pursue food.

2. In the video, why does Buck finally eat so hungrily?

   ○ A. He seems to trust and understand that John Thornton is there to help him and wants him to be happy.
   ○ B. He pulled 1,000 pounds, and that made him really hungry.
   ○ C. He has to sneak food from John Thornton, so he eats it as quickly as he can.
   ○ D. His instincts as a dog make him eat quickly.

3. What is the difference in the portrayal of these scenes in the text and in the video clip?

   ○ A. In the text, the food is rabbit, but in the video, the food is moose.
   ○ B. Buck has different reasons for seeking food. Also, he relies on Francois in the text, but he relies only on himself in the video.
   ○ C. Buck has different reasons for seeking food. Also, he relies on Thornton in the video, but he relies only on himself in the text.
   ○ D. Buck moves slowly in the text and quickly in the video.

Your Turn

Ask students to complete the Your Turn activity.

QUESTION 1

A. Incorrect. The text doesn't mention if Francois fed him well or not.

B. Incorrect. This happens in the video, not the text.

C. Incorrect. Dub "turned up a snowshoe rabbit," and Buck pursued it for food.

D. Correct. The text talks about "the blood lust, the joy to kill."

QUESTION 2

A. Correct. Thornton doesn't push Buck, he lets Buck decide to trust him.

B. Incorrect. Buck eats in the video before pulling the 1,000 pounds.

C. Incorrect. Thornton brings him the food.

D. Incorrect. The movie doesn't talk about Buck's instincts or say anything about all dogs eating quickly.

QUESTION 3

A. Incorrect. We don't know what animal the meat in the video comes from.

B. Incorrect. Buck does have different reasons for seeking food. However, he does not rely on Francois in the text, and he does not rely on Thornton in the video.

C. Correct. Buck has different motivations, and in the video he is learning to trust Thornton.

D. Incorrect. Buck moves quickly when chasing the rabbit in the text, and he moves slowly—but eats hungrily—in the video.

Close Read

Skills Focus

QUESTION 1: Theme

See paragraph 2: The author explains how much Francois wants control and tries to get it with his lash. Whenever he turns away, though, he no longer has control. I think the author is trying to say that real control comes from more than yelling and lashing out.

QUESTION 2: Language, Style, and Audience

See paragraph 5.

QUESTION 3: Media

See paragraph 2: When I read that Francois yelled and lashed at the dogs, I could tell he was angry, but when I saw it in the video it seemed really mean. The interactions between Francois and the dogs seem much harsher and abusive when I can see and hear them than they do when I am reading them.

QUESTION 4: Connect to Essential Question

See paragraph 2: After reading the excerpt and watching the video, I think Buck is taking the biggest chance. In the video, Buck takes a chance on trusting Thornton, even after he has experienced how mean a human can be through his interactions with Francois, which is shown in both the text and the video.

Close Read

Reread *The Call of the Wild* and rewatch the video clip of *The Call of the Wild* available on the StudySync site. As you reread, complete the Skills Focus questions below. Then use your answers and annotations from the questions to help you complete the Write activity.

SKILLS FOCUS

1. Reread paragraph 2. What message is the author trying to convey about control? Include important details from the text that support your answer.

2. Reread paragraph 5 and identify an analogy. Explain what the analogy means and why you think it was important for Jack London to phrase his text that way.

3. Identify a part in the excerpt where humans interact with Buck and the dogs. Explain their interaction(s), and contrast this scene with what you saw in the video. How is this scene treated differently between the two types of media?

4. Based on your observations of the video and having read the text, who was taking a bigger chance: Buck, Thornton, the pack, or Francois? Make specific references from both the video and the text to support your response.

WRITE

LITERARY ANALYSIS: In the final paragraph, Jack London writes, "such is the paradox of living, this ecstasy comes when one is most alive, and it comes as a complete forgetfulness that one is alive." Based on his language, what sort of response was he likely looking for from his audience? Is there a difference in the impact of the text and the impact of the video? Which medium is more powerful and effective? Use textual evidence as well as references from the video to support your response.

Reading & Writing Companion

85

Writer's Notebook

Connect to Essential Question: Give students time to reflect on how *The Call of the Wild* connects to the unit's essential question "Why do we take chances?" by freewriting in their Writer's Notebooks.

ELL **Beginning & Intermediate**

Read aloud the unit's essential question: "Why do we take chances?" Encourage students to draw their connections or allow students to write in their native language. Circulate the room, prompting students for their thoughts as they respond orally or through pantomime.

ELL **Advanced & Advanced High**

Allow students to share their connections orally in pairs or small groups before freewriting.

StudySyncTV

Project the StudySyncTV episode ▶ and pause at the following times to prompt discussion:

1:43 What difficulty does Jasmine have with the prompt?

4:03 What opposing interpretations do Ben and Jasmine have of the description of Buck?

7:38 What human activity does the end of the excerpt remind Ben and Alicia of? Do you think this is a valid comparison?

Collaborative Conversation

SCAFFOLDS

Break students into collaborative conversation groups to discuss the Close Read prompt. Ask students to use the StudySyncTV episode as a model for their discussion. Remind them to reference their Skills Focus annotations in their discussion.

In the final paragraph, Jack London writes, "such is the paradox of living, this ecstasy comes when one is most alive, and it comes as a complete forgetfulness that one is alive." Based on his language, what sort of response was he likely looking for from his audience? Is there a difference in the impact of the text and the impact of the video? Which medium is more powerful and effective? Use textual evidence as well as references from the video to support your response.

Use the scaffolds below to differentiate instruction for your **ELL** English Language Learners and **A** Approaching grade-level learners.

ELL **BEGINNING, INTERMEDIATE** Use the <u>discussion guide</u> and <u>speaking frames</u> to facilitate the discussion with support from the teacher.

ADVANCED, ADVANCED HIGH Use the <u>discussion guide</u> and <u>speaking frames</u> to facilitate the discussion in mixed-level groups.

A **APPROACHING** Use the <u>discussion guide</u> to facilitate the discussion in mixed-level groups.

APPROACHING
ADVANCED, ADVANCED HIGH
BEGINNING, INTERMEDIATE

Discussion Guide	Speaking Frames
1. Where does the author use language designed to get a response from the audience?	• The phrase ____ in paragraph ____ seems designed to get a response from the audience. • The response the audience is likely to have is ____.
2. What happened in the video that seems designed to get a response from the audience?	• The scene in the video that seems designed to get a response from the audience is ____.

Review Prompt and Rubric

Before students begin writing, review the writing prompt and rubric with the class.

LITERARY ANALYSIS: In the final paragraph, Jack London writes, "such is the paradox of living, this ecstasy comes when one is most alive, and it comes as a complete forgetfulness that one is alive." Based on his language, what sort of response was he likely looking for from his audience? Is there a difference in the impact of the text and the impact of the video? Which medium is more powerful and effective? Use textual evidence as well as references from the video to support your response.

ELL **PROMPT GUIDE**

A
- What is the difference between the impact of the text and the video?
- Which is more powerful?

- Which medium is more effective at getting a reaction from the audience? Why?

An additional rubric item for Language and Conventions appears in your digital teacher and student accounts.

Score	Media	Language, Style, and Audience
4	The writer clearly analyzes and explains information from different media and the advantages and disadvantages of using them. The writer provides exemplary analysis, using relevant evidence from the text and video.	The writer clearly analyzes and explains the author's word choice and tone. The writer provides exemplary analysis, using relevant evidence from the text.
3	The writer analyzes and explains information from different media and the advantages and disadvantages of using them. The writer provides sufficient analysis, using relevant evidence from the text and video most of the time.	The writer analyzes and explains the author's word choice and tone. The writer provides sufficient analysis, using relevant evidence from the text most of the time.
2	The writer begins to analyze or explain information from different media and the advantages and disadvantages of using them, but the analysis is incomplete. The writer uses relevant evidence from the text and video only some of the time.	The writer begins to analyze or explain the author's word choice and tone, but the analysis is incomplete. The writer uses relevant evidence from the text only some of the time.
1	The writer attempts to analyze or explain information from different media and the advantages and disadvantages of using them, but the analysis is not successful. The writer uses little or no relevant evidence from the text and video.	The writer attempts to analyze or explain the author's word choice and tone, but the analysis is not successful. The writer uses little or no relevant evidence from the text.
0	The writer does not provide a relevant response to the prompt or does not provide a response at all.	The writer does not provide a relevant response to the prompt or does not provide a response at all.

Write

Ask students to complete the writing assignment using textual evidence to support their answers.

Use the scaffolds below to differentiate instruction for your **ELL** English Language Learners and **A** Approaching grade-level learners.

ELL
BEGINNING With the help of the word bank, write a response using paragraph frame 1.

INTERMEDIATE With the help of the word bank, write a response using paragraph frames 1 and 2.

ADVANCED, ADVANCED HIGH Write a response of differentiated length using the sentence starters.

A
APPROACHING Write a response of differentiated length using the sentence starters.

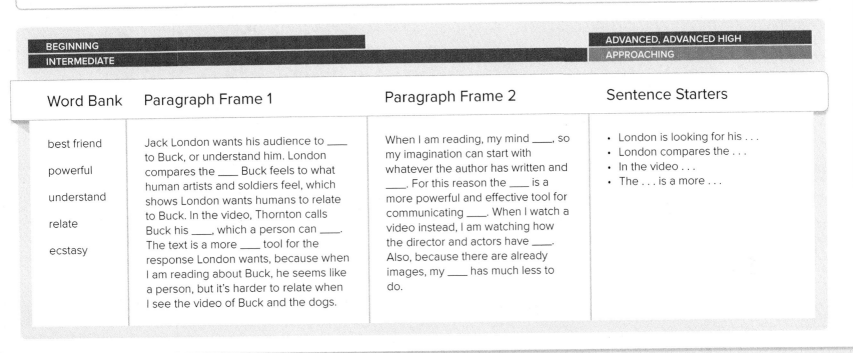

	BEGINNING INTERMEDIATE		ADVANCED, ADVANCED HIGH APPROACHING
Word Bank	Paragraph Frame 1	Paragraph Frame 2	Sentence Starters
best friend powerful understand relate ecstasy	Jack London wants his audience to ____ to Buck, or understand him. London compares the ____ Buck feels to what human artists and soldiers feel, which shows London wants humans to relate to Buck. In the video, Thornton calls Buck his ____, which a person can ____. The text is a more ____ tool for the response London wants, because when I am reading about Buck, he seems like a person, but it's harder to relate when I see the video of Buck and the dogs.	When I am reading, my mind ____, so my imagination can start with whatever the author has written and ____. For this reason the ____ is a more powerful and effective tool for communicating ____. When I watch a video instead, I am watching how the director and actors have ____. Also, because there are already images, my ____ has much less to do.	• London is looking for his . . . • London compares the . . . • In the video . . . • The . . . is a more . . .

Peer Review

Students should submit substantive feedback to two peers using the instructions below.

- How well does this response answer the prompt?
- How well does the writer analyze the differences between the text and the video?
- What did the writer do well in this response? What does the writer need to work on?

Rate

Respond to the following with a point rating that reflects your opinion.

	1 2 3 4
Ideas	
Evidence	
Language and Conventions	

ELL **A**
SENTENCE FRAMES
- You were able to (completely / partly / almost) answer the prompt.
- You could answer the prompt better by ____.
- The reference to the video that was really helpful was ____.
- I think you could work on ____.

Cocoon

POETRY
Mahvash Sabet
2013

Introduction

Mahvash Sabet (b. 1953), a leader in the Bahá'í community in Tehran, Iran, was arrested and imprisoned at Evin Prison in March of 2008 because of her faith. The Iranian government does not recognize the Bahá'í Faith as an official religion, even though it is the largest religious minority in the country. Before her arrest, Sabet worked as a teacher, collaborating with the National Literacy Committee and serving as director of the Bahá'í Institute for Higher Education for 15 years. While in prison, Sabet began writing poems, which were smuggled out by relatives and were eventually translated into English by Bahiyyih Nakhjavani. *Prison Poems*, a collection of about 70 of Sabet's poems, was published in 2013. After nearly ten years of imprisonment, Sabet was released in September of 2017. "Cocoon" depicts a speaker wrestling with contradictory feelings,

The speaker mourns for the cocoon, the chrysalis that had been smashed and destroyed before her eyes. She feels tossed to and fro, caught between compulsions, longing for both freedom and the security of her old cocoon. Initially, when her soul had broken out of the cocoon, she felt thrilled at the feeling of freedom. However, a part of her was afraid, feeling threatened by the fire that awaited her. So she wonders about contrary desires. She loves to fly and applauds bravely dying, but she also weeps for the security of how it used to be.

ELL Proficiency-leveled summaries and summaries in multiple languages are available digitally.

🔊 Audio and audio text highlighting are available with this text.

CONNECT TO ESSENTIAL QUESTION

Why do we take chances?

Poet Mahvash Sabet was a leader in the Bahá'í community in Tehran, Iran, where she was arrested for practicing her faith. She wrote poems such as "Cocoon" during her imprisonment, which were a risk in themselves to write.

Access Complex Text

LEXILE: N/A   **WORD COUNT:** 132

The following areas may be challenging for students, particularly **ELL** English Language Learners and **A** Approaching grade-level learners.

Prior Knowledge

- Some students may be unfamiliar with the Bahá'í faith, a religion that teaches the essential worth of all religions and the unity and equality of all people.

- Established in 1863, it initially grew in Iran and parts of the Middle East, where it has faced ongoing persecution since its inception.

Specific Vocabulary

- Difficult vocabulary, such as *cowering* (to crouch, or kneel-down with the upper body brought forward, usually in fear), *pining* (suffering because of a broken heart), and *demise* (a person or thing's death), may need to be explained.

- Remind students to use context clues while reading and to use a dictionary to define any unfamiliar words.

SCAFFOLDS   **ELL** ENGLISH LANGUAGE LEARNERS   **A** APPROACHING GRADE LEVEL   **B** BEYOND GRADE LEVEL

These icons identify differentiation strategies and scaffolded support for a variety of students. See the digital lesson plan for additional differentiation strategies and scaffolds.

Instructional Path

The print teacher's edition includes essential point-of-use instruction and planning tools
Complete lesson plans and program documents appear in your digital teacher account

First Read: Cocoon

Objectives: After an initial reading and discussion of the poem, students will be able to make inferences to analyze and understand the ideas presented in the poem.

Skill: Connotation and Denotation

Objectives: After rereading and discussing a model of close reading, students will be able to determine the meanings of words and phrases as they are used in a text, including connotative and denotative meanings.

Close Read: Cocoon

Objectives: After engaging in a close reading and discussion of the text, students will be able to analyze the author's use of connotations and denotations and explain the author's purpose for writing in a short, written response.

Progress Monitoring

Opportunities to Learn	Opportunities to Demonstrate Learning	Opportunities to Reteach

Connotation and Denotation

⚙ Skill: Connotation and Denotation	⚙ Skill: Connotation and Denotation • Your Turn ▭ Close Read • Complete Vocabulary Chart • Skills Focus • Write	⚙ Unit 4 Skill: Connotation and Denotation - Gettysburg Address ⚙ Unit 4 Skill: Connotation and Denotation - Blind ⚙ Spotlight Skill: Connotation and Denotation

First Read

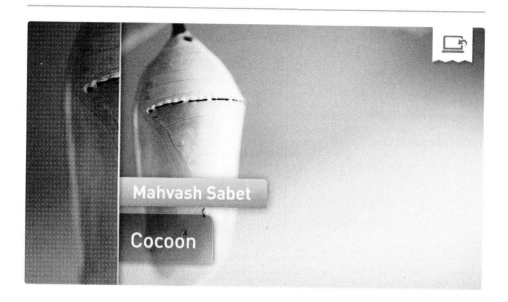

Mahvash Sabet

Cocoon

 Introduce the Text

As a class, watch the video preview 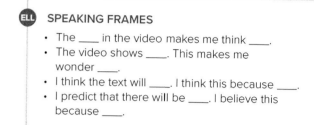 and have students read the introduction in pairs to make connections to the video preview.

To activate prior knowledge and experiences, ask students:

- What key words or images from the video do you think will be most important to the poem you are about to read?

- What behaviors would you consider to be bizarre, and why?

ELL SPEAKING FRAMES

- The _____ in the video makes me think _____.
- The video shows _____. This makes me wonder _____.
- I think the text will _____. I think this because _____.
- I predict that there will be _____. I believe this because _____.

Entry Point

As students prepare to read "Cocoon," share the following information with them to provide context.

✓ In 1979, Iran—once called Persia, and now officially the Islamic Republic of Iran—underwent a revolution that overthrew its ruler, the shah, and installed a government run by conservative Islamic clergymen according to Islamic law. Restrictions on free speech, women's activity and dress, and many social practices were instituted. Bahá'í was banned and its followers persecuted because its founder claimed to be a prophet, but Muslims believe Mohammad was the last prophet. Anyone who publicly criticizes the government may be put in jail.

✓ Women's rights are restricted in Iranian society under the Islamic government. For example, a married woman cannot leave the country without her husband's permission, and women cannot watch men play sports in stadiums.

✓ According to Sabet, writing poetry was her "means of survival" in prison. Prison poems form a subgroup of poetry. Some prisons in the United States have poetry writing programs for inmates.

"I'm tossed to and fro, from here to there . . ."

1 There's a part of me that keeps mourning
2 for the soft cocoon where I lay,
3 a part of me that keeps pining
4 for the delicate **chrysalis** smashed and destroyed
5 before my eyes that day.

6 I'm tossed to and fro, from here to there,
7 caught between **compulsions**;
8 I'm thrown left and right and back and forth,
9 longing for the freedom of flight and yet
10 **craving** those soft consolations.

11 When my soul broke free, a part of me
12 **thrilled** at the lift of its arc,
13 but another shrank back in cowering fear
14 from the threatening fires, from the lowering smoke
15 that awaited me in here.

16 All this makes me wonder greatly
17 about **contrary** desires.
18 There's something in me approves of flying,
19 applauds the thought of bravely dying,
20 yet I weep for the cocoon's demise.

From *Prison Poems*, 2013. Used by permission of George Ronald Publishing Ltd.

Skill:
Connotation and
Denotation

The denotative meaning of cocoon is a case that insect larva spin as protection when turning into an adult. The connotative meaning here seems to be a bed, a safe place that the speaker remembers before she was arrested and imprisoned.

Reading & Writing
Companion   87

 SELECTION VOCABULARY

chrysalis / la crisálida *noun* pupa of a moth or butterfly enclosed in a cocoon COGNATE

compulsion / la compulsión *noun* an urge to do or say something COGNATE

 Analyze Vocabulary Using Context Clues

In lines 1–5, focus on that part of the poem that uses the word *chrysalis*. Point out these context clues:

1. I know that *delicate* is an adjective and that it describes the word *chrysalis*. That means *chrysalis* must be a noun. In a previous line, the speaker says she is in mourning for a "soft cocoon." *Cocoon* is also a noun, because the adjective *soft* describes it.

2. The speaker says she is in mourning for the cocoon and she is pining for the chrysalis that was destroyed that day. I'm thinking that a *chrysalis* might be a synonym of *cocoon*, or maybe part of a cocoon.

3. When I look up the word in a dictionary, I see my second guess was right. A chrysalis is the hard, outer case that protects the cocoon inside of it.

 ✓ **CHECK FOR SUCCESS**

If students are unable to make predictions, revisit the Checklist section of the Grade 8 Context Clues lesson with the class. After revisiting, guide students as they make predictions about the next bold word, appearing in line 7 of the poem, using the following routine:

- Is the word a noun, a verb, an adjective, or an adverb?

- Why would someone be "thrown back and forth" when trying to make up their mind?

- How can longing for something, such as freedom or safety, become a "compulsion"?

 Connotation and Denotation

What does the author notice about the denotation of the word *cocoon* and the way the speaker uses it?

The reader notes that the denotative meaning of *cocoon* is an envelope an insect forms to change into a butterfly or moth. The way it is used in the poem gives it a positive connotation: a safe, warm place.

TEXT TALK

Why is the speaker in mourning?

See lines 1–5: She is in mourning for the "soft cocoon" where she lay, and the "chrysalis" where she felt safe.

Why does the speaker feel as if she's being tossed to and fro, and thrown left and right?

See lines 6–10: She longs for freedom, but at the same time she also longs for the safety of the "cocoon" she describes in the first part of the poem.

Skills Focus

QUESTION 1: Connotation and Denotation

See lines 1–5: Both *smashed* and *destroyed* have negative connotations. They both suggest that something has been ruined or broken. But *destroyed* has a more negative connotation than *smashed*. If something is *smashed*, like a vase, it might still be repaired. If something is destroyed, however, it no longer exists. It cannot be saved or rebuilt. For this reason, *destroyed* has a more negative connotation.

QUESTION 2: Connotation and Denotation

See lines 1–10: The word *cocoon*, which is also the title of the poem, has a very strong, positive emotional connotation. The author could have chosen a word such as *bed* or even *sofa*, but *cocoon* suggests something that surrounds you and keeps you safe. *Craving* also has a strong emotional connotation. The author could have said that she wanted soft consolations. But if you crave something, you have a very strong desire for it.

QUESTION 3: Connotation and Denotation

See lines 11–15: *Broke* is the past tense of *break*. The denotation of the word *break* is to shatter something into parts with suddenness or violence. It can have a negative connotation, if someone threatens another person with violence, but here it has a positive connotation. The poet uses broke here to mean that she has freed herself from bonds that hold her back or "imprison" her. This connotation makes sense because in the twelfth line she says that she is "thrilled" when her soul breaks free.

SELECTION VOCABULARY

crave / antojarse *verb* to have a great desire for

- What is the author longing for?
- How might *craving* be similar to *longing*?

thrill / entusiasmar *verb* to feel sudden intense sensation or emotion

- When your feelings are "lifted," are you happy or sad?
- How would you feel if you were suddenly free of something?

contrary / contrario/a *adjective* very opposed in nature, character, or purpose   COGNATE

- What two desires does the speaker have?
- How are these two desires different?

Reading Comprehension OPTIONAL

Have students complete the digital reading comprehension questions ✓ when they finish reading.

ANSWER KEY

QUESTION 1: C

QUESTION 2: B

QUESTION 3: A

QUESTION 4: D

QUESTION 5:

See chart.

First	Second	Third	Fourth
The speaker feels sorrow and longing for the security and comfort that was ripped away from her on "that day."	The speaker is experiencing an internal conflict between wanting to face the world as her true self and craving comfort and compassion.	When the speaker existed as her true self, a part of her was joyful, but a part of her was afraid of the personal costs of that freedom.	The speaker thinks it is important to be her true self even if it means she will die, but she is sad that in order to do so she must sacrifice security and comfort.

Connect and Extend OPTIONAL

CONNECT TO EXTENDED WRITING PROJECT

Students can find inspiration from "Cocoon" when writing their informational essays. Have them reflect on the denotations and connotations of words when describing the risks that some people take, why they take them, and the outcomes.

BEYOND THE BOOK

Photography: Risk Takers

Taking a risk can mean many things to many different people. For Mahvash Sabet, it meant confronting her fears about freedom. To explore the concept of "taking a risk," have students do the following:

Find a photograph in a magazine or online that they feel shows someone taking a risk. It might be an Olympic champion, or someone who pushes themselves to achieve some goal.

- The photo may be of someone famous, someone not many people know about, or someone only they know.
- The portrait may be in color or black and white.

Choose one type of brief caption to write that tells the story of the person in the photo.

- A narrative describing the person and circumstances
- Why they think this person is taking a risk.

Display the portraits and stories. To reflect, ask students:

- What do the portraits and captions make you think about?
- How might you look at the concept of taking a risk in a new way?

Think Questions

Circulate as students answer Think Questions independently. Scaffolds for these questions are shown on the opposite page.

QUESTION 1: Textual Evidence

The very first line of the poem—"There's a part of me that keeps mourning"—suggests that the author is clearly upset over something. The word *mourning* means "the expression or feeling of extreme sadness." The speaker says she mourns the "soft cocoon where I lay." A cocoon is a case spun by some insects as protection when they change into a butterfly or a moth. The speaker must be mourning a sense of security, perhaps her home.

QUESTION 2: Textual Evidence

While a part of the speaker seems to long for "the freedom of flight," she is torn between wanting that freedom and yet craving those "soft consolations." I think the "soft consolations" is another reference to the cocoon that she mentions in the first part of the poem. She seems torn between wanting freedom and, at the same time, the "consolation" of her "cocoon."

QUESTION 3: Textual Evidence

The speaker says that part of her was thrilled when her "soul broke free," but another part of her "shrank back in cowering fear." The idea of being free frightens the speaker. She imagines that "threatening fires" and "lowering smoke" wait for her now that she is free.

QUESTION 4: Context Clues

In the lines 9 and 10, the speaker says that she is "longing for the freedom of flight," but at the same time she is "craving those soft consolations." The "soft consolations" must refer to the "soft cocoon" she mentions in the first part of the poem. I know *longing* means having a great desire for something, so *craving* must have a meaning very similar to *longing* because the speaker wants both freedom and consolation.

QUESTION 5: Greek and Latin Roots and Affixes

The word *desires* is a noun used in the same line where the word *contrary* appears, so *contrary* must be an adjective that describes *desires*. I know the writer keeps saying that a part of her wants one thing and another part of her wants something else, so her desires are pitted against one another. The word *contrary* must mean "to oppose or contradict."

Cocoon

COCOON   **First Read**

Read "Cocoon." After you read, complete the Think Questions below.

☁ THINK QUESTIONS

1. In lines 1–5, what is the speaker mourning? Cite evidence from the text to support your answer.

2. What do lines 6–10 tell you about the speaker's state of mind? Support your answer with evidence from the text.

3. The speaker says in lines 11–15 that a part of her felt thrilled "when my soul broke free." What other emotion does she describe? Cite evidence from the text to support your answer.

4. What is the meaning of the word **craving** as it is used in the text? Write your best definition here, along with a brief explanation of how you arrived at its meaning, and then consult a dictionary to check your answer.

5. The Latin word *contra* means "against." With this information in mind and using context clues from the text, write your best definition of the word **contrary** here.

Think Questions

Use the scaffolds below to differentiate instruction for your **ELL** English Language Learners and **A** Approaching grade-level learners.

ELL **BEGINNING** Write a response using the word bank and sentence frames.

INTERMEDIATE Write a response using the sentence frames.

ADVANCED, ADVANCED HIGH Write a response using the Text-Dependent Question Guide.

A **APPROACHING** Write a response using the Text-Dependent Question Guide.

| | INTERMEDIATE | APPROACHING |
| BEGINNING | | ADVANCED, ADVANCED HIGH |

Word Bank	Sentence Frames	Text-Dependent Question Guide
safe consolations shrank	The speaker is sad and ____. She is mournful for the soft ____ where she lay. The speaker misses a feeling of ____.	1. • Where did the speaker lay and why did she like it? • What happened to the chrysalis? • Why is the speaker sad? • How do I know this?
mournful demise applauds against	The speaker wants to feel the ____ of flight. At the same time, she also wants the ____ of home. She wants to feel ____.	2. • How does the speaker feel about freedom? • In what ways are the "soft consolations" like the "soft cocoon" in lines 1–5? • What is the speaker caught between and why can't she make up her mind?
cocoon thrilled fear	The speaker felt ____ when her "soul broke free." But a part of her also ____ back in ____.	3. • What two feelings does the speaker describe in lines 11–15? • What does part of the author feel when her "soul breaks free"? • What is the author afraid of?
safety freedom flying	There is something in the speaker that approves of ____. She also ____ the thought of bravely dying. But she still weeps for the cocoon's ____.	4. • Read: "I'm thrown left and right and back and forth / longing for the freedom of flight and yet / **craving** those soft consolations." • What does *longing* mean? • What was smashed and destroyed before the speaker's eyes? • What else does the author want besides freedom?
	The Latin word *contra* means "____."	5. • Read: "All this makes me wonder greatly / about **contrary** desires." • What does the author approve of? • What does the author weep for? • How are these desires different?

Skill: Connotation and Dentotation

Introduce the Skill

Watch the Concept Definition video ▶ and read the following definition with your students.

The **denotation** of a word is its dictionary definition. The **connotation** of a word is the idea or feeling that a word suggests, or that our culture or our emotions give the word. A word's connotation can be positive, negative, or neutral. For example, the words *cheap* and *affordable* both denote "inexpensive." However, *cheap* connotes something that is of low quality.

To determine the connotation of a word, readers must use **context**, such as the genre or subject of a text. They also use **context clues**, or the surrounding words that help a reader determine a word's meaning. To verify the denotation of a word and check for possible connotations, readers can consult reference materials such as dictionaries, glossaries, and thesauruses. To **analyze** an author's word choices, readers consider the emotional impact of language in the text for its potential effect on readers.

TURN AND TALK

1. Can you think of a time when knowing the dictionary definition of a word might not be enough to understand how it is used in a text?

2. What words can you think of that carry different connotations depending on the context, or the way in which they are used?

ELL SPEAKING FRAMES

- I needed to know more than the dictionary definition for the word ___. The reason is ___.

- The word ___ means different things in different situations. Sometimes it means ___, and other times it means ___.

Skill: Connotation and Denotation

Cocoon

Use the Checklist to analyze Connotation and Denotation in "Cocoon." Refer to the sample student annotations about Connotation and Denotation in the text.

••• CHECKLIST FOR CONNOTATION AND DENOTATION

In order to identify the denotative meanings of words, use the following steps:

✓ first, note unfamiliar words and phrases, keywords used to describe important characters, events, and ideas, or words that inspire or cause an emotional reaction

✓ next, determine and note the denotative meaning of a word by checking a reference source, such as a dictionary, glossary, or thesaurus

To better understand the meanings of words and phrases as they are used in a text, including connotative meanings, use the following questions:

✓ How do synonyms or context help you identify the connotative meaning of the word?

✓ How could you say this word or phrase differently? Would it change or maintain the meaning of the sentence/line/paragraph?

✓ How can you note differences between words with similar denotations and their connotations?

To determine the meaning of words and phrases as they are used in a text, including connotative meanings, use the following questions:

✓ What is the meaning of the word or phrase? What is its denotation, and what connotations does the word or phrase have?

✓ If I substitute a synonym based on denotation, is the meaning the same? How does it change the meaning of the text?

Reading & Writing Companion   89

V SKILL VOCABULARY

denotation / la denotación *noun* the literal or dictionary meaning of a word, in contrast to the feelings or ideas that the word suggests   COGNATE

connotation / la connotación *noun* an idea or feeling that a word suggests in addition to its literal or primary meaning   COGNATE

context / el contexto *noun* the set of facts or circumstances that surround a situation or event   COGNATE

Skill: Connotation and Denotation

Reread lines 11–20 of "Cocoon." Then, using the Checklist on the previous page, answer the multiple-choice questions below.

⟳ YOUR TURN

1. In lines 11 and 12, the speaker writes, "When my soul broke free, a part of me / thrilled at the lift of its arc." What word could you use in place of *thrilled* that would have the same connotation and maintain, or keep, the meaning of the line?

   ○ A. When my soul broke free, a part of me / was happy at the lift of its arc

   ○ B. When my soul broke free, a part of me / was surprised at the lift of its arc.

   ○ C. When my soul broke free, a part of me / was exhilarated at the lift of its arc.

   ○ D. When my soul broke free, a part of me / was pleased at the lift of its arc.

2. *Shrank* is the past tense of *shrink*, which means "to become smaller because of cold, heat, or moisture." Does the way the speaker uses the word *shrank* in line 13 have a negative or a positive connotation?

   ○ A. Since only part of the author shrank back in cowering fear, the use of the word has a neutral connotation, neither positive nor negative.

   ○ B. The speaker shrinks because of heat from a threatening fire, so *shrank* has a negative connotation.

   ○ C. The speaker is thrilled because her soul has broken free, so the use of *shrank* in the third line has a positive connotation.

   ○ D. The speaker shrinks because of fear, not because of heat, cold, or moisture, so she uses its negative connotation.

Ⅴ SKILL VOCABULARY

context clue / la clave del contexto *noun* a hint in the surrounding text that can help a reader infer the meaning of an unfamiliar word, phrase, or description

analyze / analizar *verb* to consider in detail and discover essential features or meaning COGNATE

⚙ Your Turn

Ask students to complete the Your Turn activity.

QUESTION 1

A. Incorrect. The denotation of *happy* is contentment, which does not have the same connotation as *thrilled*, which means "a sudden feeling of excitement and pleasure."

B. Incorrect. To be *surprised* means "to come upon or encounter something suddenly and unexpectedly."

C. Correct. *Exhilarated* means "to be energized and excited" and has the same connotation as *thrilled*, so substituting this word would keep the meaning of the line.

D. Incorrect. To be *pleased* means "to be glad or satisfied," which would not have the same connotation as *thrilled*.

QUESTION 2

A. Incorrect. The fact that the author was divided about whether she felt thrilled or shrank back in fear because she was so frightened does not affect the negative connotation of *shrank*, because it only describes her reaction to the fear the speaker felt.

B. Incorrect. Although exposure to heat can cause some objects to shrink in size, in this case the fire is threatening the speaker's security and even her life, so it is not causing her to literally shrink from the heat of the fire.

C. Incorrect. The speaker says she is thrilled in the second line, yet the word *but* that opens the third line indicates that she is going to explain how her feelings have changed.

D. Correct. The speaker uses the word *shrank* to imply that she has become so frightened, she has figuratively grown small to increase the distance between herself and the source of her fear. This gives the word a negative connotation.

Close Read

Skills Focus

QUESTION 1: Connotation and Denotation

See lines 1–5.

QUESTION 2: Connotation and Denotation

See lines 1–10.

QUESTION 3: Connotation and Denotation

See lines 11–15.

QUESTION 4: Connect to Essential Question

See lines 11–20: For the speaker, the idea of freedom is frightening because she won't feel protected. She says she "weeps for the cocoon's demise," a place where she had felt safe. Though freedom is "thrilling," it brings with it the possibility of danger. To enjoy freedom, the speaker had to overcome her fear and take a chance even though there is the possibility of "bravely dying."

CHECK FOR SUCCESS

If students struggle to respond to Skills Focus question 1, ask them the following questions:

1. What is the denotation for *smashed*? What is the denotation for *destroyed*? Which word has more connotations?

2. Which word do you think has a stronger connotation? Why?

COCOON   Close Read

Reread "Cocoon." As you reread, complete the Skills Focus questions below. Then use your answers and annotations from the questions to help you complete the Write activity.

◎ SKILLS FOCUS

1. The words *smashed* and *destroyed* in the first stanza (lines 1–5) have similar denotations. Which word has a stronger connotation, and why?

2. Reread lines 1–10. Identify words the author uses that have specific emotional connotations. Explain why you think the author chose these specific words.

3. Reread lines 11 and 12 in the third stanza. Does the word *broke* have a positive or a negative connotation the way it is used here? How could it be used so that it has a different connotation?

4. Why does the speaker consider the idea of freedom as taking a chance?

✏ WRITE

LITERARY ANALYSIS: In this poem, Mahvash Sabet describes the conflicting emotions she feels when she is arrested in her home and watches as it is destroyed. She then reflects on why she should feel torn between desiring freedom and wanting the security she once had. Some of the words she chooses to describe her feelings have powerful connotations that help her describe her experience. Write an analysis of at least 250 words in which you explain Sabet's purpose for telling this story about her personal experience. Use textual evidence to support your response, including the author's use of connotation and denotation.

Reading & Writing Companion   91

Writer's Notebook

Connect to Essential Question: Give students time to reflect on how "Cocoon" connects to the unit's essential question "Why do we take chances?" by freewriting in their Writer's Notebooks.

 Beginning & Intermediate

Read aloud the unit's essential question: "Why do we take chances?" Encourage students to draw their connections or allow students to write in their native language. Circulate the room, prompting students for their thoughts as they respond orally or through pantomime.

 Advanced & Advanced High

Allow students to share their connections orally in pairs or small groups before freewriting.

Collaborative Conversation

Break students into collaborative conversation groups to discuss the Close Read prompt. Ask students to use the StudySyncTV episode as a model for their discussion. Remind them to reference their Skills Focus annotations in their discussion.

In this poem, Mahvash Sabet describes the conflicting emotions she feels when she is arrested in her home and watches as it is destroyed. She then reflects on why she should feel torn between desiring freedom and wanting the security she once had. Some of the words she chooses to describe her feelings have powerful connotations that help her to describe her experience. Write an analysis of at least 250 words in which you explain Sabet's purpose for telling this story about her personal experience. Use textual evidence to support your response, including the author's use of connotation and denotation.

Use the scaffolds below to differentiate instruction for your **ELL** English Language Learners and **A** Approaching grade-level learners.

ELL **BEGINNING, INTERMEDIATE** Use the discussion guide and speaking frames to facilitate the discussion with support from the teacher.

ADVANCED, ADVANCED HIGH Use the discussion guide and speaking frames to facilitate the discussion in mixed-level groups.

A **APPROACHING** Use the discussion guide to facilitate the discussion in mixed-level groups.

APPROACHING
ADVANCED, ADVANCED HIGH
BEGINNING, INTERMEDIATE

Discussion Guide	Speaking Frames
1. What is the author's purpose for telling her story?	• A part of the author keeps ____ for the soft ____ where she once felt safe. • Another part of the author wants ____, but she also ____ it. • The author wants people to know how hard it is to have ____ desires.
2. How did the author use connotations and denotations to describe this experience?	• ____ is one word the author uses that has a more powerful connotation than *wanting*. • When the speaker says she is "cowering in fear," it is a stronger connotation than just saying she is ____.

Review Prompt and Rubric

Before students begin writing, review the writing prompt and rubric with the class.

LITERARY ANALYSIS: In this poem, Mahvash Sabet describes the conflicting emotions she feels when she is arrested in her home and watches as it is destroyed. She then reflects on why she should feel torn between desiring freedom and wanting the security she once had. Some of the words she chooses to describe her feelings have powerful connotations that help her to describe her experience. Write an analysis of at least 250 words in which you explain Sabet's purpose for telling this story about her personal experience. Use textual evidence to support your response, including the author's use of connotation and denotation.

ELL **PROMPT GUIDE**

A • What conflicting emotions does the speaker feel?
• What powerful words does the speaker use to explain how she feels?

• How does the speaker feel at the end of the poem?

Score	Connotation and Denotation	Language and Conventions
4	The writer clearly and effectively identifies the connotations and denotations of words from the poem. The writer provides exemplary analysis of connotations and denotations, using relevant evidence from the text all of the time.	The writer demonstrates a consistent command of grammar, punctuation, and usage conventions. Although minor errors may be evident, they do not detract from the fluency or the clarity of the writing.
3	The writer identifies the connotations and denotations of words from the poem. The writer provides sufficient analysis of connotations and denotations, using relevant evidence from the text most of the time.	The writer demonstrates an adequate command of grammar, punctuation, and usage conventions. Although some errors may be evident, they create few (if any) disruptions in the fluency or clarity of the writing.
2	The writer begins to analyze or explain the connotations and denotations of words from the poem. The writer provides an incomplete analysis, using relevant evidence from the text only some of the time.	The writer demonstrates a partial command of grammar, punctuation, and usage conventions. Some distracting errors may be evident, at times creating minor disruptions in the fluency or clarity of the writing.
1	The writer attempts to analyze or explain the connotations and denotations of words from the poem. The writer provides an unsuccessful analysis, using little or no relevant evidence from the text.	The writer demonstrates little or no command of grammar, punctuation, and usage conventions. Serious and persistent errors create disruptions in the fluency of the writing and sometimes interfere with meaning.
0	The writer does not provide a relevant response to the prompt or does not provide a response at all.	Serious and persistent errors overwhelm the writing and interfere with the meaning of the response as a whole, making the writer's meaning impossible to understand.

Write

Ask students to complete the writing assignment using textual evidence to support their answers.

Use the scaffolds below to differentiate instruction for your **ELL** English Language Learners and **A** Approaching grade-level learners.

ELL **BEGINNING** With the help of the <u>word bank</u>, write a response using <u>paragraph frame 1</u>.

INTERMEDIATE With the help of the <u>word bank</u>, write a response using <u>paragraph frames 1 and 2</u>.

ADVANCED, ADVANCED HIGH Write a response of differentiated length using the <u>sentence starters</u>.

A **APPROACHING** Write a response of differentiated length using the <u>sentence starters</u>.

| BEGINNING | | ADVANCED, ADVANCED HIGH |
| INTERMEDIATE | | APPROACHING |

Word Bank	Paragraph Frame 1	Paragraph Frame 2	Sentence Starters
freedom inform safe experiences protected	The author's purpose is to ____ the reader about her ____. She was arrested in Iran because she was a member of the Bahá'í faith. She describes an experience when she saw a place she felt ____ "smashed and destroyed." These are words with negative connotations. Now the author is confused. She likes the idea of ____. But a part of her sees it as a threatening fire where she is cowering in fear. "The Cowering" and "threatening" also have negative connotations. She also misses the "cocoon" where she was ____. The author wonders how she can have two different emotions at the same time.	The author uses words with strong ____. Instead of just being afraid, she is "____ in fear." She is not caught between two choices or decisions. She is caught between "____." Each of these word choices helps the reader to know how strong her ____ are.	• In the opening, stanza the author . . . • When the speaker's soul "breaks free," she is afraid of . . . • The speaker questions . . . • The speaker's purpose for writing seems to be . . .

Peer Review

Students should submit substantive feedback to two peers using the instructions below.

- How well does this response answer the prompt?
- Does the writer support the analysis with textual evidence?
- What did the writer do well in his or her literary analysis? What does the writer need to work on?

Rate

Respond to the following with a point rating that reflects your opinion.

	1 2 3 4
Ideas	▪▪▪▫
Evidence	▪▪▪▪
Language and Conventions	▪▪▫▫

Submit

ELL **A** **SENTENCE FRAMES**

- You were able to (completely / partly / almost) answer the prompt.
- You could answer the prompt better by ____.

- Your use of textual evidence to support the author's purpose was ____.
- I thought the best part of your analysis was ____.

No Risk, No Reward

Blast: A Single Line

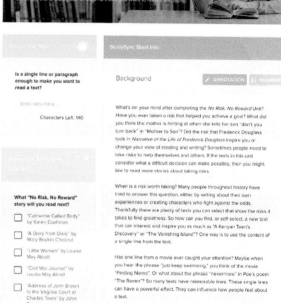

TEXT TALK

What are you thinking after finishing the *No Risk, No Reward* unit? What is your opinion of this genre based on the unit's selections? Answers may vary.

What is one strategy you can use for self-selecting a new text? How does it work? I can use the content of a single line from the text.

What should you do once you choose a text that interests you? Start reading the text to confirm my interest. If I like it, I should keep reading.

Create Your Own Blast

Ask students to write a 140-character Blast after they complete the QuikPoll.

Use the scaffolds below to differentiate instruction for your **ELL** English Language Learners.

ELL **BEGINNING** Write a response using the <u>word bank</u> to complete the <u>sentence frame</u>.

INTERMEDIATE Write a response using the <u>sentence frame</u>.

ADVANCED, ADVANCED HIGH Write a response using the <u>sentence starter</u>.

SCAFFOLDS

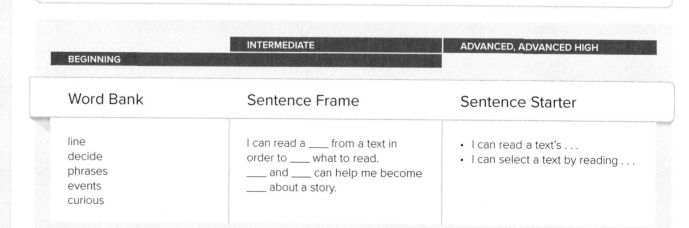

BEGINNING	INTERMEDIATE	ADVANCED, ADVANCED HIGH
Word Bank	**Sentence Frame**	**Sentence Starter**
line decide phrases events curious	I can read a ____ from a text in order to ____ what to read. ____ and ____ can help me become ____ about a story.	• I can read a text's . . . • I can select a text by reading . . .

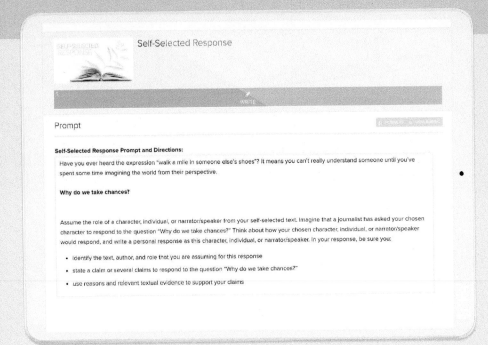

Self-Selected Response

Prompt

Self-Selected Response Prompt and Directions:

Have you ever heard the expression "walk a mile in someone else's shoes"? It means you can't really understand someone until you've spent some time imagining the world from their perspective.

Why do we take chances?

Assume the role of a character, individual, or narrator/speaker from your self-selected text. Imagine that a journalist has asked your chosen character to respond to the question "Why do we take chances?" Think about how your chosen character, individual, or narrator/speaker would respond, and write a personal response as this character, individual, or narrator/speaker. In your response, be sure you:

- identify the text, author, and role that you are assuming for this response
- state a claim or several claims to respond to the question "Why do we take chances?"
- use reasons and relevant textual evidence to support your claims

Self-Selected Response

Introduce the Prompt

Read aloud the prompt. Ask students to discuss:

- What is the prompt asking you to do?
- Why might it be helpful to think about the world from another person's point of view?

Write

Ask students to complete the writing assignment using text evidence to support their answers.

Use the scaffolds below to differentiate instruction for your **ELL** English Language Learners and **A** Approaching grade level readers.

ELL **BEGINNING** With the help of the word bank, write a response using paragraph frame 1.

INTERMEDIATE With the help of the word bank, write a response using paragraph frames 1 and 2.

ADVANCED, ADVANCED HIGH Write a response of differentiated length using the sentence starters.

A **APPROACHING** Write a response of differentiated length using the sentence starters.

	BEGINNING INTERMEDIATE	INTERMEDIATE	ADVANCED, ADVANCED HIGH APPROACHING
Word Bank	**Paragraph Frame 1**	**Paragraph Frame 2**	**Sentence Starters**
care wounded effort working brave injured ill allowed soldiers suffering	I am writing as (character/individual/narrator/speaker) ____ from the text ____. I took a chance by ____. I took that chance because ____. I risked losing ____. Still, I thought that this risk was important to take because ____.	I am writing as (character/individual/narrator/speaker) ____ from the text ____. I took a chance by ____. I took that chance because ____. I risked losing ____. Still, I thought that this risk was important to take because ____. I also took that chance because ____. Taking this risk taught me that ____.	• I am . . . from the text . . . • I took a chance by . . . • I took that chance because . . . • I risked losing . . . • Still, I thought that this risk was important to take because . . . • I also took that chance because . . . • Taking this risk taught me that . . .

Extended Writing Project

EXTENDED WRITING PROJECT
INFORMATIVE WRITING

The Extended Writing Project (EWP) in Grade 8, Unit 3 focuses on informative writing. The students probe the unit's essential question—Why do we take chances?—as they write an informative text about what happens when people take risks. The multiple informative texts in the unit, as well as fiction and poetry, serve as resources for students in crafting their writing. Specific skill lessons teach developing ideas, thesis statements, organization, and conventions, while other skill lessons focus on supporting details, introductions, and conclusions to help students craft a strong informative text. Directed revision leads students through the process of revising for clarity, development, organization, word choice, and sentence variety. Throughout the EWP, students have the opportunity to practice using created student writing, authentic texts, and their own work.

CONNECT TO ESSENTIAL QUESTION

Why do we take chances?

After finishing the texts in this unit, students have read about many characters and subjects who took risks to achieve rewards. Students will explore how authors inform readers about risk-taking subjects and characters through an informative essay that requires a controlling idea or thesis.

Audio and audio text highlighting are available in select lessons in the Extended Writing Project.

Extended Writing Project Prompt

What happens when we take risks?

Choose three informative texts from this unit, including research links in the Blasts, and explain how the authors inform readers about their risk-taking subjects. Identify the risks individuals take and the outcomes of those risks. Include a clear main idea or thesis statement, and cite evidence from each text to explain your conclusions.

 SCAFFOLDS    **ELL** ENGLISH LANGUAGE LEARNERS    **A** APPROACHING GRADE LEVEL    **B** BEYOND GRADE LEVEL

These icons identify differentiation strategies and scaffolded support for a variety of students. See the digital lesson plan for additional differentiation strategies and scaffolds.

Instructional Path

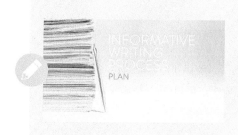

Informative Writing Process: Plan

Objectives: After learning about genre characteristics and craft, students will analyze a sample Student Model and plan a meaningful informative essay in response to a prompt.

Skill: Thesis Statement

Objectives: After reading and discussing a model of student writing, students will develop and clearly introduce a main idea about a topic.

Skill: Organizing Informative Writing

Objectives: After reading and discussing a model of student writing, students will develop their drafts by organizing ideas, concepts, and information effectively.

Skill: Supporting Details

Objectives: After reading and discussing a model of student writing, students will develop their drafts by using supporting details.

Informative Writing Process: Draft

Objectives: After reading a Student Model draft and reviewing a writing checklist, students will draft a meaningful informative essay in response to a prompt.

The print teacher's edition includes essential point-of-use instruction and planning tools.
Complete lesson plans and program documents appear in your digital teacher account.

Skill: Introductions

Objectives: After reading and discussing a model of student writing, students will develop their drafts by improving their introductions.

Skill: Transitions

Objectives: After reading and discussing a model of student writing, students will develop their drafts by using appropriate and varied transitions to create cohesion and clarify the relationships among ideas and concepts.

Skill: Precise Language

Objectives: After reading and discussing a model of student writing, students will develop their drafts by using precise language and domain-specific vocabulary to inform about or explain the topic.

Skill: Style

Objectives: After reading and discussing a model of student writing, students will develop their drafts by establishing and maintaining a formal style.

Skill: Conclusions

Objectives: After reading and discussing a model of student writing, students will develop their drafts by improving their conclusions.

Instructional Path

The print teacher's edition includes essential point-of-use instruction and planning tools
Complete lesson plans and program documents appear in your digital teacher account

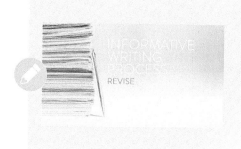

Informative Writing Process: Revise

Objectives: Students will use a revision guide to revise the draft of their informative essay for clarity, development, organization, style, diction, and sentence effectiveness.

Grammar: Participles

Objectives: After learning about participles and seeing how they are used in text examples, students will practice using participles correctly.

Grammar: Gerunds

Objectives: After learning about gerunds and seeing how they are used in text examples, students will practice using gerunds correctly.

Grammar: Infinitives

Objectives: After learning about infinitives and seeing how they are used in text examples, students will practice using infinitives correctly.

Informative Writing Process: Edit and Publish

Objectives: After seeing an example of editing in the Student Model and reviewing an editing checklist, students will edit and publish the final draft of their informative essay.

Progress Monitoring

Opportunities to Learn	Opportunities to Demonstrate Learning	Opportunities to Reteach

Informative Writing Process: Plan

Opportunities to Learn	Opportunities to Demonstrate Learning	Opportunities to Reteach
Informative Writing Process: Plan	Informative Writing Process: Plan • Write	Units 4–6 Process: Plan

Informative Writing Process: Draft

Opportunities to Learn	Opportunities to Demonstrate Learning	Opportunities to Reteach
Informative Writing Process: Draft	Informative Writing Process: Draft • Write	Units 4–6 Process: Draft

Informative Writing Process: Revise

Opportunities to Learn	Opportunities to Demonstrate Learning	Opportunities to Reteach
Informative Writing Process: Revise	Informative Writing Process: Revise • Write	Units 4–6 Process: Revise

Informative Writing Process: Edit and Publish

Informative Writing Process: Edit and Publish

Informative Writing Process: Edit and Publish
• Write

Units 4, 6
Process: Edit and Publish

Unit 5
Process: Edit and Present

Thesis Statement

Skill: Thesis Statement

Skill: Thesis Statement
• Your Turn

Informative Writing Process: Draft

Unit 4
Skill: Thesis Statement

Spotlight Skill: Thesis Statement

Organizing Informative Writing

Skill: Organizing Informative Writing

Skill: Organizing Informative Writing
• Your Turn

Informative Writing Process: Draft

Spotlight Skill: Organizing Informative Writing

Supporting Details

Skill: Supporting Details

Skill: Supporting Details
• Your Turn

Informative Writing Process: Draft

Spotlight Skill: Supporting Details

Introductions

Skill: Introductions

Skill: Introductions
• Your Turn

Informative Writing Process: Revise

Unit 4
Skill: Introductions

Spotlight Skill: Introductions

Transitions

Skill: Transitions

Skill: Transitions
• Your Turn

Informative Writing Process: Revise

Unit 4
Skill: Transitions

Spotlight Skill: Transitions

Precise Language

⚙ Skill: Precise Language	⚙ Skill: Precise Language	⚙ Spotlight Skill: Precise Language
	• Your Turn	
	✏ Informative Writing Process: Revise	

Style

⚙ Skill: Style	⚙ Skill: Style	⚙ Unit 4 Skill: Style
	• Your Turn	
	✏ Informative Writing Process: Revise	⚙ Spotlight Skill: Style

Conclusions

⚙ Skill: Conclusions	⚙ Skill: Conclusions	⚙ Unit 4 Skill: Conclusions
	• Your Turn	
	✏ Informative Writing Process: Revise	⚙ Spotlight Skill: Conclusions

Participles

⚙ Grammar: Participle	⚙ Grammar: Participle	⚙ Grammar: Commas—With Introductory Phrases
	• Your Turn	
	✏ Informative Writing Process: Edit and Publish	

Gerunds

⚙ Grammar: Gerunds	⚙ Grammar: Gerunds	⚙ Grammar: Verbs—Progressive Tense
	• Your Turn	
	✏ Informative Writing Process: Edit and Publish	

Infinitives

⚙ Grammar: Infinitives	⚙ Grammar: Infinitives	⚙ Grammar: Verbs—Regular Verbs
	• Your Turn	
	✏ Informative Writing Process: Edit and Publish	

Informative Writing Process: Plan

Introduce the Extended Writing Project

- What is the prompt asking you to do?

- Which characteristics of informative writing will you need to learn more about in order to respond to the prompt?

- What are the five characteristics of informative writing?

- What elements of craft do informative writers use?

 DIFFERENTIATED QUESTIONS

- What does **risk-taking subjects** mean?

- What kinds of risks do people take in the texts you read?

- What can the outcomes or results of the risks teach us?

Informative Writing Process: Plan

PLAN	DRAFT	REVISE	EDIT AND PUBLISH

In a variety of genres, the authors of the texts in this unit explore the value of taking risks to achieve rewards. Whether one is learning to read, overcoming a terrible tragedy, or simply getting on with life, any decision can involve a risk. While there is always a chance that something will go wrong, often great, unforeseen opportunities come from risk-taking.

WRITING PROMPT

What happens when we take risks?

Choose three informational texts from this unit, including research links in the Blasts, and explain how the authors inform readers about their risk-taking subjects. Identify the risks individuals take and the outcomes of those risks. Include a clear main idea or thesis statement, and cite evidence from each text to explain your conclusions. Regardless of which sources you choose, be sure your essay includes the following:

- an introduction
- a main idea or thesis statement
- a clear text structure
- supporting details
- a conclusion

Copyright © BookheadEd Learning, LLC

Introduction to Informative Writing

Informative writing informs readers about real people, places, things, and events. It includes ideas, concepts, and information that needs to be organized in a logical way such as definition, classification, compare/contrast, and cause/effect. Good informative writing also includes a clear thesis statement or main idea of the essay, and the writer develops that main idea with supporting details, such as descriptions, examples, reasons, quotations, and relevant facts. The characteristics of informative writing include:

- an introduction with a thesis statement or main idea
- supporting details that develop the thesis statement or main idea
- a clear and logical text structure
- a formal style
- a conclusion that wraps up your ideas

As you continue with this Extended Writing Project, you'll receive more instruction and practice at crafting each of the characteristics of informative writing to create your own informative essay.

Review the Rubric

Have students examine the "Informative Writing Rubric—Grade 8" grading rubric. Inform students that this is the same rubric that will be used to evaluate their completed Informative Extended Writing Project.

Reading & Writing Companion

Read and Annotate

As students read, have them use the Annotation Tool to identify and label the genre characteristics and craft of informative writing, including:

- an introduction with a thesis statement or main idea
- supporting details that develop the thesis statement or main idea
- a clear and logical text structure
- a formal style
- a conclusion that wraps up your ideas

When students finish reading, ask them to share their annotations in small groups.

ELL ANNOTATION GUIDE

Find the following quotes in the Student Model. Then, use the Annotation Tool to label each quote as an example of introduction, main idea or thesis statement, clear text structure, supporting detail, or conclusion.

- People take risks every day.
- Even though these risks and the outcomes of these risks differ, they all teach essential lessons.
- Douglass recalls the rage: "I have had her rush at me with a face made all up of fury, and snatch from me a newspaper, in a manner that fully revealed her apprehension."
- In his speech "Address to the Nation on the Explosion of the Space Shuttle *Challenger*," President Ronald Reagan reminds Americans that the crew was willing to do a dangerous job.
- As a result, many members of the tribe will risk giving up their land and homes to relocate the community.
- They set examples that readers can follow when they need to decide if they want to take a risk for an important goal.

A READ AND ANNOTATE

Pair students with on-grade-level peers to complete the annotation activity.

Before you get started on your own informative essay, read this essay that one student, Aiko, wrote in response to the writing prompt. As you read the Model, highlight and annotate the features of informative writing that Aiko included in her essay.

☰ STUDENT MODEL

NOTES

Risks Teach Valuable Lessons

1   People take risks every day. Many risks are small, such as trying a new type of food. Other risks are bigger, such as moving across the country. Whether big or small, all risks have something in common. People can never be certain of how a risk will turn out. Every time a person takes a risk, there is a chance that they will lose something valuable. Frederick Douglass, the crew of the *Challenger*, and members of the Biloxi-Chitimacha-Choctaw Native American tribe are examples of people who have risked devastating losses to pursue worthy goals. Even though these risks and the outcomes of these risks differ, they all teach essential lessons.

2   In his autobiography *Narrative of the Life of Frederick Douglass, an American Slave*, Douglass describes dangerous risks that he took on the road to freedom. Born into slavery, Douglass was legally denied an education. When he was young, however, the mistress of one house started to teach him how to read until her husband told her to stop. She then became angry and violent when Douglass tried to learn on his own. Douglas recalls the rage: "I have had her rush at me with a face made all up of fury, and snatch from me a newspaper, in a manner that fully revealed her apprehension." Douglass knew that there could be serious personal and legal consequences if he were caught, but he decided that knowledge was worth the risk. Douglass saw knowledge as part of his long-term plan to escape slavery. He explains, "I looked forward to a time at which it would be safe for me to escape. I was too young to think of doing so immediately; besides, I wished to learn how to write, as I might have occasion to write my own pass." Douglass's efforts gave him a way to pursue freedom. After several years, he learned how to read and write. The risks Douglass took in pursuit of his goal also teach readers valuable lessons. His success teaches the values of perseverance and faith in one's own abilities.

Reading & Writing Companion 95

💬 TEXT TALK

Structure and Organization

What is the purpose of Aiko's essay?

See paragraph 1: Aiko states that she will compare informative texts about risks that historical figures have taken. She will use those texts to show what we can learn from them.

Organization and Focus

Where does Aiko identify her thesis or main idea?

See paragraph 1: The thesis or main idea is stated in the last sentence of the introduction: "Even though these risks and the outcomes of these risks differ, they all teach essential lessons."

NOTES

3 However, failure teaches lessons, too. In 1986, the crew of the space shuttle *Challenger* set out to make new discoveries in space, but they lost their lives in a space shuttle disaster. In his speech "Address to the Nation on the Explosion of the Space Shuttle *Challenger*," President Ronald Reagan reminds Americans that the crew was willing to do a dangerous job. They wanted to travel into space because they believed that the mission would be worth the risk. He says, "They had a hunger to explore the universe and discover its truths." The *Challenger* crew was well prepared and planning to study important questions about the universe. Unfortunately, they never had a chance to achieve that goal because the space shuttle exploded after takeoff. Despite this tragic end, Americans can still learn a valuable lesson from the *Challenger* crew. Reagan explains that "the future doesn't belong to the fainthearted; it belongs to the brave. The *Challenger* crew was pulling us into the future, and we'll continue to follow them." The crew was willing to risk their lives in search of knowledge about the universe. Their efforts teach the values of selflessness and bravery.

4 The risks that one needs to take to pursue a goal can also change over time. This is evident in "Vanishing Island," an informational article by Anya Groner. In the early 1800s, many members of the Biloxi-Chitimacha-Choctaw Native American tribe established a community on a small island off the coast of Louisiana, and it became a "cultural homeland." The island is called Isle de Jean Charles. Since the mid-twentieth century, however, the land on the island has been rapidly eroding, or wearing away. Storms, river engineering, and pollution are causing this to happen, and the landform may not even exist by 2050. As a result, many members of the tribe will risk giving up their land and homes to relocate the community. Chief Naquin, the current chief of the Biloxi-Chitimacha-Choctaw Native American tribe, compared the loss of this island to "the loss of a family member." Leaving that land will be painful, but members are dedicated to preserving their history, community, and culture on the new site. For example, tribal secretary Chantel Comardelle envisions a museum that guides visitors through the history of the island. Many members of the community also value family. To encourage interactions among family members on the new site, they want to build groups of houses with shared backyards. These plans address important issues, but many residents on Isle de Jean Charles will

TEXT TALK

Organization and Coherence

Where does Aiko use a transition to connect ideas from one paragraph to another?

Answers will vary. Sample answer: Aiko uses the word "risks" at the end of paragraph 1 and in the first sentence of paragraph 2 to connect her main idea to a text.

Development of Ideas and Details

How does Aiko use specific details to contribute to the development of her essay?

Answers will vary. Sample answer: In paragraph 2, Aiko quotes passages from *Narrative of the Life of Frederick Douglass, an American Slave* to support her ideas.

Development of Ideas

In what ways does Aiko connect the texts to the world and life in general?

Answers will vary. Sample answer: In paragraph 3, Aiko states, "However, failure teaches lessons, too." In this way, she engages readers by showing them that this informative text is still relevant.

Word Choice

Where do you find Aiko's word choice especially strong or expressive?

Answers will vary. Sample answer: In paragraph 3, Aiko uses the word "selflessness" to describe a quality of the *Challenger* crew and their sacrifice.

NOTES

still need to endure a difficult move. Their sacrifices teach readers the values of determination and resilience, the ability to recover from a loss.

5   *Narrative of the Life of Frederick Douglass, an American Slave,* "Address to the Nation on the Explosion of the Space Shuttle *Challenger,*" and "Vanishing Island" inform readers about historic risks that people have taken to pursue their goals. They show that each person faced hardships as a result of their decisions, and the *Challenger* crew tragically lost their lives. However, their stories continue to teach lessons about honorable qualities. They set examples that readers can follow when they need to decide if they want to take a risk for an important goal.

Reading & Writing Companion   97

TEXT TALK

Sentence Fluency

Choose one sentence that you think is really effective. Why do you think it's so strong?

Answers will vary. Sample answer: I think that this sentence from paragraph 4 is strong: "Storms, river engineering, and pollution are causing this to happen, and the landform may not even exist by 2050." The facts in this sentence surprised me because I did not realize that there are a number of reasons why water can take over land, and I was stunned to read that this island could completely vanish in a few decades.

Conventions

Did Aiko use verbals in a logical and correct way? Find one verbal that Aiko used correctly and identify what kind of verbal it is.

Answers will vary. Sample answer: In paragraph 4, Aiko writes, "Leaving that land will be painful." In this clause, "leaving" is a gerund because it ends in "-ing," and it acts like a noun. It is the subject of this independent clause.

✏ WRITE

Writers often take notes about their ideas before they sit down to write. Think about what you've learned so far about informative writing to help you begin prewriting.

- What are your ideas about what happens when people take risks? Is risk-taking positive or negative behavior? Why?
- Which three informational texts in the unit best reflect your ideas? Why?
- What risks do the people in those texts take?
- What do the outcomes of their risks tell you about risk-taking?
- How do the authors of those texts express their ideas about risk-taking?
- What textual evidence might you use to support your ideas?

Response Instructions

Use the questions in the bulleted list to write a one-paragraph summary. Your summary should describe the ideas that you want to share and how the texts support them.

Don't worry about including all of the details now; focus only on the most essential and important elements. You will refer back to this short summary as you continue through the steps of the writing process.

Write

Circulate as students use the questions in the bulleted list to plan their writing. See the instructions for scaffolding and differentiation that follow.

CHECK FOR SUCCESS

If students struggle to come up with answers for the questions in the lesson, work with students to provide an answer to one question and then help them build from there.

For example, start by asking students, "Do you think risk-taking is good or bad?" or "What happens as a result of the risks taken in the unit?" Once students have answered one question, help them to work through a second question until they've begun to build some momentum. It may be helpful to start with a different question than the one that's listed first in the lesson.

Review Prompt and Rubric

Before students begin writing, review the writing prompt and rubric with the class.

Response Instructions

Use the questions in the bulleted list to write a one-paragraph summary. Your summary should describe the ideas that you want to share and how the texts support them.

Don't worry about including all of the details now; focus only on the most essential and important elements. You will refer back to this short summary as you continue through the steps of the writing process.

Score	Plan	Language and Conventions
4	The writer responds to the questions, and the writing is clear and focused.	The writer demonstrates a consistent command of grammar, punctuation, and usage conventions. Although minor errors may be evident, they do not detract from the fluency or clarity of the writing.
3	The writer responds to the questions, but the writing is not always clear or focused.	The writer demonstrates an adequate command of grammar, punctuation, and usage conventions. Although some errors may be evident, they create few (if any) disruptions in the fluency or clarity of the writing.
2	The writer responds to the questions, but the writing is somewhat unclear and unfocused.	The writer demonstrates a partial command of grammar, punctuation, and usage conventions. Some distracting errors may be evident, at times creating minor disruptions in the fluency or clarity of the writing.
1	The writer responds to the questions, but the writing is very unclear and unfocused.	The writer demonstrates little or no command of grammar, punctuation, and usage conventions. Serious and persistent errors create disruptions in the fluency of the writing and sometimes interfere with meaning.
0	The writer fails to respond to the questions.	Serious and persistent errors overwhelm the writing and interfere with the meaning of the response as a whole, making the writer's meaning impossible to understand.

Write

Use the scaffolds below to differentiate instruction for your **ELL** English Language Learners and **A** Approaching grade-level learners.

SCAFFOLDS

ELL **BEGINNING, INTERMEDIATE** With the help of the <u>word bank</u>, write a response using the <u>paragraph frame</u>.

ADVANCED, ADVANCED HIGH Write a response using the <u>sentence starters</u>.

A **APPROACHING** Write a response using the <u>sentence starters</u>.

BEGINNING	ADVANCED, ADVANCED HIGH
INTERMEDIATE	APPROACHING

Word Bank	Paragraph Frame	Sentence Starters
resilience Anya Groner Frederick Douglass Ronald Reagan perseverance lessons selflessness	The main idea or thesis is that risks teach valuable ____. In his autobiography, ____ takes a risk when he teaches himself how to read. His risk teaches readers about ____. In his speech about the *Challenger* explosion, ____ explains that the crew was willing to risk their lives for science. The story of the *Challenger* crew teaches about ____. In the article "Vanishing Island," the author ____ describes how many residents on Isle de Jean Charles are about to risk losing their home and historic land to preserve their history and continue to develop as a culture. Their risk teaches readers the importance of ____.	• My essay will be about . . . • When people take risks . . . • In the text . . . by . . . • One person who takes a risk is . . . • The outcome of the risk is . . . • This shows readers that . . .

Peer Review

Students should submit substantive feedback to two peers using the review instructions below.

- How well does this response answer the prompt?
- What part of the informative essay are you most interested in reading?
- Are there any ideas that could be improved on? How so?

Rate

Respond to the following with a point rating that reflects your opinion.

	1 2 3 4
Ideas	▪ ▪ ▪ ☐
Evidence	▪ ▪ ▪ ▪
Language and Conventions	▪ ▪ ☐ ☐

Submit

ELL **A** **SENTENCE FRAMES**

- The response does a good job of addressing ____ from the prompt.
- The response would improve by addressing ____ from the prompt.

- I am most interested in reading about ____.
- I think you could improve ____ by (adding / clarifying / describing) ____.

Skill: Thesis Statement

Introduce the Skill

Watch the Concept Definition video ▶ and read the following definition with your students.

In an essay, a **thesis statement** expresses the writer's main idea about a topic. The thesis statement usually appears in the **introduction**, or opening paragraph of your essay, and is often the last sentence of the introduction. The **body paragraphs** of the essay should offer a thorough explanation of the thesis statement as well as supporting details, reasons, and relevant evidence. The thesis is often restated in the **conclusion** of an essay.

Skill:
Thesis Statement

••• CHECKLIST FOR THESIS STATEMENT

Before you begin writing your thesis statement, ask yourself the following questions:

- What is the prompt asking me to write about?
- What is the topic of my essay? How can I state it clearly for the reader?
- What claim do I want to make about the topic of this essay? Is my statement clear to my reader?
- Does my thesis statement introduce the body of my essay?
- Where should I place my thesis statement?

Here are some methods to introduce and develop your claim and topic clearly:

- Think about the topic and central idea of your essay.
  - > The central idea of an argument is stated as a claim, or what will be proven or shown to be true.
  - > Identify as many claims as you intend to prove.
- Write a clear statement about the central idea or claim. Your thesis statement should:
  - > let the reader anticipate the body of your essay
  - > respond completely to the writing prompt
- Consider the best placement for your thesis statement.
  - > If your response is short, you may want to get right to the point. Your thesis statement may be presented in the first sentence of the essay.
  - > If your response is longer (as in a formal essay), you can build up your thesis statement. In this case, you can place your thesis statement at the end of your introductory paragraph.

Copyright © BookheadEd Learning, LLC

Reading & Writing Companion   **99**

TURN AND TALK

Turn to your partner and discuss online articles you have read that have interesting thesis statements or main ideas. Discuss how using a version of the thesis statement as the headline draws your attention.

ELL SPEAKING FRAMES
- An article I read with an interesting thesis statement is ____.
- The headline caught my attention by ____.

  SKILL VOCABULARY

thesis statement / la presentación de la tesis **noun** a statement that shares the main idea of an argumentative or informational essay

introduction / la introducción **noun** the opening paragraph or section of an essay COGNATE

body paragraph / el párrafo del cuerpo **noun** a paragraph that appears between the introduction and the conclusion of an essay

conclusion / la conclusión **noun** the closing paragraph or section of an essay; a closing argument in an argumentative text COGNATE

Extended Writing Project

YOUR TURN

Read the phrases below. Then, complete the chart by sorting them into those that are thesis statements and those that are supporting details.

Phrases	
A	I lived in Master Hugh's family about seven years. During this time, I succeeded in learning to read and write. —From *Narrative of the Life of Frederick Douglass*
B	I immediately walked over, picked up the shark and placed him back into the water and told him to live free. I swear the shark looked at me with gratitude. He was alive because I spoke up for him and he knew it. —From "The Day I Saved a Life"
C	Today is a day for mourning and remembering. —From "Address to the Nation on the Explosion of the Space Shuttle *Challenger*"
D	If I was in a separate room any considerable length of time, I was sure to be suspected of having a book, and was at once called to give an account of myself. —From *Narrative of the Life of Frederick Douglass*
E	And perhaps we've forgotten the courage it took for the crew of the shuttle. But they, the *Challenger* Seven, were aware of the dangers, but overcame them and did their jobs brilliantly. —From "Address to the Nation on the Explosion of the Space Shuttle *Challenger*"
F	Movies like Jaws, Day of The Shark, Shark Night, Deep Blue Sea etc., give us the impression of a mindless killing machine out to kill all human beings. Well, I've seen another side of the shark and I've seen it up close and personal. —From "The Day I Saved a Life"

Your Turn

Ask students to complete the Your Turn activity.

Thesis Statement	Supporting Details
A	D
C	E
F	B

Writer's Notebook

Ask students to pretend that they are writing an article for a class newsletter that tells about local places to visit. Have them write a thesis statement about a local place to visit.

ELL TURN AND TALK

Allow students to share their ideas orally in pairs or small groups before writing.

Write

Ask students to complete the writing assignment.

ELL **REWRITE CHECKLIST**

A **Main Idea**

☐ What selections will you write about?

☐ What is the main idea of each selection?

☐ How are the main ideas related?

Responding to the Prompt

☐ How do the main ideas of each selection relate to the prompt?

☐ What makes the risks in each selection different?

☐ What makes the risks in each selection similar?

☐ How can you clearly state your ideas?

Placement

☐ Is there information that you need to share before stating your thesis?

☐ Where will your thesis statement appear in your essay?

☐ Why will it work best in that location?

Thesis Statement	Supporting Details

✎ **WRITE**

Use the questions in the checklist to revise the beginning of your informative essay.

Reading & Writing
Companion   101

Skill:
Organizing Informative Writing

Skill: Organizing Informative Writing

Introduce the Skill

Watch the Concept Definition video and read the following definition with your students.

The purpose of **informative writing** is to inform readers about real people, places, things, and events, so authors need to organize their ideas, concepts, and information in a logical way. Experienced authors carefully choose an **organizational structure**, such as definition, classification, compare/contrast, and cause/effect, that best suits their material. Writers often use an outline to decide which organizational structure will help them express their ideas. For example, texts about historical topics might need a cause/effect structure to explain why something happened. **Headings** that divide a series of paragraphs can make organization obvious. They tell readers how information is arranged and presented. A reader can scan a document and find specific information. Some writers also use **graphics**, such as charts and tables, or **multimedia**, such as video, sound, and hypertext links, to make complex information easier to understand. The organizational structure should always be appropriate for the writing purpose.

••• CHECKLIST FOR ORGANIZING INFORMATIVE WRITING

As you consider how to organize your writing for your informative essay, use the following questions as a guide:

- What is my topic? How can I summarize the main idea?
- How can I organize the information from the text into broad categories?
- What is the logical order of my ideas, concepts, and information? Do I see a pattern that is similar to a specific text structure?
- Which organizing structure should I use to present my information?
- How might using graphics, headings, or some form of multimedia help to present my information?

Here are some broader categories that can help you organize ideas, concepts, and information and aid comprehension:

- topic or main idea
- definitions, including restatements and examples
- classifications, including subcategories of a topic
- comparisons of ideas or concepts
- cause-and-effect relationships

 TURN AND TALK

Turn to your partner and discuss a time you followed directions to complete a task, such as cooking with a recipe or assembling something with an instruction manual.

 SKILL VOCABULARY

informative writing / la escritura informativa *noun* nonfiction writing that presents information about real people, places, things, and events

organizational structure / la estructura organizativa *noun* the order or pattern that a writer uses to organize information, such as cause-and-effect or compare-and-contrast **COGNATE**

heading / el título *noun* the title given to a particular section of text

---

ELL SPEAKING FRAMES

- I followed directions to ____.
- The structure of the directions was / was not clear because ____

⚙ Your Turn

Ask students to complete the Your Turn activity.

"What Is Ornithology?"	definition
"On Puffins and Penguins: An Exclusive Look at Their Similarities and Differences"	compare/contrast
"Why Can't Ostriches Fly?"	cause and effect
"A Guide to Flightless Birds"	classification

⚙ Your Turn

Ask students to complete the Your Turn activity. Answers will vary.

Introduction:	Richard Turere, Frederick Douglass, and the *Challenger* crew show that taking risks brings out the best in people.
Body Paragraph 1:	Richard Turere took a risk when he used a flashlight to scare away lions. This risk gave him an idea for a set of lights that scare away lions. These lights protect people, the livestock that lions hunt, and the lions themselves.
Body Paragraph 2:	Like Richard Turere, Frederick Douglass helped a lot of people because he secretly learned how to read and write even though he could have been punished. His success changed his own life, and it continues to inspire others.
Body Paragraph 3:	The *Challenger* crew also inspired many people even though their story ended in tragedy. In his speech about the disaster, President Reagan says that people will follow their example because they took a risk for important reasons.
Conclusion:	Taking risks can help people develop bravery and strength. It can also inspire others to do the same.

Extended Writing Project

⟳ YOUR TURN

Read the informational text titles below. Then, complete the chart by writing the organizational structure that would best convey the ideas of each text.

Organizational Structure Options			
compare/contrast	definition	classification	cause and effect

Informational Text Title	Organizational Structure
"What Is Ornithology?"	
"On Puffins and Penguins: An Exclusive Look at Their Similarities and Differences"	
"Why Can't Ostriches Fly?"	
"A Guide to Flightless Birds"	

⟳ YOUR TURN

Complete the chart below by writing a short summary of what you will focus on in each paragraph of your essay.

Outline	Summary
Introduction:	
Body Paragraph 1:	
Body Paragraph 2:	
Body Paragraph 3:	
Conclusion:	

Reading & Writing Companion   103

🗀 SKILL VOCABULARY

graphics / las gráficas *noun* charts or tables that can make complex information easier to understand COGNATE

multimedia / multimedia *adjective* using several communications media at the same time COGNATE

Extended Writing Project

SUPPORTING | DETAILS

•Skills

Skill:
Supseorting Details

Introduce the Skill

Watch the Concept Definition video and read the following definition with your students.

In informative and argumentative writing, writers develop their thesis statements or claims with information called **supporting details**. These details can include any kind of textual evidence, such as descriptions, examples, reasons, quotations that reveal expert opinions, facts, and statistics. Supporting details help explain key ideas and are closely related to the topic.

Supporting details that develop a thesis statement or claim must be relevant, necessary, or concrete. **Relevant** supporting details are appropriate and logically related to the topic. **Necessary** details are essential and required for developing a writer's thesis statement or proving a writer's claim. A **concrete detail** is very specific. It helps readers visualize and understand the topic or the idea in the writer's mind.

Though information is plentiful, the writer must be careful to **evaluate**, or judge, the quality of information to determine what is most important and most closely related to the thesis statement or claim.

••• CHECKLIST FOR SUPPORTING DETAILS

As you look for supporting details to develop your topic, claim, or thesis statement, ask yourself the following questions:

- What is my main idea about this topic?
- What does a reader need to know about the topic in order to understand the main idea?
- What details will support my thesis statement?
- Is this information necessary to the reader's understanding of the topic?
- Does this information help to develop and refine my key concept or idea?
- Does this information relate closely to my thesis statement or claim?
- Where can I find better evidence that will provide stronger support for my point?

Here are some suggestions for how you can develop your topic:

- Review your thesis statement or claim.
- Consider your main idea.
- Note what the reader will need to know in order to understand the topic.
- Be sure to consult credible sources.
- Use different types of supporting details, such as:
  - > well-chosen facts that are specific to your topic and enhance your discussion to establish credibility with your reader and build information
  - > definitions to explain difficult concepts, terms, or ideas in your topic, claim, or thesis statement
  - > concrete details that will add descriptive and detailed material to your topic
  - > quotations to directly connect your thesis statement or claim to the text
  - > examples and other information to deepen your claim, topic, or thesis statement

TURN AND TALK

Turn to your partner and share a "fun fact" about the natural world. It could relate to an animal species, the human body, space, or another topic. Discuss how that fun fact would make a strong supporting detail in a paper on that topic.

ELL SPEAKING FRAMES

- A "fun fact" I know is ____.
- This fact relates to the topic of ____.
- This fact would make a good supporting detail because ____.

⚙ Your Turn

Ask students to complete the Your Turn activitiy.

QUESTION 1

A. Incorrect. This quotation does not support the idea that teaching was also risky.

B. Incorrect. This quotation does not support the idea that teaching was also risky.

C. Correct. This quotation supports the idea that teaching was also risky.

D. Incorrect. This quotation does not support the idea that teaching was also risky.

QUESTION 2

A. Incorrect. This quotation does not support Aiko's idea that failure is part of success.

B. Correct. This quotation best supports Aiko's idea that failure is part of success, "part of the process."

C. Incorrect. This quotation does not support Aiko's idea that failure is part of success.

D. Incorrect. This quotation states that more work is to be done, but it does not support Aiko's idea that failure is part of success.

Extended Writing Project

🔁 YOUR TURN

Choose the best answer to each question.

1. Aiko wants to improve the supporting details of a previous draft of her informative essay. How can she rewrite the underlined sentence to provide more support?

> In his autobiography *Narrative of the Life of Frederick Douglass, an American Slave*, Douglass describes many risks he took. However, Douglass is not the only person who took risks. <u>Some kids helped him</u>. This shows that it was also risky to agree to teach an enslaved person at the time.

○ A. Douglass knew some white children, and he says, "As many of these as I could, I converted into teachers."

○ B. Douglass gave bread to some boys, "who, in return, would give me that more valuable bread of knowledge."

○ C. Even though it was "almost an unpardonable offence to teach slaves to read in this Christian country," some local boys agreed to teach him.

○ D. Douglass recalls chatting with some white boys about slavery: "These words used to trouble them; they would express for me the liveliest sympathy."

2. Aiko would like to add a supporting detail to a previous draft of her paragraph on "Address to the Nation on the Explosion of the Space Shuttle *Challenger*." Which quotation could best follow and provide support for her last sentence?

> Failure can have a great impact on people, too. For example, when the crew of the *Challenger* died on their mission, the American people were deeply affected by the loss. The tragedy was a reminder that failure is part of success.

○ A. "Nineteen years ago, almost to the day, we lost three astronauts in a terrible accident on the ground. But we've never lost an astronaut in flight; we've never had a tragedy like this. And perhaps we've forgotten the courage it took for the crew of the shuttle."

○ B. "I know it is hard to understand, but sometimes painful things like this happen. It's all part of the process of exploration and discovery. It's all part of taking a chance and expanding man's horizons."

○ C. "I've always had great faith in and respect for our space program, and what happened today does nothing to diminish it. We don't hide our space program."

○ D. "We'll continue our quest in space. There will be more shuttle flights and more shuttle crews and, yes, more volunteers, more civilians, more teachers in space. Nothing ends here; our hopes and our journeys continue."

Reading & Writing Companion   105

Ⅴ SKILL VOCABULARY

supporting detail / el detalle de apoyo *noun* a piece of text evidence, a description, an example, a reason, an expert opinion, a fact, or a statistic that further explains a key idea and closely relates to the thesis or claim

relevant / relevante *adjective* appropriate and logically related to the topic COGNATE

necessary / necesario/a *adjective* essential and required COGNATE

concrete detail / el detalle concreto *noun* a specific detail that helps readers visualize or understand the topic or the idea in the writer's mind COGNATE

evaluate / evaluar *verb* to judge or decide; to estimate the quality of COGNATE

Extended Writing Project

↻ YOUR TURN

Complete the chart below by identifying evidence from each text you've chosen. Identifying evidence will help you develop your own thesis statement.

Text	Evidence
Selection #1:	
Selection #2:	
Selection #3:	

⚙ Your Turn

Ask students to complete the Your Turn activity. Answers will vary.

Selection #1:	Taking a risk to walk outside near wild animals at night led Richard Turere to come up with an invention that helped a lot of people.
Selection #2:	Because asking for help was too risky, Frederick Douglass came up with a way to trick other boys into helping him when he challenged them to write as well as he could.
Selection #3:	The *Challenger* crew reminded hard-to-impress Americans that space is still a new frontier for exploration and discovery.

📓 Writer's Notebook

Ask students to think of a topic they know a lot about, such as their favorite class, TV show, or sport. Ask them to pretend they are writing a study guide on that topic. Have students write a list of supporting details that are important to understanding the topic.

TURN AND TALK

Allow students to share their topics and list of supporting details orally in pairs or small groups.

Informative Writing Process: Draft

Write

Ask students to complete the writing assignment.

✓ CHECK FOR SUCCESS

If students struggle to begin drafting their informative essay, ask them the following questions:

- What is your thesis statement or the main idea of your informative essay?
- What is your main idea about each selection that you chose?
- How do those ideas support your thesis statement or the main idea of your essay?
- What supporting details help explain key ideas and are closely related to your topic?

 DRAFT CHECKLIST

- ☐ Does your introduction clearly include your thesis statement or main idea of the essay?
- ☐ Do the main ideas in your body paragraphs help develop your thesis statement?
- ☐ Does your conclusion wrap up your ideas?

Extended Writing Project

Informative Writing Process: Draft

| PLAN | DRAFT | REVISE | EDIT AND PUBLISH |

You have already made progress toward writing your informative essay. Now it is time to draft your informative essay.

✏ WRITE

Use your plan and other responses in your Binder to draft your informative essay. You may also have new ideas as you begin drafting. Feel free to explore those new ideas as you have them. You can also ask yourself these questions:

- Does my thesis statement or main idea of the essay clearly respond to the prompt?
- Does the organization of my essay make sense?
- Have I developed my thesis statement by using supporting details that help explain key ideas and are closely related to my topic?
- Have I made my ideas clear to readers?

Before you submit your draft, read it over carefully. You want to be sure that you've responded to all aspects of the prompt.

Peer Review

Students should submit substantive feedback to two peers using the review instructions below.

- Has the writer stated a thesis that clearly responds to the prompt?
- What suggestions can you make to help the writer improve the organization of this informative essay?
- Are there any ideas that could be improved on? How so?
- Does the writer use relevant supporting details to develop the thesis statement? Are there any supporting details that could be added or improved?

 SENTENCE FRAMES

- You clearly stated your thesis that ____.
- Your thesis does / does not respond to the entire prompt because ____.

- Each supporting detail does / does not help develop your thesis because ____.
- I would suggest improving your ____ by ____.

Extended Writing Project

Here is Aiko's informative essay draft. As you read, identify Aiko's main ideas. As she continues to revise and edit her essay, she will find and improve weak spots in her writing, as well as correct any language or punctuation mistakes.

NOTES

Skill:
Introductions

Aiko adds more information about the people she will write about to clarify why she chose to analyze their stories in her essay. After reviewing these changes, Aiko sees that she still needs to engage readers at the beginning of her paragraph, so she adds a new sentence as a hook. After making those changes, Aiko then revises her thesis statement so that it flows from her new ideas.

☰ STUDENT MODEL: FIRST DRAFT

Risks Teach Valuable Lessons

~~Everybody takes risks even through they can never be certain of how a risk will turn out. Some risks are small. Some are big. Every time a person takes a risk, risking losing something. Frederick Douglass, the crew of the Challenger, and members of the Biloxi-Chitimacha-Choctaw Native American tribe all risked losses in to pursue their goals. The risks that they took were very different, but they all show that risk-taking can help people learn lessons.~~

People take risks every day. Many risks are small, such as trying a new type of food. Other risks are bigger, such as moving across the country. Whether big or small, all risks have something in common. People can never be certain of how a risk will turn out. Every time a person takes a risk, there is a chance that they will lose something valuable. Frederick Douglass, the crew of the *Challenger*, and members of the Biloxi-Chitimacha-Choctaw Native American tribe are examples of people who have risked devastating losses to pursue worthy goals. Even though these risks and the outcomes of these risks differ, they all teach essential lessons.

In his autobiography *Narrative of the Life of Frederick Douglass, An American Slave*, Douglass describes many dangerous risks taking. Born into slavery, Douglass was legaly denied an education. When he was young, the mistress of one house started to teach him how to read until her husband telling her to stop. She then got angry and violent when Douglass tried to learn on his own. Douglass says, "I have had her rush at me with a face made all up of fury, and snatch from me a newspaper, in a manner that fully revealed her apprehension." Still, Douglass, wanting to learn, he explains, "All this, however, was too late. The first step had been taken. Mistress, in teaching me the alphabet, had given me the *inch*, and no precaution could prevent me from taking the *ell*." Douglass's efforts made a difference. After several years, he learned how to read and writing.

Copyright © BookheadEd Learning, LLC

108 🖥 Reading & Writing Companion

Please note that excerpts and passages in the StudySync® library and this workbook are intended as touchstones to generate interest in an author's work. The excerpts and passages do not substitute for the reading of entire texts, and StudySync® strongly recommends that students seek out and purchase the whole literary or informational work in order to experience it as the author intended. Links to online resellers are available in our digital library. In addition, complete works may be ordered through an authorized reseller by filling out and returning to StudySync® the order form enclosed in this workbook.

Ⓑ **GRAPHIC ORGANIZER**

Before students write their draft, have them think about the Student Model (and process) and the prompt. Challenge students to create an original graphic organizer to help plan their thoughts before beginning their draft. Students can share/compare their graphic organizers with their peers.

✏️ ## Analyze Student Model

Have students discuss the questions in the lesson as well as the Student Model draft. Ask:

- What thesis statement or main idea does Aiko present in the introduction?
- What main idea does Aiko share in her first body paragraph?
- How does the main idea in the body paragraph support her thesis statement or the main idea of the essay?

Encourage students to share ideas for their own informative essays based on the questions in the lesson.

ELL SPEAKING FRAMES

- The writer's thesis statement or main idea of the essay is ____.
- The main idea in the writer's first body paragraph is ____.
- The writer uses the main idea of the first body paragraph to develop her thesis statement by ____.

⚙️ ## Introductions

Discuss the Model

1. Why does Aiko replace the first sentence in her introduction? Answers will vary. Sample answer: Her original sentence was not engaging, so Aiko decides to add a stronger hook. She writes a short sentence that shows how the topic of risk-taking is an important part of everyone's life.

2. Why does Aiko decide to revise her thesis statement? Aiko has revised some information in her introduction, so she needs to make sure that her thesis statement flows from her updated set of ideas.

ELL SPEAKING FRAMES

- Aiko replaces the first sentence in her introduction because ____.
- Aiko revises her thesis statement because ____.

Transitions

Discuss the Model

1. What is Aiko searching for as she rereads her draft? any unclear relationships among ideas and concepts

2. What is an example of a transition that Aiko adds to create cohesion? What relationship does it show among ideas in her draft? Answers will vary. Sample answer: Aiko uses the word "however" to show the difference in outcomes for Douglass and the *Challenger* crew.

ELL SPEAKING FRAMES

- As Aiko rereads her draft, she searches for ____.
- Aiko uses the transition ____ to show the relationship between ____ and ____.

Style

Discuss the Model

1. How does Aiko revise the language in her draft to make it more formal? She uses a third-person instead of a second-person pronoun. She replaces a conversational phrase with a more formal one.

2. How does domain-specific vocabulary improve Aiko's essay? Answers will vary. Sample answer: Domain-specific vocabulary shows readers that Aiko is knowledgeable about her topic, and it makes the information that she shares more accurate.

Style

Connect to Mentor Text

Project the following example of style and discuss with your students:

Then it happened. I hit the jackpot! I discovered in my scoop the largest tooth I had ever seen. It was four inches long and black in color. Its edges were serrated and you could still see the gum line. The great white teeth I found paled in comparison to this massive tooth. It was a Megalodon tooth! ("The Day I Saved a Life")

Ask students:

- Which style of writing does the example show?

- Which style will be appropriate for your informative essay?

~~The risks Douglass took in pursuit of his goal also teach readers valuable lessons. His success teaches the values of perseverance and faith in one's own abilities.~~

~~In 1986, The crew of the space shuttle *Challenger* set out to making new discoveries in space. They lost they're lives in a space shuttle disaster. In his speech, "Address to the Nation on the Explosion of the Space Shuttle *Challenger*," President Ronald Reagan reminds Americans that the crew was willed to do a dangerous job. Believing that their mission would be worth the risk.~~

The risks Douglass took in pursuit of his goal also teach readers valuable lessons. His success teaches the values of perseverance and faith in one's own abilities.

However, failure teaches lessons, too. In 1986, the crew of the space shuttle *Challenger* set out to make new discoveries in space, but they lost their lives in a space shuttle disaster. In his speech "Address to the Nation on the Explosion of the Space Shuttle *Challenger*," President Ronald Reagan reminds Americans that the crew was willing to do a dangerous job. They wanted to travel into space because they believed that the mission would be worth the risk.

And well prepared, there were important questions about the universe that the *Challenger* crew was planning to study. Unfortunately, they never had a chance to acheive that goal because the Space Shuttle exploded after takeoff despite this tragic end, Americans are still to learn a valuable lessen from the *Challenger* crew. Reagan's explaining "The future doesn't belong to the fainthearted; it belongs to the brave. The *Challenger* crew was pulling us into the future, and we'll continue to follow them." The crew was willing to risk their lives to find out new information about the universe. The crew also teaches the values of putting others before yourself and bravery.

~~The risks that you need to take to go after a goal aren't always the same over time. This is evident in "Vanishing Island," an informational article by Anya Groner. In the early 1800s, many members of the Biloxi-Chitimacha-Choctaw Native American tribe established a community on a small island off the coast of Louisiana called Isle de Jean Charles, and it became a "cultural homeland." Since the~~

Skill: Transitions

Aiko sees that the ideas in this paragraph do not logically follow from the ideas in the first body paragraph about Frederick Douglass's risk. She searches for a way to use a transition word and a clear topic sentence to show the relationship between the two paragraphs. She uses the linking word "However" to show readers that the outcome of the Challenger crew's risk contrasts with the successful outcome of Frederick Douglass's risk.

 SPEAKING FRAMES

- Aiko revises the language in her draft to make it more formal by ____.
- Domain-specific vocabulary improves Aiko's essay because ____.

NOTES

Skill: Style

Aiko starts by looking for sentences that sound conversational, and she finds three issues in her first sentence: It includes a second-person pronoun, the conversational phrase "go after a goal," and a contraction. Since this sentence needs several changes, she decides to rewrite it by using third-person pronouns, replacing the conversational phrase, and avoiding contractions.

Skill: Precise Language

Aiko searches for other language that needs to be more specific and vivid. For example, she replaces "wants" with "envisions" and elaborates on the purpose of the museum that the tribal secretary describes.

~~mid-twentieth century, however, the land on the Island been disappearing into the water that's around the Island at a fast rate. It may not even exist by 2050. As a result, many members of the tribe will risk to give up their land and homes to relocate the community.~~

The risks that one needs to take to pursue a goal can also change over time. This is evident in "Vanishing Island," an informational article by Anya Groner. In the early 1800s, many members of the Biloxi-Chitimacha-Choctaw Native American tribe established a community on a small island off the coast of Louisiana, and it became a "cultural homeland." The island is called Isle de Jean Charles. Since the mid-twentieth century, however, the land on the island has been rapidly eroding, or wearing away. Storms, river engineering, and pollution are causing this to happen, and the landform may not even exist by 2050.

~~Chief Naquin, the current chief of the Biloxi-Chitimacha-Choctaw Native American tribe, compared the loss of this island to "the loss of a family member." But the members' not giving up and dedicated to preserving their history, community, and culture on the new site. The tribal secretary Chantel Comardelle wants a museum that guides visitor's through the history of the island. Many members of the community also value family. And building houses that give extended families shared backyards. These plans address important issues, but many residents on Isle de Jean Charles will still need to go through a major move, and that teaches readers a lot.~~

Chief Naquin, the current chief of the Biloxi-Chitimacha-Choctaw Native American tribe, compared the loss of this island to "the loss of a family member." Leaving that land will be painful, but members are dedicated to preserving their history, community, and culture on the new site. For example, tribal secretary Chantel Comardelle envisions a museum that guides visitors through the history of the island. Many members of the community also value family. To encourage interactions among family members on the new site, they want to build groups of houses with shared backyards. These plans address important issues, but many residents on Isle de Jean Charles will still need to endure a difficult move. Their sacrifices teach readers the values of determination and resilience, the ability to recover from a loss.

Precise Language

Discuss the Model

1. In this section of her draft, why doesn't Aiko successfully convey information to readers? Vague, general, and overused language makes the information in this section unclear.

2. What is one example of precise language that Aiko adds to the draft? Answers will vary. Sample answer: Aiko replaces "wants a museum" with "envisions a museum."

3. How does that change improve her essay? Answers will vary. Sample answer: This change makes the sentence more accurate. It shows that Chantel Comardelle is imagining and designing a museum that has not been built yet.

ELL SPEAKING FRAMES

- In this section of her draft, Aiko doesn't successfully convey information because ___.
- One example of precise language that Aiko adds to the draft is ___.
- That change improves her essay because ___.

Precise Language

Connect to Mentor Text

Project the following excerpt from "A Night to Remember" as an example of precise language and discuss with your students:

For the next 37 seconds, Fleet and Lee stood quietly side by side, watching the ice draw nearer. Now they were almost on top of it, and still the ship didn't turn. The berg towered wet and glistening far above the forecastle deck, and both men braced themselves for a crash. Then, miraculously, the bow began to swing to port. At the last second the stem shot into the clear, and the ice glided swiftly by along the starboard side. It looked to Fleet like a very close shave.

Ask students:

- What information is the author trying to convey?

- What is one example of precise language that the author uses?

- What domain-specific vocabulary does the author use?

⚙ Conclusions

Discuss the Model

1. Why does Aiko delete the first sentence in her conclusion? Aiko sees that the first sentence in her conclusion is not clearly related to her thesis statement or the information that she presents in her essay.

2. Why does Aiko update the thesis statement or main idea in her conclusion? Aiko has already revised the thesis statement or main idea in her introduction, so she needs to revise the main idea in her conclusion as well. She wants to make sure that both statements convey the same ideas.

3. Aiko wanted to motivate readers with her last line. How well did she do? Can you suggest any ways to improve the last line? Answers will vary.

⚙ Conclusions

Connect to Mentor Text

Project the following example of a conclusion from "Vanishing Island" and discuss with your students:

Perhaps, years from now, Comardelle's children will recall these trips to Isle de Jean Charles, an island homeland that no longer exists. Sitting on a back porch, they'll tell their children about how they caught crabs in the bayou. How they listened to their grandparents speak in Cajun French about weddings in general stores and waiting out hurricanes in their daddy's boats. Around them the egrets will take flight as Spanish moss sways in the breeze. Relatives might wave from nearby porches. After all, history isn't just what happened a long time ago. The creation of a new homeland, the tribe's relocation, and the council's efforts to maintain culture are all history in action. If the relocation works, Comardelle, the Naquins, and the other members of the Biloxi-Chitimacha-Choctaw tribe will achieve something amazing. Their people and their culture will have a safe home in coastal Louisiana for centuries to come.

Ask students:

• What do you notice about this conclusion?

• Did the author restate the thesis or main idea of this essay?

• What important ideas from the article did the author include in this conclusion?

• What impression might the author have wanted to make on you as a reader? How do you know?

~~People need to consider when risks are worth taking and when they are not worth taken.~~ *Narrative of the Life of Frederick Douglass, An American Slave,* "Address to the Nation on the Explosion of the Space Shuttle *Challenger*," and "Vanishing Island" ~~are stories about people who took major risks. The risks that they took were very different, but they all show that risk-taking can help people learn lessons.~~

Narrative of the Life of Frederick Douglass, an American Slave, "Address to the Nation on the Explosion of the Space Shuttle *Challenger*," and "Vanishing Island" inform readers about historic risks that people have taken to pursue their goals. They show that each person faced hardships as a result of their decisions, and the *Challenger* crew tragically lost their lives. However, their stories continue to teach lessons about honorable qualities. They set examples that readers can follow when they need to decide if they want to take a risk for an important goal.

⚙ Skill:
Conclusions

Aiko's revision brings her essay to a close by clearly reviewing her thesis statement and supporting details. To leave her readers with a lasting impression, she also tried to motivate them by adding the final line. It reminds readers that they can use the information in this essay when they need to decide whether or not to take a risk.

Reading & Writing Companion   111

⟨ELL⟩ SPEAKING FRAMES

• Aiko deletes the first sentence in her conclusion because ____.
• Aiko updates the thesis statement in her conclusion because ____.
• Aiko's last line (did / did not) motivate me because ____.
• Aiko could improve the last line by ____.

Skill:
Introduction

••• CHECKLIST FOR INTRODUCTIONS

Before you write your introduction, ask yourself the following questions:

- What is my claim?
- How can I introduce my topic clearly?
- How will you "hook" your reader's interest? You might:
  - > start with an attention-grabbing statement
  - > begin with an intriguing question
  - > use descriptive words to set a scene

Below are two strategies to help you introduce your claim and topic clearly in an introduction:

- Peer Discussion
  - > Talk about your topic with a partner, explaining what you already know and your ideas about your topic.
  - > Write notes about the ideas you have discussed and any new questions you may have.
  - > Review your notes and think about what will be your claim or main idea.
  - > Briefly state your claim or thesis statement.
  - > Write ways you can give readers a "preview" of what they will read in the rest of your essay.
  - > Write a possible "hook."

- Freewriting
  - > Freewrite for ten minutes about your topic. Don't worry about grammar, punctuation, or having fully formed ideas. The point of freewriting is to discover ideas.
  - > Review your notes and think about what will be your claim or main idea.
  - > Briefly state your claim or thesis.
  - > Write ways you can give readers a "preview" of what they will read in the rest of your essay.
  - > Write a possible "hook."

SKILL VOCABULARY

introduction / la introducción *noun* the opening paragraph or section of an essay COGNATE

topic / el tema *noun* the subject of a literary work, usually expressed as a single word or phrase in the form of a noun

thesis statement / la presentación de la tesis *noun* a statement that shares the main idea of an argumentative or informational essay

claim / la afirmación *noun* the writer's or speaker's position on a debatable issue or problem

---

⚙ Skill: Introductions

Introduce the Skill

Watch the Concept Definition video ▶ and read the following definition with your students.

The **introduction** is the opening paragraph or section of an essay or other nonfiction text. To begin an argumentative essay, writers identify the **topic**, or what the essay will be about. The most important part of the introduction in an argumentative essay is the **thesis statement**. This statement contains the writer's **claim**, or main argument, and it states something that the writer believes to be true.

In an informative/explanatory text, the introduction should provide readers with necessary information in order to introduce a topic. It should state the thesis, which in an informative/explanatory essay is a short statement that summarizes the main point of the essay and previews the ideas that will follow in the text. In an informative/explanatory essay, many writers also include one or two sentences that are called a "hook." They are intended to engage readers' interest and grab their attention so they keep reading.

⚙ TURN AND TALK

Turn to your partner and discuss the last time you had to introduce someone new to a friend or family member. Tell how you chose which details to include in your introduction.

ELL SPEAKING FRAMES
- I introduced ____ to ____.
- A detail I chose to include was ____ because ____.

Your Turn

Ask students to complete the Your Turn activity.

QUESTION 1

A. Correct. Asking an intriguing question is a good way to grab readers' attention.

B. Incorrect. This sentence states the writer's opinion. It does not introduce her main ideas.

C. Incorrect. This sentence does not reflect the main ideas of the essay.

D. Incorrect. This sentence introduces a supporting detail, not the main idea of the essay.

QUESTION 2

A. Incorrect. The word "teachers" could cause confusion. Although each person's story teaches a valuable lesson, the people whom the writer mentions are not all teachers.

B. Incorrect. This sentence does not add information that shows readers why these people are noteworthy.

C. Incorrect. The thesis statement that follows this sentence already makes this point, so it does not add new information.

D. Correct. Their stories teach readers why difficult risks are sometimes important to take.

Copyright © BookheadEd Learning, LLC

Extended Writing Project

🔁 YOUR TURN

Choose the best answer to each question.

1. The following introduction is from a previous draft of Aiko's essay. Aiko would like to replace the underlined sentence with a sentence that better grabs readers' attention and introduces her main idea. Which of these would be the BEST replacement for the underlined sentence?

> <u>Lots of different people take risks.</u> Even if a risk leads to failure, there is always a lesson to learn. There are lessons for the people who have taken the risks, but there are also lessons for people who learn about them. Frederick Douglass, the *Challenger* crew, and the Biloxi-Chitimacha-Choctaw Native American tribe are examples of risk-takers. Their risks and the outcomes of their risks differ, but their stories all teach valuable lessons.

- A. Have you ever taken a risk that didn't work out?
- B. I don't like taking risks.
- C. Sometimes people should not take risks.
- D. Members of the Biloxi-Chitimacha-Choctaw Native American tribe are taking a risk.

2. The following introduction is from a previous draft of Aiko's essay. Aiko would like to replace the underlined sentence with a sentence that explains why she has chosen Frederick Douglass, the *Challenger* crew, and the Biloxi-Chitimacha-Choctaw Native American tribe as examples of risk-takers. Which of these would be the BEST replacement for the underlined sentence?

> Lots of different people take risks. Even if a risk leads to failure, there is always a lesson to learn. There are lessons for the people who have taken the risks, but there are also lessons for people who learn about them. <u>Frederick Douglass, the *Challenger* crew, and the Biloxi-Chitimacha-Choctaw Native American tribe are examples of risk-takers.</u> Their risks and the outcomes of their risks differ, but their stories all teach valuable lessons.

- A. Frederick Douglass, the *Challenger* crew, and the Biloxi-Chitimacha-Choctaw Native American tribe are risk-takers and teachers.
- B. Frederick Douglass, the *Challenger* crew, and the Biloxi-Chitimacha-Choctaw Native American tribe are risk-takers who are noteworthy.
- C. Frederick Douglass, the *Challenger* crew, and the Biloxi-Chitimacha-Choctaw Native American tribe are examples of people who took risks with different outcomes.
- D. Frederick Douglass, the *Challenger* crew, and the Biloxi-Chitimacha-Choctaw Native American tribe are examples of people who took difficult risks for important causes.

Reading & Writing Companion   113

Writer's Notebook

Ask students to imagine that they are writing an informative article about a game for the school newspaper. That could include a board game, a video game, a sports game, or a game played in class. Have them write the introduction of the article. Remind them to use the questions in the checklist as a guide.

ELL TURN AND TALK

Allow students to share their ideas orally in pairs or small groups before writing.

Extended Writing Project

✏️ WRITE

Use the steps in the checklist to revise the introduction of your informative essay.

✏️ Write

Ask students to complete the writing assignment.

ELL REWRITE CHECKLIST

A Hook

☐ What attention-grabbing statement could you include?

☐ How might an intriguing question grab your readers' attention?

☐ How could descriptive details establish a scene that introduces your ideas?

Development

☐ Have you provided readers with the information necessary to introduce your claim?

☐ Does the introduction show readers how you will organize your ideas?

Thesis Statement

☐ Does your thesis statement answer all parts of the prompt?

☐ Does your thesis statement summarize the main point of the essay?

☐ Does your thesis statement preview the ideas that will follow in the text?

Skill: Transitions

Introduce the Skill

Watch the Concept Definition video ▶ and read the following definition with your students.

Transitions are connecting words, phrases, and clauses that writers use to **clarify** the relationships among ideas and details in a text. Transitions have different functions depending on whether the text is argumentative, informative, or narrative.

In an argumentative essay, writers state claims and provide reasons and evidence for their claims. To clarify a relationship between a claim and a reason or supporting evidence, transitions such as *although* and *on the other hand* help make connections clear.

For informative essays, transitions such as *however, in addition,* and *for example* may help create **cohesion** among ideas and concepts.

In narrative writing, authors use a variety of words, phrases, and clauses to signal shifts in time, setting, and action. Transitions such as *until now, meanwhile,* and *once it was over* may make narrative events more **coherent**.

Transitions also help to connect ideas both within and across paragraphs and between major sections of text.

Copyright © BookheadEd Learning, LLC

TURN AND TALK

Turn to your partner and inform your partner about one routine you follow to complete homework or a project at home. Use a variety of transitions to describe your routine.

ELL   **SPEAKING FRAMES**

- One routine I follow to complete (my homework / a project) is ____.
- When I follow this routine, I ____.
- If we needed to show the class how our routines are related, we could use this transition: ____.
- For example, we could say ____.

Extended Writing Project

Skill:
Transitions

•••   **CHECKLIST FOR TRANSITIONS**

Before you revise your current draft to include transitions, think about:

- the key ideas you discuss in your body paragraphs
- how your paragraphs connect together to support your claim(s)
- the relationships among your ideas and concepts
- the logical progression of your ideas

Next, reread your current draft and note areas in your essay where:

- the relationships among your ideas and concepts are unclear, identifying places where you could add linking words or other transitional devices to make your essay more cohesive. Look for:
  - > sudden jumps in your ideas
  - > breaks between paragraphs where the ideas in the next paragraph are not logically following from the previous one

Revise your draft to use words, phrases, and clauses to create cohesion and clarify the relationships among your ideas and concepts, using the following questions as a guide:

- Are there unifying relationships between the ideas I present in my essay?
- Have I clarified, or made clear, these relationships?
- What linking words (such as conjunctions), phrases, or clauses could I add to my essay to clarify the relationships among the ideas and concepts I present?

Reading & Writing Companion   **115**

V   **SKILL VOCABULARY**

transition / la transición *noun* a connecting word or phrase that a writer may use to clarify the relationship between ideas in a text; set off with a comma COGNATE

clarify / aclarar *verb* to make clear and more comprehensible

cohesion / la cohesión *noun* the quality of parts working together as a whole COGNATE

coherent / coherente *adjective* marked by being orderly and logical; easy to understand COGNATE

Extended Writing Project

YOUR TURN

Choose the best answer to each question.

1. Below is an excerpt from a previous draft of Aiko's informative essay. Aiko notices that her introduction and first body paragraphs are not clearly connected to one another, so she wants to revise the underlined sentence. Which of the following sentences clearly shows how the main idea of the first body paragraph relates to the topic of the essay?

> Frederick Douglass, the crew of the *Challenger*, and members of the Biloxi-Chitimacha-Choctaw Native American tribe all risked losses in pursuit of their goals. Even though their risks and the outcomes of their risks differ, they all required courage.
>
> Douglass describes a major risk that he took in his autobiography. Born into slavery, Douglass was legally denied an education. At first, his mistress started teaching him how to read, but after she changed her mind about teaching him, she became angry and violent when he tried to learn on his own.

- A. In Frederick Douglass's autobiography, Douglass described how he learned to read and write while risking severe punishment.
- B. In Frederick Douglass's autobiography, Douglass described his effort to learn how to read and write, and the outcome of this risk was positive.
- C. As an example, Frederick Douglass described major risks that he took while learning how to read and write.
- D. As an example, Frederick Douglass wrote about acts of courage in his autobiography.

2. Below is a body paragraph from a previous draft of Aiko's informative essay. Aiko would like to add a transition word or phrase to help readers move from sentence 2 to sentence 3. Which transition will work best?

> (1) Risks can also have tragic outcomes. (2) For example, the space shuttle *Challenger* exploded after takeoff in 1986. (3) After the disaster occurred, President Reagan reflected on this tragedy in his speech "Address to the Nation on the Explosion of the Space Shuttle *Challenger*." (4) He mourned the loss of the crew and emphasized that their risks took great courage. (5) He said, "And perhaps we've forgotten the courage it took for the crew of the shuttle. (6) But they, the *Challenger* Seven, were aware of the dangers, but overcame them and did their jobs brilliantly."

- A. Similarly,
- B. For example,
- C. In addition to that detail,
- D. As a result,

Your Turn

Ask students to complete the Your Turn activity.

QUESTION 1

A. Correct. This sentence indicates which text this paragraph will focus on, and it clearly describes an example of a risk that requires courage.

B. Incorrect. This sentence indicates which text this paragraph will focus on, but the main idea does not clearly relate to the thesis statement.

C. Incorrect. This sentence relates to the thesis statement, but it does not clearly indicate which text this paragraph will focus on.

D. Incorrect. This sentence mentions courage, but it does not clearly relate to the thesis statement about risks that require courage.

QUESTION 2

A. Incorrect. "Similarly" is a word used to show how one idea relates to another idea that is like it.

B. Correct. "For example" introduces a supporting detail that helps develop the topic sentence.

C. Incorrect. "In addition to that detail" adds evidence to information that has already been presented.

D. Incorrect. "As a result" is a phrase that shows the relationship between a cause and its effect.

Writer's Notebook

In one paragraph, write about a risk that you once took and the outcome. Write one thesis statement about what you learned from that risk in a sentence and use supporting details to develop that claim. Then, look for ways to use a variety of transitions to show how your ideas and/or concepts are connected.

 TURN AND TALK

Allow students to share their paragraphs orally in pairs or small groups before writing.

✏ Write

Ask students to complete the writing assignment.

✏ WRITE

Use the questions in the checklist to revise one of your body paragraphs. Look for a variety of ways to use words, phrases, and clauses to create cohesion and clarify the relationships among ideas in this section. Those ideas may include your claim, counterclaims, reasons, and evidence.

ELL REWRITE CHECKLIST

A Logical Progression of Your Argument

☐ Is there a clear relationship among all paragraphs in this essay, including this one?

☐ Is there a clear connection between this paragraph and the paragraph before it?

☐ Is there a clear flow of information from one idea to another within the paragraph?

☐ Do you use a variety of transition words, phrases, or clauses to make those connections clear?

Relationships Among the Topic and Supporting Details

☐ What is your thesis statement about the topic of your essay?

☐ How does the topic sentence relate to that thesis statement?

☐ Do you clearly show readers the relationship between the topic sentence and each supporting detail?

☐ Is there a clear relationship among the supporting details?

☐ Do you use a variety of transition words, phrases, or clauses to show those connections?

Reading & Writing
Companion   117

Skill:
Precise Language

sync•skills

••• CHECKLIST FOR PRECISE LANGUAGE

As you consider precise language and domain-specific vocabulary related to a subject or topic, use the following questions as a guide:

- What information am I trying to convey or explain to my audience?
- Are there any key concepts that need to be explained or understood?
- What domain-specific vocabulary is relevant to my topic and explanation?
- Where can I use more precise vocabulary in my explanation?

Here are some suggestions that will help guide you in using precise language and domain-specific vocabulary to inform about or explain a topic:

- Determine the topic or area of study you will be writing about.
- Identify key concepts that need explanation in order to inform readers.
- Research any domain-specific vocabulary that you may need to define.
- Substitute precise, descriptive, and domain-specific language for vague, general, or overused words and phrases.
- Reread your writing to refine and revise if needed.

SKILL VOCABULARY

precise language / el lenguaje preciso **noun** exact language that includes specific nouns and action verbs COGNATE

domain-specific vocabulary / el vocabulario específico de un campo **noun** words and phrases that are limited to specific domains, or fields of study, such as law or medicine

---

Skill: Precise Language

Introduce the Skill

Watch the Concept Definition video and read the following definition with your students.

Precise language refers to clear and direct words or phrases that have very specific meanings. **Domain-specific vocabulary** are words and phrases that are used to explain concepts that are related to a particular subject or topic. A scientist writing about astronomy might use terms such as "airglow," for example, which is a glow in the night sky caused by radiation from the upper atmosphere.

When writers have to explain a complicated subject or topic, using precise language allows readers to develop a deeper understanding of the text and make connections between facts and other information. For example, the word *observe* is a synonym for the words *notice* or *see*, but it has a more precise meaning. To observe something means "to notice something and recognize it as significant." This difference, when used to describe a scientific experiment, can help readers develop their own ideas about the subject matter.

TURN AND TALK

Turn to your partner and practice using precise language and domain-specific vocabulary to describe a song that you heard, a photo that you viewed, or an object that you observed this past week.

> **(ELL) SPEAKING FRAMES**
> - One memorable (song / object / photo) I (heard / observed / viewed) this past week is ____.
> - I chose that (song / object / photo) because ____.
> - One observation I want to convey is ____.
> - I can convey that observation by saying, ____.

Your Turn

Ask students to complete the Your Turn activity.

QUESTION 1

A. Incorrect. This sentence includes domain-specific vocabulary, but some of the language is vague and unclear.

B. Incorrect. No domain-specific vocabulary is evident, and some of the language in this sentence is unclear.

C. Incorrect. No domain-specific vocabulary is evident, and some of the language in this sentence is unclear.

D. Correct. This sentence includes domain-specific vocabulary and precise language.

QUESTION 2

A. Incorrect. The language in this sentence is still vague and unclear.

B. Correct. This sentence includes more precise language.

C. Incorrect. The language in this sentence is still vague and unclear.

D. Incorrect. The language in this sentence is still vague and unclear.

YOUR TURN

Choose the best answer to each question.

1. Aiko wants to improve the underlined sentence from a previous draft that included a paragraph about "The Day I Saved a Life." How can she use domain-specific vocabulary and more precise language in the underlined sentence?

> In "The Day I Saved a Life," Thomas Ponce took a risk by dedicating himself to protecting a shark. Due to their roles in horror movies like *Jaws*, sharks are often seen as evil predators who do not need to be saved. <u>However, Ponce pointed out that sharks are necessary in the ocean, and they are often hurt by human beings.</u> He used that knowledge to speak on behalf of a shark that a fisherman had caught, and Ponce saved the shark's life as a result. That risk took courage because Ponce decided to do something difficult that needed to be done quickly.

- ○ A. However, Ponce informs readers that sharks are needed in oceans, and human beings often cause harm to them.
- ○ B. However, Ponce adds that they are very important in the ocean, and they are often unnecessarily removed from it or hurt by human beings.
- ○ C. However, Ponce says that sharks are absolutely necessary in the ocean, and they are often the victims.
- ○ D. However, Ponce explains that sharks are vital parts of their ecosystems, and they are often victims of cruelty by human beings.

2. Aiko wants to improve the underlined sentence from one of her previous drafts by revising and refining the language. How can she use more precise language in the underlined sentence?

> In "The Day I Saved a Life," Thomas Ponce took a risk by dedicating himself to protecting a shark. Due to their roles in horror movies like *Jaws*, sharks are often seen as evil predators who do not need to be saved. However, Ponce pointed out that sharks are necessary in the ocean, and they are often hurt by human beings. He used that knowledge to speak on behalf of a shark that a fisherman had caught, and Ponce saved the shark's life as a result. <u>That risk took courage because Ponce decided to do something difficult that needed to be done quickly.</u>

- ○ A. That risk took courage because Ponce took action, and he could have done nothing instead.
- ○ B. That risk took courage because the situation was urgent, and Ponce's goal was difficult to achieve.
- ○ C. That risk took courage because Ponce could have failed to do something difficult.
- ○ D. That risk took courage because it involved a shark and someone else achieving his goal of catching that shark.

Reading & Writing Companion   119

Writer's Notebook

Ask students to use precise language to describe one risk that a person has taken for a cause that is important to him or her. Students should look for opportunities to add domain-specific vocabulary to their descriptions as well.

ELL TURN AND TALK

Allow students to share the information they want to convey orally in pairs or small groups before freewriting.

Extended Writing Project

YOUR TURN

Identify at least five sentences from your draft that need more precise language and write them in the first column. Then, complete the chart by writing a revised sentence in the second column.

Draft Sentence	Revised Sentence

Your Turn

Ask students to complete the Your Turn activity. Answers will vary.

Draft Sentence	Revised Sentence
Richard Turere, Thomas Ponce, and Tom Sawyer are examples of young people who learn new things while taking risks.	Richard Turere, Thomas Ponce, and Tom Sawyer are examples of young people who make discoveries while taking risks.
The articles about Richard Turere and Thomas Ponce are true, while the passage about Tom Sawyer is not.	The articles about Richard Turere and Thomas Ponce are informative articles, while the passage about Tom Sawyer is from a work of fiction.
"Lion lights" aren't that expensive to make, and they're a solution that works.	"Lion lights" are an inexpensive and effective solution.
To get the fisherman to let the baby bonnethead shark go, Thomas Ponce shared several facts that he knew about sharks.	To persuade the fisherman to release the baby bonnethead shark, Thomas Ponce shared several facts about the need to save sharks.
Tom did not want to spend the day doing work for Aunt Polly, so he tried to think of ways to get out of it.	Tom dreaded spending the day doing work for his Aunt Polly, so he brainstormed ways to avoid it.

Skill: Style

Introduce the Skill

Watch the Concept Definition video and read the following definition with your students.

Style is the way a writer uses language to express ideas and convey information. It is revealed through the writer's choice of words and sentence construction. Style also involves being aware of the rules for writing standard English.

Choosing an appropriate style depends on the audience and the purpose for writing. Different subjects require different styles of writing. For both argumentative and informative writing, writers must use a formal style. With a **formal style**, a writer chooses **academic** language—the type of vocabulary used in school texts, for example—rather than informal or conversational language. The writer might also use special vocabulary unique to a particular topic, sometimes called **domain-specific** language.

Finally, to help maintain a formal style, writers must be sure to follow conventional rules for grammar, spelling, capitalization, and punctuation.

TURN AND TALK

Turn to your partner and brainstorm situations in which a speaker or writer should use formal language and situations in which a speaker or writer should use informal language. For each example, explain which style would work best and why it would work best.

ELL SPEAKING FRAMES

- A (speaker / writer) should use an informal style when ____.
- This style would work well because ____.
- A (speaker / writer) should use a formal style when ____.
- This style would work well because ____.

Skill:
Style

••• CHECKLIST FOR STYLE

First, reread the draft of your informative essay and identify the following:

- places where you use slang, contractions, abbreviations, and a conversational tone
- areas where you could use subject-specific or academic language in order to help persuade or inform your readers
- moments where you use first person (*I*) or second person (*you*)
- areas where sentence structure lacks variety
- incorrect uses of the conventions of standard English for grammar, spelling, capitalization, and punctuation

Establish and maintain a formal style in your essay, using the following questions as a guide:

- Have I avoided slang in favor of academic language?
- Did I consistently use a third-person point of view, using third-person pronouns (*he, she, they*)?
- Have I varied my sentence structure and the length of my sentences? Apply these specific questions where appropriate:
  - > Where should I make some sentences longer by using conjunctions to connect independent clauses, dependent clauses, and phrases?
  - > Where should I make some sentences shorter by separating any independent clauses?
- Did I follow the conventions of standard English, including:
  - > grammar?
  - > spelling?
  - > capitalization?
  - > punctuation?

V SKILL VOCABULARY

style / el estilo **noun** a way of expressing something that is characteristic of the person or time period COGNATE

formal style / el estilo formal **noun** a writing style or way of writing for academic essays

academic / académico/a **adjective** having to do with school COGNATE

domain-specific / específico/a del campo **adjective** having to do with a particular topic

xtended Writing Project

↻ YOUR TURN

Choose the best answer to each question.

. Below is a section from a previous draft of Aiko's informative essay. She sees that she needs to revise the language in the underlined sentence to make sure that it is written in a formal style. Which of the following sentences is a successful revision that is written in a formal style?

> A resettlement committee is working on a design for the new site, and their plan should help the community achieve their goals. To preserve the community's history on Isle de Jean Charles, the site may include a museum. <u>It'd guide us through information about the island and what it was like to live on it.</u> Many members of the community also value family, and they'd like to build houses that give extended families a shared backyard.

- ○ A. It would guide you through information about the island and what it was like to live on it.
- ○ B. It guides you through information about the island and what it was like to live on it.
- ○ C. It would guide visitors through information about the island and the community's experiences on it.
- ○ D. It guides visitors through information about the island and the communitys experiences on it.

2. Below is a section from a previous draft of Aiko's informative essay. Aiko wants to vary the length of her sentences, so she decides to rewrite the underlined sentence as two separate independent clauses. Which of the following sentences successfully divide the underlined sentence into separate independent clauses that are written in a formal style?

> A resettlement committee is working on a design for the new site, and their plan should help the community achieve their goals. To preserve the community's history on Isle de Jean Charles, the site may include a museum. It'd guide us through information about the island and what it was like to live on it. <u>Many members of the community also value family, and they'd like to build houses that give extended families a shared backyard.</u>

- ○ A. Many members of the community also value family and would like to build houses for them. They'll give extended families a shared backyard.
- ○ B. Many members of the community also value family and would like to build houses for them. Giving extended families backyards to share.
- ○ C. Many members of the community also value family. And they would like to build houses that give extended families a shared backyard.
- ○ D. Many members of the community also value family. For this reason, they would like to build houses that give extended families a shared backyard.

122 Reading & Writing Companion

⚙ Your Turn

Ask students to complete the Your Turn activity.

QUESTION 1

A. Incorrect. This sentence uses the second-person point of view, and "what it was like" is written in a conversational tone.

B. Incorrect. This sentence is not accurate since the museum had not been built when the article was written. In addition, the sentence also uses the second-person point of view, and "what it was like" is written in a conversational tone.

C. Correct. This sentence uses the third-person point of view and a formal tone. It also avoids using contractions.

D. Incorrect. This sentence is not accurate since the museum had not been built when the article was written. In addition, "community's" needs an apostrophe before the "s."

QUESTION 2

A. Incorrect. The noun that "They" represents is not clear, and "They'll" is a contraction.

B. Incorrect. The second sentence is a sentence fragment, not an independent clause.

C. Incorrect. In formal writing, a sentence should not start with a conjunction like "and."

D. Correct. The sentence has been divided into two independent clauses, and the contraction "they'd" has been spelled out as "they would." This change makes the sentence more formal.

📖 Writer's Notebook

Can you switch your writing style? Rewrite one paragraph from your draft for different audiences. Use an informal style to write the first version for students in your class. Then, use a formal style to write the second version for an audience that is made of leaders in the community.

 TURN AND TALK

Allow students to share both versions of a sentence orally in pairs or small groups before writing.

Write

Ask students to complete the writing assignment.

ELL **REWRITE CHECKLIST**

A **Language**

☐ Can you find examples of slang in this paragraph?

☐ How can you replace those words or phrases with more formal language?

☐ Do you see opportunities to add academic language to this paragraph?

Sentence Structure

☐ Do all of your sentences follow the same pattern, or do they have different structures?

☐ Where can you make some sentences longer and clearer?

☐ Where can you make some hard-to-follow sentences shorter?

Conventions

☐ Did you follow the conventions of standard English, including:

   ☐ grammar?

   ☐ spelling?

   ☐ capitalization?

   ☐ punctuation?

Extended Writing Project

WRITE

Use the steps in the checklist to add to or revise the language of one paragraph from your draft by establishing and maintaining a formal style.

Reading & Writing
Companion

123

Skill:
Conclusions

••• CHECKLIST FOR CONCLUSIONS

Before you write your conclusion, ask yourself the following questions:

- How can I restate the thesis or main idea in my concluding section or statement? What impression can I make on my reader?
- How can I write my conclusion so that it supports and follows logically from my argument?
- How can I conclude with a memorable comment?

Below are two strategies to help you provide a concluding statement or section that follows from and supports the argument presented:

- Peer Discussion

  > After you have written your introduction and body paragraphs, talk with a partner and tell him or her what you want readers to remember, writing notes about your discussion.

  > Review your notes and think about what you wish to express in your conclusion.

  > Do not simply restate your claim or thesis statement. Rephrase your main idea to show the depth of your knowledge and the importance of your idea.

  > Write your conclusion.

- Freewriting

  > Freewrite for ten minutes about what you might include in your conclusion. Don't worry about grammar, punctuation, or having fully formed ideas. The point of freewriting is to discover ideas.

  > Review your notes and think about what you wish to express in your conclusion.

  > Do not simply restate your claim or thesis statement. Rephrase your main idea to show the depth of your knowledge and the importance of your idea.

  > Write your conclusion.

Copyright © BookheadEd Learning, LLC

V SKILL VOCABULARY

conclusion / la conclusión *noun* the closing paragraph or section of an essay; a closing argument in an argumentative text COGNATE

thesis statement / la presentación de la tesis *noun* a statement that shares the main idea of an argumentative or informational essay

claim / la afirmación *noun* the writer's or speaker's position on a debatable issue or problem

narrative / la narración *noun* a story, real or imagined, consisting of connected events

---

Skill: Conclusions

Introduce the Skill

Watch the Concept Definition video ▶ and read the following definition with your students.

A **conclusion** is the closing paragraph or section of an essay, argument, or narrative. It is where the writer brings an essay to a close by restating the main idea or **thesis statement** or the **claim** in an argument. It also summarizes the evidence and research that support the claim or thesis. The conclusion should follow logically from the information, explanations, or claim that has been presented. A conclusion is a good way to suggest to your readers that you have accomplished what you set out to do. In addition, try to leave readers with an interesting final impression. This might be accomplished by closing with a quote, an anecdote, or a call to action.

In a **narrative**, a conclusion should follow logically from the events of the plot and what the characters have experienced. It might include characters reflecting on events, why they matter, and how they feel about them.

⚙ TURN AND TALK

Turn to your partner and brainstorm ways to end an article that informs readers about after-school activities for students in your community.

ELL SPEAKING FRAMES

- If I were writing a conclusion for an article about after-school activities, I would start by ____.
- I would then ____ because ____.
- I would also want my readers to remember ____.
- So, I might end the paragraph with a(n) ____.

Your Turn

Ask students to complete the Your Turn activity.

QUESTION 1

A. Correct. This sentence rephrases the thesis statement and includes each part of it.

B. Incorrect. This sentence does not follow from the sentence before it, and the writer is discussing three risks, not every risk.

C. Incorrect. This sentence rephrases a part of the thesis statement, but it leaves out some important information.

D. Incorrect. This sentence restates the topic sentence of this paragraph instead of the thesis statement.

QUESTION 2

A. Incorrect. This sentence comments on one text, rather than on all three.

B. Incorrect. This sentence asks a question, rather than bringing Aiko's ideas to a close.

C. Incorrect. This sentence states a personal connection, rather than bringing Aiko's ideas to a close.

D. Correct. This sentence brings Aiko's ideas to a close and conveys the information that she wants readers to remember.

⟳ YOUR TURN

Choose the best answer to each question.

1. The following conclusion is from a previous draft of Aiko's essay. Aiko sees that she copied the thesis statement from the introduction and pasted it at the end of her conclusion. As a result, she would like to rephrase the underlined sentence so that it engages readers. Which of the following sentences would be the BEST replacement for the underlined sentence?

> Frederick Douglass, the *Challenger* crew, and members of the Biloxi-Chitimacha-Choctaw Native American tribe all took risks to pursue important goals. Frederick Douglass found ways to learn how to read and write even though it was illegal for him to get an education at the time. The *Challenger* crew wanted to explore space, but they lost their lives just after their shuttle took off. Members of the Biloxi-Chitimacha-Choctaw Native American tribe wanted to reestablish their homes and culture on new land, and the outcome of their work was not known when "Vanishing Island" was published. Even though these risks and their outcomes differ, they all teach essential lessons.

○ A. These risks and their outcomes widely vary, but they all teach valuable lessons.
○ B. It is also evident that every risk teaches readers a valuable lesson.
○ C. Readers can learn valuable lessons from each risk.
○ D. These are the risks that each person took to pursue an important goal.

2. The following conclusion is from a previous draft of Aiko's essay. Aiko would like to add a sentence to bring her essay to a more effective close. Which sentence could she add after the last sentence to help achieve this goal?

> Frederick Douglass, the *Challenger* crew, and members of the Biloxi-Chitimacha-Choctaw Native American tribe all took risks to pursue important goals. Frederick Douglass found ways to learn how to read and write even though it was illegal for him to get an education at the time. The *Challenger* crew wanted to explore space, but they lost their lives just after their shuttle took off. Members of the Biloxi-Chitimacha-Choctaw Native American tribe wanted to reestablish their homes and culture on new land, and the outcome of their work was not known when "Vanishing Island" was published. Even though these risks and their outcomes differ, they all teach essential lessons.

○ A. The lesson from the Biloxi-Chitimacha-Choctaw Native American tribe is the most recent example.
○ B. What is an example of a lesson that you learned from each selection?
○ C. I think that the lessons I learned from each story apply to my life and my classmates' lives as well.
○ D. Each story shows readers personal qualities that everyone can work to develop.

Reading & Writing Companion   125

Extended Writing Project

✏ WRITE

Use the steps in the checklist to revise the conclusion of your informative essay.

✎ Write

Ask students to complete the writing assignment.

ELL REWRITE CHECKLIST

A **Restated Thesis Statement or Main Idea**

☐ Have you clearly restated the thesis or main idea of this informative essay?

☐ Is the main idea in your introduction the same as the main idea that you restated in your conclusion?

☐ Does the thesis statement in your conclusion show a deeper understanding of the main idea?

Coherence

☐ Does your conclusion bring your essay to a close in a logical way?

☐ Does your conclusion review important information from your essay?

Impression

☐ Does the information in your conclusion show readers that your main idea is important?

☐ Have you concluded this paragraph with a memorable comment?

  Reading & Writing Companion

📓 Writer's Notebook

Ask students to imagine that they are writing an informative article about a game for the school newspaper. That could include a board game, a video game, a sports game, or a game played in class. Have them write the conclusion of the article. Remind them to use the questions in the checklist as a guide.

 TURN AND TALK

Allow students to share their ideas orally in pairs or small groups before writing.

Informative Writing Process: Revise

Review Revision Guide

Break the class into five groups, and assign each group a category of the revision guide. Ask:

- What is the purpose of this section of the guide?

- How did it improve Aiko's writing?

- How will it help to improve your writing?

Allow groups to share their ideas with the class.

ELL SPEAKING FRAMES

- I think ____ (clarity / development / organization / word choice / sentence variety) improved Aiko's writing by ____.

- I think ____ (clarity / development / organization / word choice / sentence variety) will improve my writing because ____.

Informative Writing Process: Revise

| PLAN | DRAFT | REVISE | EDIT AND PUBLISH |

You have written a draft of your informative essay. You have also received input from your peers about how to improve it. Now you are going to revise your draft.

← REVISION GUIDE

Examine your draft to find areas for revision. Keep in mind your purpose and audience as you revise for clarity, development, organization, and style. Use the guide below to help you review:

Review	Revise	Example
Clarity		
Identify the information you want to convey and any concepts that need to be explained. Annotate places where you can add domain-specific vocabulary to clarify information or explain a concept.	Clarify information or explain a concept by using domain-specific vocabulary. Remember to think about whether or not you need to define a term for your audience.	Since the mid-twentieth century, however, the land on the island has been rapidly eroding, or wearing away;. It Storms, river engineering, and pollution are causing this to happen, and the landform may not even exist by 2050.

Extended Writing Project

Review	Revise	Example
Development		
Identify your main idea about the topic. Annotate places where you need to add, replace, or remove supporting details. Each detail should clearly help develop the main idea.	Make sure to include textual evidence from the selections that you have read, and use quotation marks when you are quoting a source directly.	In his speech "Address to the Nation on the Explosion of the Space Shuttle *Challenger*," President Ronald Reagan reminds Americans that the crew was willing to do a dangerous job. They wanted to travel into space because they believed that the mission would be worth the risk. He says, "They had a hunger to explore the universe and discover its truths."
Organization		
Review your body paragraphs. Identify and annotate any sentences that don't flow in a clear and logical way.	Rewrite the sentences so that the information flows from one idea to another. Make sure that you have clearly expressed the relationships between ideas.	Leaving that land will be painful. ~~On the new site~~, but members are dedicated to preserving their history, community, and culture on the new site. ~~The~~ For example, tribal secretary Chantel Comardelle envisions a museum that guides visitors through the history of the island.
Style: Word Choice		
Identify weak or repetitive words or phrases that do not clearly express your ideas to the reader.	Replace weak and repetitive words and phrases with more descriptive ones that better convey your ideas.	The crew was willing to risk their lives ~~to find out new information~~ In search of knowledge about the universe. ~~The crew also~~ Their efforts teach the values of ~~putting others before yourself~~ selflessness and bravery.

Please note that excerpts and passages in the StudySync® library and this workbook are intended as touchstones to generate interest in an author's work. The excerpts and passages do not substitute for the reading of entire texts, and StudySync® strongly recommends that students seek out and purchase the whole literary or informational work in order to experience it as the author intended. Links to online resellers are available in our digital library. In addition, complete works may be ordered through an authorized reseller by filling out and returning to StudySync® the order form enclosed in this workbook.

Revise

Students should start this activity with a copy of their drafts either printed on paper or open in a word-processing program, such as Google Docs. Allow students time to revise their drafts using the instructions in the revision guide. Once students have finished revising their narrative, have them submit their work.

CHECK FOR SUCCESS

Circulate around the room to spend time with individual students. Ask:

- What category are you working on?
- Why are you revising this specific section?
- How are you revising it?
- How does this change support your purpose?
- Does this change make your writing appropriate for your audience?

If students struggle while revising their drafts, choose an exemplary revision to share with the class while the student talks through the process. You could also invite a student to share a dilemma in the revision process and allow the class to offer feedback or suggestions.

 ORGANIZATION

Revise your draft, focusing on organization. One way to clarify the organization of ideas in your text is by using transitions.

 ORGANIZATION

Tell students to revise their drafts using the revision guide, focusing on organization and development.

Write

Ask students to complete their writing assignment.

ELL REWRITE CHECKLIST

☐ Find ideas that are not clearly connected.

☐ Identify the relationship between those ideas.

☐ Clarify the relationship by using a transition word, phrase, or clause.

Review	Revise	Example
Style: Sentence Variety		
Read your informational essay aloud. Annotate places where you have too many long or short sentences in a row.	Revise short sentences by linking them together. Shorten longer sentences for clarity of emphasis.	Many members of the community also value family;. To encourage interactions among family members on the new site, so they want to build groups of houses with shared backyards.

✎ WRITE

Use the guide above, as well as your peer reviews, to help you evaluate your informative essay to determine areas that should be revised.

Extended Writing Project

Grammar: Participles

A present participle is formed by adding -ing to a verb. As part of a verb phrase, the present participle is used with forms of the helping verb to be.

A past participle is usually formed by adding -ed to a verb. The past participle of some verbs has other endings, as in broken. When a participle acts as the main verb in a verb phrase, it is used with forms of the helping verb to have.

A present or past participle can also act as an adjective to describe, or modify, a noun or a pronoun. When a participle acts as an adjective, it is called a verbal.

Participle as a Verb	Participle as an Adjective
They looked the same as the other people from Africa who had been **coming** over, who had dark skin. The People Could Fly: American Black Folktales	A poor, bare, miserable room it was, with **broken** windows, no fire, ragged bedclothes, a sick mother, **wailing** baby, and a group of pale, hungry children **cuddled** under one old quilt, **trying** to keep warm. Little Women

Both present and past participles can function as either verbs or adjectives.

Text	Function	Explanation
But Coach had **spoken**, and his word was law on the court. Middle School Madness	verb	**Spoken** is a past participle. It works with the helping verb had to tell what Coach had done.
The magical time of childhood stood still, and the pulse of the **living** earth pressed its mystery into my **living** blood. A Celebration of Grandfathers	adjective	**Living** is a present participle. It modifies the nouns earth and blood.

 Reading & Writing Companion

Grammar: Participles

Introduce the Skill

Review the image and definition for participles as a class.

- participle (verb phrase) - a form of a verb used with a helping verb
- present participle - formed by adding -ing to a verb; can act as an adjective
- past participle - usually formed by adding -ed to a verb; can act as an adjective

Discuss the Model

1. How is a present participle formed? To form a present participle, add -ing to a verb. For example, "try" becomes "trying."

2. How is a past participle formed? To form a past participle, you can usually add -ed to a verb. For example, "cuddle" becomes "cuddled." However, there are past participles with other endings as well. For example, "speak" becomes "spoken."

3. How can a participle be used as a verb? Both past and present participles follow helping verbs. Present participles follow a version of "to be," as in "I am climbing"; past participles follow a version of "to have," as in "I have climbed."

4. How can a participle be used as an adjective? You may be able to use a present participle or a past participle to describe a noun, as in "the wailing baby" and "the broken window."

Your Turn

Ask students to complete the Your Turn activity.

QUESTION 1

A. Incorrect.

B. Incorrect.

C. Correct. *Rising* is used as an adjective to modify *sun*.

D. Incorrect.

QUESTION 2

A. Incorrect.

B. Correct. *Chirping* is used as an adjective to modify *crickets*.

C. Incorrect.

D. Incorrect.

QUESTION 3

A. Incorrect.

B. Incorrect.

C. Incorrect.

D. Correct. *Pleasing* is used as an adjective to modify *star*.

QUESTION 4

A. Incorrect.

B. Incorrect.

C. Correct. *Challenging* is used as an adjective to modify *time*.

D. Incorrect.

⟳ YOUR TURN

1. Choose the revision that uses a participle as an adjective.

> The sun rises slowly, and its light spreads along the horizon.

- ○ A. The sun rises slowly, and its light is spreading along the horizon.
- ○ B. The sun has been rising slowly, and its light spreads along the horizon.
- ○ C. The rising sun spreads light slowly along the horizon.
- ○ D. No change needs to be made to this sentence.

2. Choose the revision that uses a participle as an adjective.

> Ruby struggled to sleep through the sound of the crickets that chirped all night.

- ○ A. Ruby struggled to sleep through the sound of the crickets that were chirping all night.
- ○ B. All night, Ruby struggled to sleep through the sound of the chirping crickets.
- ○ C. Ruby was struggling to sleep through the sound of the crickets that chirped all night.
- ○ D. No change needs to be made to this sentence.

3. Choose the revision that uses a participle as an adjective.

> The pleasing film star has smiled and posed for pictures with fans all day.

- ○ A. The film star is pleasing her fans by smiling and posing for pictures.
- ○ B. The film star has smiled and posed for pictures to please her fans.
- ○ C. Smiling and posing for pictures are good ways for a film star to please fans.
- ○ D. No change needs to be made to this sentence.

4. Choose the revision that uses a participle as an adjective.

> The Civil War challenged Americans and reshaped their ideas about freedom.

- ○ A. The Civil War was challenging to Americans and reshaped their ideas about freedom.
- ○ B. The Civil War is challenging to Americans and has been reshaping their ideas about freedom.
- ○ C. The Civil War was a challenging time for Americans and reshaped their ideas about freedom.
- ○ D. No change needs to be made to this sentence.

Reading & Writing
Companion

Grammar: Gerunds

A gerund is a noun that is formed from the present participle of a verb.

A present participle is formed by adding -ing to the base form of a verb. When used as verbs, present participles always follow a form of the verb to be (for example, We are going to the car). Without a helping verb, present participles can be used as adjectives.

A gerund is determined by its use in a sentence. A gerund can be the subject of a sentence, the direct object of a verb, or the object of a preposition.

Remember that gerunds are used as nouns and present participles are used as adjectives.

Text	Explanation
High in the crow's-nest of the New White Star Liner Titanic, Lookout Frederick Fleet peered into a **dazzling** night. A Night to Remember	*Dazzling* is the present participle of the verb *to dazzle*. Here it is used as an adjective modifying the noun *night*.
"Yes," I replied, answering for her, "I paid her for everything, and the **eating** was the worst I ever tried." Ten Days in a Mad-House	The gerund *eating* is used as the subject of the last clause. Note that *answering* is part of the participial phrase *answering for her*, used as an adjective modifying *I*.
He never stopped **growling**. Cujo	The gerund *growling* is used as the direct object of the verb *stopped*.
The ringing became more distinct: it continued and became more distinct; I talked more freely to get rid of the **feeling**: but it continued and gained definitiveness--until, at length, I found that the noise was *not* within my ears. The Tell-Tale Heart	The gerund *feeling* is the object of the preposition *of*.

 Reading & Writing Companion

 ## Grammar: Gerunds

Introduce the Skill

Review the image and definition for gerunds as a class.

- present participle - formed by adding -ing to a verb; can act as an adjective
- gerund - a verb form that ends in -ing and is used as a noun

Discuss the Model

1. How is a gerund formed? A gerund is formed from the present participle of a verb, so -ing is added to a verb.

2. What is the difference between a present participle and a gerund? A present participle is an adjective, while a gerund is a noun. As a result, a gerund may be the subject of a sentence, direct object of a verb, or object of a preposition.

Your Turn

Ask students to complete the Your Turn activity.

QUESTION 1

A. Incorrect.

B. Correct. *Viewing* is the gerund form of the verb to *view*.

C. Incorrect.

D. Incorrect.

QUESTION 2

A. Correct. *Coping* is the gerund of the verb to *cope*.

B. Incorrect.

C. Incorrect.

D. Incorrect.

QUESTION 3

A. Incorrect.

B. Incorrect.

C. Correct. *Delivering* is the gerund form of the verb to *deliver*.

D. Incorrect.

QUESTION 4

A. Correct. *Reading* is the gerund form of the verb to *read*.

B. Incorrect.

C. Incorrect.

D. Incorrect.

↻ YOUR TURN

1. Replace the words in bold with a gerund.

   > A study by six leading medical organizations concludes that "**to view** entertainment violence can lead to an increase in aggressive attitudes, values, and behavior, particularly in children."

   ○ A. viewer
   ○ B. viewing
   ○ C. viewed
   ○ D. None of the above

2. Replace the word in bold with a gerund.

   > The young man's **cope** with impossible situations such as those in the Japanese internment camps took an amazing amount of strength along with a positive attitude.

   ○ A. coping
   ○ B. coped
   ○ C. is coping
   ○ D. None of the above

3. Replace the word in bold with a gerund.

   > I think Reanna is training to be a spy—no one could be more discreet in **deliver** secret messages!

   ○ A. delivers
   ○ B. delivered
   ○ C. delivering
   ○ D. None of the above

4. Replace the words in bold with a gerund.

   > Mia prefers **to read** about real-life unsolved mysteries, while most of her friends choose to read mind-bending science fiction or engaging crime novels.

   ○ A. reading
   ○ B. to read
   ○ C. has read
   ○ D. None of the above

Grammar:
Infinitives

The function of a verb is to name an action or state of being, or to describe "having." An infinitive is a verb form that may function as a noun, an adjective, or an adverb. An infinitive is formed from the word *to* followed by the base form of a verb. The word *to* is not a preposition when it is used immediately before a verb.

An infinitive used as a noun can be the subject of a sentence or the direct object of a verb.

Infinitives Are Not Prepositions	Example
When the word *to* appears before a noun or a pronoun, it is a preposition. When *to* appears before the base form of a verb, the two words form an infinitive.	Then, miraculously, the bow began **to swing** to port. A Night to Remember

Infinitives Used as Nouns	Example
The infinitive can be the subject of a sentence.	**To resist** takes courage.
The infinitive can be the direct object of a verb.	I smiled,—for what had I **to fear**? The Tell-Tale Heart

Infinitives Used as Adjectives or Adverbs	Example
The infinitive can be used as an adjective to modify a noun or a pronoun.	That's the worst of living so far out," bawled Mr. White, with sudden and unlooked-for violence; "of all the beastly, slushy, out-of-the-way places **to live** in, this is the worst. . . ." The Monkey's Paw
The infinitive can be used as an adverb to modify a verb, an adjective, or another adverb.	But I guess she deserves some kind of award for having had ten kids and survived **to tell** about it. Abuela Invents the Zero

Copyright © BookheadEd Learning, LLC

Reading & Writing Companion

Grammar: Infinitives

Introduce the Skill

Review the image and definition for infinitives as a class.

- prepositional phrase - group of words that begins with a preposition and ends with a noun or pronoun called the object of the preposition

- verb - a word that names an action or state of being or having

- infinitive - a verb that is usually preceded by the word *to*; functions as a noun, adjective, or adverb

Discuss the Model

1. **How are infinitives formed?** Infinitives are formed by adding the word *to* in front of a base form of a verb. One example of an infinitive is *to go*. The word *to* has been added before the base form of the verb *go*.

2. **What is the difference between an infinitive and a prepositional phrase?** An infinitive and a prepositional phrase are different because they end with words that function in different ways. A prepositional phrase may start with the word *to*, but it always ends with a noun. In contrast, an infinitive always starts with the word *to* and ends with a verb.

3. **When an infinitive is used as a noun, how can it function in a sentence?** When used as a noun, an infinitive can act as a subject or direct object.

4. **What other functions can an infinitive have in a sentence?** An infinitive can also act as an adjective or adverb in a sentence.

Your Turn

Ask students to complete the Your Turn activity.

QUESTION 1

A. Incorrect.

B. Correct. The word *to* is followed by the base form of a verb, so this is an infinitive.

C. Incorrect.

D. Incorrect.

QUESTION 2

A. Correct. The word *to* is followed by the base form of a verb, so this is an infinitive.

B. Incorrect.

C. Incorrect.

D. Incorrect.

QUESTION 3

A. Incorrect.

B. Correct. The word *to* is followed by the base form of a verb, so this is an infinitive.

C. Incorrect.

D. Incorrect.

QUESTION 4

A. Incorrect.

B. Correct. The word *to* is followed by the base form of a verb, so this is an infinitive.

C. Incorrect.

D. Incorrect.

⟳ YOUR TURN

1. Identify the infinitive in this sentence.

   > We went to the park to find the bench that she usually went to when she needed time to herself.

   ○ A. to the park
   ○ B. to find
   ○ C. to herself
   ○ D. There is no infinitive in this sentence.

2. Identify the infinitive in this sentence.

   > To develop her ear for music, she went to as many free concerts as possible, while also adhering to her daily practice schedule.

   ○ A. To develop
   ○ B. to as many
   ○ C. to her daily practice schedule
   ○ D. There is no infinitive in this sentence.

3. Identify the infinitive in this sentence.

   > From eight to ten candidates have registered to participate in the debates that have been assigned to Ellen for scheduling.

   ○ A. to ten
   ○ B. to participate
   ○ C. to Ellen
   ○ D. There is no infinitive in this sentence.

4. Identify the infinitive in this sentence.

   > Why would I bow to her demand for another cake to serve when she did not invite me to the party?

   ○ A. to her demand
   ○ B. to serve
   ○ C. to the party
   ○ D. There is no infinitive in this sentence.

Reading & Writing
Companion

Informative Writing Process: Edit and Publish

| PLAN | DRAFT | REVISE | EDIT AND PUBLISH |

You have revised your informative essay based on your peer feedback and your own examination.

Now, it is time to edit your informative essay. When you revised, you focused on the content of your informative essay. You probably looked at your essay's introduction, supporting ideas, and conclusion. When you edit, you focus on the mechanics of your essay, paying close attention to things like grammar and punctuation.

Use the checklist below to guide you as you edit:

☐ Have I used participles correctly?

☐ Have I used gerunds correctly?

☐ Have I used infinitives correctly?

☐ Do I have any sentence fragments or run-on sentences?

☐ Have I spelled everything correctly?

Notice some edits Aiko has made:

- Rewrote a sentence with a participle that did not clearly describe a noun, adjective, or adverb.

- Corrected a spelling mistake.

- Fixed a run-on sentence by dividing it into two separate sentences.

- Replaced an infinitive that did not make sense with a verb.

- Fixed a sentence fragment by replacing a gerund with a verb.

Informative Writing Process: Edit and Publish

Practice with Student Model (optional)

Provide groups with a different section of Aiko's draft. Each group should practice editing Aiko's model using the checklist in the lesson. Has she:

☐ used participles correctly?

☐ used gerunds correctly?

☐ used infinitives correctly?

☐ corrected any sentence fragments or run-on sentences?

☐ spelled everything correctly?

After the groups have finished, call on volunteers from each group to make edits until all the mistakes have been found and edited, pausing to discuss points of disagreement.

ELL A SPEAKING FRAMES

- Aiko did / did not find a (participle / gerund / infinitive) that was used incorrectly ____.
- Aiko did / did not successfully revise the sentence with that error by ____.
- ____ is an example of a run-on sentence that Aiko has / has not corrected.
- ____ is an example of a sentence fragment that Aiko has / has not corrected.
- ____ is spelled incorrectly. The correct spelling is ____.

Write

After students finish editing, suggest, if there's time, that they set their essays aside for a few minutes, and that they then proofread them one more time. Once students have completed their writing, have them submit their work.

CHECK FOR SUCCESS

If students struggle to edit successfully, help them determine where edits are needed and what changes need to be made.

Direct students to the grammar lessons in this unit if they are uncertain about the rules for specific concepts.

ELL READ ALOUD

Encourage students to read their stories aloud to themselves or to a partner in order to catch any remaining mistakes.

A READ ALOUD

Encourage students to read their stories aloud to themselves or to an on-grade-level peer in order to catch any remaining mistakes.

B PLAY CRITIC

Have students review their writing for any potential weaknesses or places in which they might have gone in different directions. Invite them to operate as their own critics—how might the ending of their creative piece be resolved differently? How might someone with an opposing point of view challenge a point made in their essay? What other piece of evidence might have been included in their research paper? Have students critically analyze an aspect of their own work from an outsider's perspective.

Extended Writing Project

~~And~~ The *Challenger* crew was well prepared~~, there were important questions about the universe~~ ~~that the *Challenger* crew was~~ and planning to study important questions about the universe. Unfortunately, they never had a chance to ~~acheive~~ achieve that goal because the space shuttle exploded after takeoff ~~despite~~. Despite this tragic end, Americans can ~~are~~ still ~~to~~ learn a valuable ~~lessen~~ lesson from the *Challenger* crew. Reagan's ~~explaining~~ explains that "the future doesn't belong to the fainthearted; it belongs to the brave. The *Challenger* crew was pulling us into the future, and we'll continue to follow them." The crew was willing to risk their lives in search of knowledge about the universe. Their efforts teach the values of selflessness and bravery.

✎ WRITE

Use the questions on the previous page, as well as your peer reviews, to help you evaluate your informative essay to determine areas that need editing. Then edit your essay to correct those errors.

Once you have made all your corrections, you are ready to publish your work. You can distribute your writing to family and friends, hang it on a bulletin board, or post it on your blog. If you publish online, share the link with your family, friends, and classmates.

English Language Learner Resources

::studysync

GRADE 8 > UNIT

USERS   ASSIGNMENTS

No Risk, No Reward
Core ELA
Grade 8
30 Days

Unit Overview

Integrated Reading and Writing

Extended Writing Project

ELL Resources

Novel Study

End-of-Unit Assessment

Instructional Path

Add to book

The History of the Space Shuttle

Narrative of the Life of Ada Lee, an American Farm Girl

Skill: Classroom Vocabulary

Students will learn and recognize classroom
vocabulary words and practice using them in a variety
of contexts.

Assign

Skill: Making Connections

Students will learn and practice the skill of making
connections when reading in order to demonstrate
and improve comprehension.

Teacher Resources: Lesson Plan

Assign

Lessons in the English Language Learner Resources section offer explicit ELL instruction. These lessons share a thematic and genre focus with all other lessons in the Core ELA unit.

The twenty ELL Resources are developed around two texts, "The History of the Space Shuttle" and "Narrative of the Life of Ada Lee, an American Farm Girl," and an Extended Oral Project. Each text is written at four distinct levels. For ELLs, these texts serve as structural and thematic models of authentic texts in the Integrated Reading and Writing section of the unit. Thus, teachers may use the ELL texts in place of or as extensions for "Address to the Nation on the Explosion of the Space Shuttle *Challenger*" and *Narrative of the Life of Frederick Douglass, an American Slave*.

ELL lessons modify the routines used with texts in the Integrated Reading and Writing section. Explicit vocabulary instruction is emphasized, and reading and writing Skills lessons focus strongly on language acquisition and reading comprehension.

After reading texts about risks people have taken and why they chose to take them, students will complete an Extended Oral Project that can be used in place of or as an extension to the Extended Writing Project. In this unit, students will plan and present advice for risk-takers in the form of an informational presentation.

Focus on English Language Proficiency Levels

ADVANCED HIGH
ADVANCED
INTERMEDIATE
BEGINNING

ELL Resources provide targeted support for four levels of proficiency: Beginning, Intermediate, Advanced, and Advanced High. Instruction and scaffolds, as well as the texts themselves, are differentiated based on these levels.

Additional differentiated scaffolds include visual glossaries, speaking and writing frames, and suggested grouping for peer and teacher support. Lessons also include suggested extension activities to challenge Advanced and Advanced High students as they progress through the year.

ELL Resources

ELL TEXTS

The History of the Space Shuttle

- Skill: Sight Vocabulary and High-Frequency Words
- Skill: Using Prereading Supports
- First Read
- Skill: Analyzing Expressions
- Skill: Main Ideas and Details
- Skill: Spelling Patterns and Rules
- Close Read

The Narrative of Ada Lee

- Skill: Classroom Vocabulary
- Skill: Making Connections
- First Read
- Skill: Language Structures
- Skill: Comparing and Contrasting
- Skill: Main and Helping Verbs
- Close Read

EXTENDED ORAL PROJECT

- Introduction
- Skill: Acquiring Vocabulary
- Plan

- Skill: Sentence Types
- Practice
- Present

The History of the Space Shuttle

INFORMATIONAL TEXT

Introduction

Through great achievements and heartbreaking losses, NASA's Space Shuttles and the crews that flew them into space and back captured America's hearts and minds. The Space Shuttle was a reusable vehicle that allowed NASA to carry out 135 missions as well as send more than 350 people and 3 million pounds of cargo into space. Although the program ended in 2011, its

NASA's Space Shuttle program lasted for more than thirty years. There were 135 space missions, and 350 people went into space. The program started in 1958. The goal was to compete with the Soviet space program. Americans were very interested in space exploration. There were many successes. The most famous achievement was the 1969 moon landing. Later, NASA scientists created a reusable space vehicle. By the early 1980s, NASA built the *Columbia, Challenger,* and *Discovery* space crafts. However, in 1986, NASA experienced a very big failure. The *Challenger* exploded. Despite this loss, the Space Shuttle program continued. The astronauts worked on the Hubble Space Telescope and the International Space Station. Unfortunately, there was another disaster in 2003. The space shuttle *Columbia* broke into pieces as it returned to Earth. This was one reason that the Space Shuttle program ended in 2004.

ELL Summaries in multiple languages are available digitally.

🔊 Audio and audio text highlighting are available with this text.

CONNECT TO ESSENTIAL QUESTION

Why do we take chances?

This informational text explores the triumphs and tragedies of NASA's Space Shuttle program. Many brave astronauts flew over 100 space shuttle missions, but not everyone survived to return home to Earth. Knowing the dangers, why would astronauts continue to risk their lives on the space shuttle?

Core ELA Connections

Texts	Theme	Genre
"Address to the Nation on the Explosion of the Space Shuttle Challenger"	NASA's space shuttle was a reusable vehicle that completed 135 missions in space. This text builds on ideas of space travel, achievements, and losses.	An informational text, "The History of the Space Shuttle" provides a thorough background of the NASA vehicle.

Differentiated Text Levels

ELL LEVEL	BEGINNING	INTERMEDIATE	ADVANCED	ADVANCED HIGH
WORD COUNT	377	416	467	545
LEXILE	540L	620L	770L	810L

Instructional Path

The print teacher's edition includes essential point-of-use instruction and planning tools. Complete lesson plans and program documents appear in your digital teacher account.

Skill: Sight Vocabulary and High-Frequency Words

Objectives: Students will be able to learn and recognize sight vocabulary and high-frequency words in English.

Objectives: Students will be able to recognize sight vocabulary and high-frequency words when listening and reading, and produce sight vocabulary and high-frequency words when speaking and writing.

Skill: Using Prereading Supports

Objectives: Students will be able to learn and practice the skill of using prereading supports when reading a new text.

Objectives: Students will be able to read a new or unfamiliar text using prereading supports such as graphic organizers, illustrations, and topic vocabulary.

First Read: The History of the Space Shuttle

Objectives: Students will be able to perform an initial reading of a text using the strategy of using prereading supports.

Objectives: Students will be able to demonstrate comprehension of a text by responding to questions orally and in writing using textual evidence.

Skill: Analyzing Expressions

Objectives: Students will be able to analyze expressions.

Objectives: Students will be able to analyze expressions when reading.

Skill: Main Ideas and Details

Objectives: Students will be able to distinguish between main ideas and details.

Objectives: Students will be able to distinguish between main ideas and details when reading and justify their decision when speaking.

Skill: Spelling Patterns and Rules

Objectives: Students will be able to recognize and apply spelling patterns and rules.

Objectives: Students will be able to recognize spelling patterns and rules when reading and apply spelling patterns and rules when writing

Close Read: The History of the Space Shuttle

Objectives: Students will be able to perform a close reading of a text in order to analyze main ideas and details.

Objectives: Students will be able to demonstrate analysis of main ideas and details by participating in a collaborative conversation and writing a short constructed response.

Progress Monitoring

Opportunities to Learn	Opportunities to Demonstrate Learning	Opportunities to Reteach
Sight Vocabulary and High-Frequency Words		
⚙ Skill: Sight Vocabulary and High-Frequency Words	⚙ Skill: Sight Vocabulary and High-Frequency Words • Your Turn 💻 First Read • Sight Vocabulary and High-Frequency Words Focus	⚙ Spotlight Skill: Sight Vocabulary and High-Frequency Words
Using Prereading Supports		
⚙ Skill: Using Prereading Supports	⚙ Skill: Using Prereading Supports • Your Turn 💻 First Read • Practice Prereading Skill	⚙ Spotlight Skill: Using Prereading Supports
Analyzing Expressions		
⚙ Skill: Analyzing Expressions	⚙ Skill: Analyzing Expressions • Your Turn	⚙ Spotlight Skill: Analyzing Expressions
Main Ideas and Details		
⚙ Skill: Main Ideas and Details	⚙ Skill: Main Ideas and Details • Your Turn 💻 Close Read • Skills Focus • Write	⚙ Spotlight Skill: Main Ideas and Details
Spelling Patterns and Rules		
⚙ Skill: Spelling Patterns and Rules	⚙ Skill: Spelling Patterns and Rules • Your Turn 💻 Close Read • Write	⚙ Spotlight Skill: Spelling Patterns and Rules

First Read

StudySync

The History of the Space Shuttle

Introduce the Text

As a class, watch the video preview ▶ and have students read the introduction in pairs to make connections to the video preview. Ask students various "wh" questions such as:

- What did you see in the video? How does it make you feel?
- What do you think the text will be about?
- Is there something in the video or introduction that surprised you?

ELL Beginning & Intermediate

SPEAKING FRAMES
- I see ____. I feel ____.
- I think the text will be about ____.
- I was surprised by ____.

Practice Prereading Skill

Remind students that Using Prereading Supports:

helps you prepare to read a text. An example of this is learning topic vocabulary to prepare to read a text. When you scan a text and discover words that are important to the topic, you can look them up in a dictionary or ask your teacher or peers for support.

Have students work in small, mixed-level groups to skim the passage looking for topic vocabulary related to space exploration. Prompt students to use a dictionary, context clues, and each other to define unknown words.

As students are working in small groups, circulate to listen for sample questions such as:

- *What does this word mean?*
- *What meaning does the dictionary give?*

Activate Prior Knowledge and Experiences OPTIONAL

Have students make connections while practicing their oral language by discussing what they know about space exploration.

Generate a list (on the board or on paper) of any information or ideas your students have about space exploration.

Ask students to share where their background knowledge came from. For example, did their ideas come from a movie, friend, television show, book, or family member?

V VOCABULARY

satellite
an object that follows a consistent course around a larger object

fleet
a group of vehicles that are owned and operated by the same company

orbit
to revolve around a large object in a curved path

disintegrate
to fall apart or separate into pieces

clear
to approve or give official permission

≡ READ

NOTES

1 The Space Shuttle program ran for three decades and 135 missions. It launched more than 350 people and 3 million pounds of cargo into space. Some of these missions ended in joyful celebrations. Others led to tragedy. Overall, the Space Shuttle program was an impressive achievement.

2 The National Aeronautics and Space Administration (NASA) was founded in 1958. Americans wanted to enter the Space Race. The Soviet Union launched the world's first made-man **satellite** in 1957. Interest in space exploration grew. In 1962, President John F. Kennedy said that NASA would put a man on the Moon. On July 20, 1969, Neil Armstrong achieved that goal.

3 With the success of the Moon landing behind them, NASA's scientists needed a new goal. A task force wanted to design a reusable space vehicle. They also wanted to build a space station and launch missions to Mars. President Richard Nixon told them to focus on the vehicle. The Space Shuttle program was born.

Reading & Writing Companion **133**

◀)) AUDIO TEXT HIGHLIGHTING

Allow students to use the audio text highlight feature to follow along as they read. Alternately, you may wish to work directly with students or group them in twos or threes for partner reading or choral reading.

Preteach Vocabulary

Model the first word and example for the class.

1. The first word is *satellite,* and its meaning is "an object that follows a consistent course around a larger object."

2. When I hear the word *satellite*, I think of devices in space that send information to Earth. These devices gather information by moving around the Earth in a set path.

3. For example: The weather is predicted using *satellites* in space.

4. This is an example of something that is a *satellite* because it works by traveling around the planet and sending information to Earth.

Continue this exercise with each word in the glossary, calling on individuals or groups of students to share out.

 Beginning

PRETEACH VOCABULARY
Use the gestures to clarify meanings.

- **satellite** (Use a balled-up piece of paper and a smaller object, such as an eraser, to show how satellites orbit Earth.)

- **orbit** (Walk around your desk two or three times.)

- **clear** (Nod your head and give a thumbs up.)

- **fleet** (Use several objects of the same type, such as books, to model a fleet.)

- **disintegrate** (Put your hands together and then wiggle your fingers in a downward motion as your hands separate, to model something coming apart as it falls.)

Sight Vocabulary and High-Frequency Words Focus

Remind students of the sight vocabulary and high-frequency words that they studied at the beginning of the unit. Point out that some of the words may be useful as they think about and discuss the text. For example:

- goes (The crew **goes** into space to . . .)
- first (The **first** Space Shuttle . . .)
- about (I learned **about** . . .)
- show (The reactions to the tragic accidents **show** that people . . .)
- keep (I don't know if NASA should **keep** . . .)

4   Each shuttle has three main parts. The orbiter is the astronauts' home in space. There are two solid rocket boosters (SRBs). The SRBs create the force needed to launch. They break off. The last piece of the puzzle is the external fuel tank (ET). The ET provides fuel for launch. It also separates. The orbiter carries fuel for the mission and reentry.

5   The first shuttle, *Enterprise*, was never **cleared** for space. In April 1981, *Columbia* **orbited** the Earth 37 times before its arrival home. *Challenger* was built in 1983. *Discovery* followed in 1984. *Atlantis* joined the **fleet** a year later. With many successes under their belt, NASA had a failure. The shuttles were not reliable. On January 28, 1986, *Challenger* exploded 73 seconds after liftoff. The crew was killed. The likelihood of the disaster seemed low. America wept. NASA didn't launch another mission for two years.

6   The Space Shuttle program continued. *Challenger's* replacement, *Endeavour*, was built in 1992. The shuttles' crews worked to put satellites into orbit. They launched and repaired the Hubble Space Telescope. They worked on the International Space Station.

7   Another tragedy struck on February 1, 2003. *Columbia* **disintegrated** coming back to Earth. The crew was killed. The loss shook the nation. The program carried on.

8   The end of the historic Space Shuttle program was announced in 2004. NASA's budget grew smaller. Its priorities changed. The orbiters and SRBs were reusable, but they were expensive to maintain. The final mission ended on July 21, 2011. *Atlantis* landed safely. It joined the other shuttles in retirement.

TEXT TALK

1. What is the text about?
2. What is the author mainly discussing?
3. What are some examples that the author gives?
4. Does the text change the way you think about the topic?

ELL   All Levels

SPEAKING FRAMES

Giving Information:

- This text is about ____.
- The main idea is ____.
- Some examples the author gives about ____ include ____.
- This text makes me think ____.

Asking for Information:

- Can you explain ____?
- What do you think about ____?
- Why do you think ____?

First Read

Read the text. After you read, answer the Think Questions below.

THINK QUESTIONS

1. When and why was NASA founded?

   NASA was founded in _____ .

   It was founded because _____ .

2. What are the parts of a Space Shuttle?

   The parts of the Space Shuttle are _____

   _____ .

3. What type of work did crews use Space Shuttles to do?

   Crews used the Space Shuttle to _____

   _____ .

4. Use context to confirm the meaning of the word *fleet* as it is used in "The History of the Space Shuttle." Write your definition of *fleet* here.

   Fleet means _____ .

   A context clue is _____ .

5. What is another way to say that someone has *cleared* a plan?

   Someone has _____ .

Reading & Writing Companion **135**

Think Questions

Circulate as students answer Think Questions independently. Answers will vary.

QUESTION 1: Comprehension

NASA was founded in 1958. NASA was founded because there was a lot of interest in space.

QUESTION 2: Comprehension

The Space Shuttle has three parts: the orbiter, the solid rocket boosters, and the external fuel tank.

QUESTION 3: Comprehension

Answers will vary, but may include the following examples:

- "The Space Shuttles' crews put satellites into orbit."
- "They launched and repaired the Hubble Space Telescope."
- "They worked on the International Space Station."

Student responses should provide an example from the text and an explanation that describes how crews used the Space Shuttle to do tasks in space.

QUESTION 4: Language

The author uses the word *fleet* to explain when each of NASA's Space Shuttles was built. Together, the Space Shuttles make a fleet. A definition for *fleet* is "a group of vehicles."

QUESTION 5: Language

Someone has approved a plan.

Skill: Analyzing Expressions

Introduce the Skill

Watch the Concept Definition video ▶ and read the definition for Analyzing Expressions.

Skill: Analyzing Expressions

★ DEFINE

When you read, you may find English expressions that you do not know. An **expression** is a group of words that communicates an idea. Three types of expressions are idioms, sayings, and figurative language. They can be difficult to understand because the meanings of the words are different from their **literal**, or usual, meanings.

An idiom is an expression that is commonly known among a group of people. For example: "It's raining cats and dogs" means it is raining heavily. **Sayings** are short expressions that contain advice or wisdom. For instance: "Don't count your chickens before they hatch" means do not plan on something good happening before it happens. **Figurative** language is when you describe something by comparing it with something else, either directly (using the words *like* or *as*) or indirectly. For example, "I'm as hungry as a horse" means I'm very hungry. None of the expressions are about actual animals.

••• CHECKLIST FOR ANALYZING EXPRESSIONS

To determine the meaning of an expression, remember the following:

✓ If you find a confusing group of words, it may be an expression. The meaning of words in expressions may not be their literal meaning.

   • Ask yourself: Is this confusing because the words are new? Or because the words do not make sense together?

✓ Determining the overall meaning may require that you use one or more of the following:

   • context clues

   • a dictionary or other resource

   • teacher or peer support

✓ Highlight important information before and after the expression to look for clues.

TURN AND TALK

1. What does it mean to analyze expressions?

2. Why might it be difficult to understand expressions?

3. What can you do if you are struggling to analyze expressions?

ELL Beginning & Intermediate

SPEAKING FRAMES

• To analyze expressions means to understand ____.

• You may not be able to ____.

• You could look at ____.

• You could think about ____.

ELL Advanced & Advanced High

SPEAKING FRAMES

• To analyze expressions means to ____.

• You may not be able to ____ because ____.

• You could look at ____, such as ____.

• You could think about ____. For example, ____.

V   SKILL VOCABULARY

expression / la expresión **noun** a phrase used to express an idea   COGNATE

literal / literal **adjective** describing the usual meaning of a word   COGNATE

idiom / el modismo **noun** a common expression that cannot be taken literally

saying / el dicho **noun** an expression that contains advice or wisdom

YOUR TURN

Read paragraphs 4–7 from the text. Then, complete the multiple-choice questions below.

---

from "The History of the Space Shuttle"

Each shuttle has three main parts. The orbiter is the astronauts' home in space. There are two solid rocket boosters (SRBs). The SRBs create the force needed to launch. They break off. The last piece of the puzzle is the external fuel tank (ET). The ET provides fuel for launch. It also separates. The orbiter carries fuel for the mission and reentry.

The first shuttle, *Enterprise*, was never cleared for space. In April 1981, *Columbia* orbited the Earth 37 times before its arrival home. *Challenger* was built in 1983. *Discovery* followed in 1984. *Atlantis* joined the fleet a year later. With many successes under their belt, NASA had a failure. The shuttles were not reliable. On January 28, 1986, *Challenger* exploded 73 seconds after liftoff. The crew was killed. The likelihood of the disaster seemed low. America wept. NASA didn't launch another mission for two years.

The Space Shuttle program continued. *Challenger's* replacement, *Endeavour*, was built in 1992. The shuttles' crews worked to put satellites into orbit. They launched and repaired the Hubble Space Telescope. They worked on the International Space Station.

Another tragedy struck on February 1, 2003. *Columbia* disintegrated coming back to Earth. The crew was killed. The loss shook the nation. The program carried on.

---

1. In paragraph 4, the sentence "The last piece of the puzzle is the external fuel tank (ET)" means that the ET:

   ○ A. was hard to put together.
   ○ B. had a lot of parts.
   ○ C. was part of the shuttle.
   ○ D. was hard to understand.

2. In paragraph 5, the phrase "With many successes under their belt" means that NASA:

   ○ A. got new uniforms.
   ○ B. had many achievements.
   ○ C. made a mistake.
   ○ D. discovered an asteroid belt.

Reading & Writing Companion **137**

 Discuss the Skill Model

1. **What is the student trying to understand?**

   The student is trying to understand the sentence "With the success of the Moon landing behind them, NASA's scientists needed a new goal."

2. **Why is the student struggling?**

   The student does not understand the meaning of the words in the sentence.

3. **What strategies does the student use?**

   The student asks for help.

ELL **Beginning & Intermediate**

Have students use the <u>speaking frames</u> and <u>helpful terms</u> to participate in the group discussion. If beginning students are hesitant to participate in a discussion, encourage them by prompting with *yes* or *no* questions.

Advanced & Advanced High

Have students use the <u>speaking frames</u> to participate in the group discussion.

SPEAKING FRAMES

- The student is trying to ____.
- The student is struggling because ____.
- The student ____ in order to ____.
- The teacher's response helps him understand ____.

HELPFUL TERMS FOR DISCUSSION

- literal
- figurative
- expression
- describes
- asks
- help

Your Turn   Ask students to complete the Your Turn activity.

QUESTION 1:   C) This meaning is supported by the passage. The ET was part of the shuttle.

QUESTION 2:   B) This meaning is supported by the passage. NASA had many achievements.

QUESTION 3:   A) This meaning is supported by the passage. Americans felt very sad after the accident.

QUESTION 4:   B) This meaning is supported by the passage. Americans had a strong reaction to the accident.

3. In paragraph 5, the sentence "America wept" means that Americans felt:

    ○ A. sad.

    ○ B. mad.

    ○ C. joyful.

    ○ D. surprised.

4. In paragraph 7, the sentence "The loss shook the nation" means that Americans:

    ○ A. had an earthquake.

    ○ B. had a strong reaction.

    ○ C. did not support NASA.

    ○ D. felt strong winds.

Reading & Writing Companion

The History of the Space Shuttle

Skill:
Main Ideas and Details

★ DEFINE

The **main ideas** are the most important ideas of a paragraph, a section, or an entire text. The **supporting details** are details that describe or explain the main idea.

To **distinguish** between the main ideas and the supporting details, you will need to decide what information is the most important and supports or explains the main ideas.

••• CHECKLIST FOR MAIN IDEAS AND DETAILS

In order to distinguish between main ideas and supporting details, do the following:

✓ Preview the text. Look at headings, topic sentences, and boldface vocabulary.

  • Ask yourself: What seem to be the main ideas in this text?

✓ Read the text.

  • Ask yourself: What are the most important ideas? What details support or explain the most important ideas?

✓ Take notes or use a graphic organizer to distinguish between main ideas and supporting details.

Reading & Writing Companion **139**

Ⓥ SKILL VOCABULARY

main idea / la idea principal *noun* the most important idea of a paragraph, a section, or an entire text

supporting details / los detalles que desarrollan la idea central *noun* details that describe or explain the main idea

distinguish / distinguir *verb* to determine the difference between two things COGNATE

 # Skill: Main Ideas and Details

Introduce the Skill

Watch the Concept Definition video and read the definition for Main Ideas and Details.

⚙ TURN AND TALK

1. How do you distinguish between the main idea and supporting details?

2. How do supporting details relate to the main idea?

3. What can you do if you are struggling to identify a main idea?

ⓔ Beginning & Intermediate

SPEAKING FRAMES

• A main idea is ____.
• Supporting details ____ a main idea.
• You could look at ____.
• You could also scan ____.

ⓔ Advanced & Advanced High

SPEAKING FRAMES

• A main idea is ____.
• Supporting details ____ a main idea because ____.
• You could look at ____, such as ____.
• You could also try using strategies like ____ or ____.

Discuss the Skill Model

1. What is the student looking for?

   The student is looking for main ideas and supporting details.

2. What strategy does the student use to identify a main idea?

   The student reads the topic sentence of the paragraph.

3. What strategy does the student use to identify supporting details?

   The student looks for details that develop the main idea.

ELL **Beginning & Intermediate**

Have students use the <u>speaking frames</u> and <u>helpful terms</u> to participate in the group discussion. If beginning students are hesitant to participate in a discussion, encourage them by prompting with *yes* or *no* questions.

Advanced & Advanced High

Have students use the <u>speaking frames</u> to participate in the group discussion.

SENTENCE FRAMES

- The student is looking for ____.
- First, the student reads ____ because ____.
- Then, the student looks for ____ in order to ____.
- The student also thinks about ____ to help him ____.

HELPFUL TERMS FOR DISCUSSION

- identify
- supporting
- highlight
- topic
- details
- consider

The History of the Space Shuttle

 YOUR TURN

Read paragraphs 7–8 from the text. Then, complete the multiple-choice questions below.

> **from "The History of the Space Shuttle"**
>
> Another tragedy struck on February 1, 2003. *Columbia* disintegrated coming back to Earth. The crew was killed. The loss shook the nation. The program carried on.
>
> The end of the historic Space Shuttle program was announced in 2004. NASA's budget grew smaller. Its priorities changed. The orbiters and SRBs were reusable, but they were expensive to maintain. The final mission ended on July 21, 2011. Atlantis landed safely. It joined the other shuttles in retirement.

1. The main idea of paragraph 7 is that NASA:

   ○ A. kept going.
   ○ B. had an accident.
   ○ C. was shocked.
   ○ D. did not know what to do.

2. A supporting detail that best develops this main idea is:

   ○ A. "Another tragedy struck on February 1, 2003."
   ○ B. "*Columbia* disintegrated coming back to Earth."
   ○ C. "The loss shook the nation."
   ○ D. "The program carried on."

3. The main idea of paragraph 8 is that the Space Shuttle program:

   ○ A. was expensive.
   ○ B. reused some parts.
   ○ C. had many shuttles.
   ○ D. came to an end.

4. A supporting detail that best develops this main idea is:

   ○ A. "NASA's budget grew smaller. Its priorities changed."
   ○ B. "The orbiters and SRBs were reusable, but they were expensive to maintain."
   ○ C. "The final mission ended on July 21, 2011."
   ○ D. "Atlantis landed safely."

 Your Turn   Ask students to complete the Your Turn activity.

QUESTION 1: B) This is the main idea of the paragraph.

QUESTION 2: B) This detail supports the main idea that NASA had an accident.

QUESTION 3: D) This is the main idea of the paragraph.

QUESTION 4: C) This detail supports the main idea that the Space Shuttle program came to an end.

Close Read

✏ WRITE

ARGUMENTATIVE: Should NASA restart the Space Shuttle program? Why or why not? Write a short paragraph in which you state your opinion on this topic. Support your claim with details from the text. Pay attention to correctly spelling words with suffixes as you write.

Use the checklist below to guide you as you write.

☐ Do you think NASA should restart the Space Shuttle program?

☐ Why do you feel that way?

☐ What details in the text support your opinion?

Use the sentence frames to organize and write your argument.

NASA (should / should not) restart the Space Shuttle program.

Restarting the Space Shuttle program would be _____.

I think this because _____.

Overall, the Space Shuttle program was _____,

but it was also _____.

Details that support this opinion are _____ and _____.

Reading & Writing Companion **141**

Close Read

Model Skills Focus

Remind students of the Reading Skill Main Ideas and Details. Tell students that one way you can identify main ideas and details is to determine what information is most important and how the text supports it. Direct students to the Skills Focus and remind them to track as you read aloud.

Find the main ideas and details of the text.

Model Main Ideas and Details for students:

- I am going to focus on the first paragraph.

- I reread the paragraph and look at my annotations. I notice that I highlighted the last sentence.

- *Overall* seems like an important key word. I think the words that follow tell the author's main idea: *the Space Shuttle program was an impressive achievement.*

- With this idea in mind, I look at the paragraph again and look for supporting details. The author gives facts about the Space Shuttle program. The paragraph says there were 135 missions in 30 years. That seems like a lot! It also says that 350 people went into space. That also seems like a big number. These details support the main idea that the program was "an impressive achievement."

Complete Skills Focus

Use a Jigsaw strategy to have students complete the Skills Focus. Divide students into three groups. Assign each group the beginning, middle, or end of the text (paragraphs 1–3, 4 and 5, and 6–8). Prompt groups to:

- Find the main ideas and details of each paragraph in their section.

- Decide on the main idea of the section as a whole.

Circulate and monitor groups as they work.

Rearrange students so they have at least one representative from each of the original groups. Prompt partners to combine the main ideas and details they found to better understand the whole text.

- How did you determine the main ideas?
- How did you determine supporting details?

- How did distinguishing main ideas from details help you better understand the text?

Collaborative Conversation

 BEGINNING, INTERMEDIATE Use the <u>word bank</u> to participate in the group discussion.

ADVANCED Use the <u>speaking frames</u> to participate in the group discussion.

BEGINNING, INTERMEDIATE	ADVANCED
Word Bank	**Speaking Frames**
• helped me identify • phrase • now I understand • main idea • key word • supporting detail	• Key words and phrases helped me because ____. • Looking for supporting details helped me because ____. • Identifying main ideas helped me better understand the text because ____.

SCAFFOLDS

Write

Ask students to complete the writing assignment. Remind students to pay attention to spelling patterns in words.

ELL **BEGINNING** Write a response using the <u>paragraph frames</u> and <u>word bank</u>.

INTERMEDIATE Write a response using the <u>paragraph frames</u>.

INTERMEDIATE

BEGINNING

Paragraph Frames

- NASA should / should not restart the Space Shuttle program.
- Restarting the Space Shuttle program would be ____. I think this because ____.

- Overall, the Space Shuttle program was ____, but it was also ____. Details that support this opinion are ____ and ____.

Word Bank

- wrong
- good
- helpful
- expensive
- successful

Narrative of the Life of Ada Lee

FICTION

Introduction

The title of "Narrative of the Life of Ada Lee, an American Farm Girl" hints at the autobiography *Narrative of the Life of Frederick Douglass, an American Slave*. This work of historical fiction makes connections between Douglass's efforts to educate himself despite laws that forbade slaves from doing so and Ada's own struggle to pursue a career despite legal and cultural unfairness to women.

Narrative of the Life of Ada Lee, an American Farm Girl

Ada Lee is sitting in her barn. She is whispering a secret to the family's dairy cow. She will soon leave for college. Women are not allowed to attend most colleges. But Ada found one on the East Coast that accepted her. She is worried that the work will be hard. Ada taught herself to read. So she thinks that she can do the work. When she gets to the college, the work is very difficult. Ada has a tall pile of books. The books are filled with legal terminology. Ada meets another student named John Wilson. John offers to tutor Ada. In exchange, Ada will give him some home-cooked meals. John and Ada spend a lot of time studying together. They earn their law degrees. They decide to get married. Ada wants to start a law practice with John. However, the state does not allow women to practice law. As a result, Ada tries to change the law. She believes that women can do anything they put their minds to.

ELL Summaries in multiple languages are available digitally.

🔊 Audio and audio text highlighting are available with this text.

CONNECT TO ESSENTIAL QUESTION

Why do we take chances?

In this short story, young women do not receive much education or have careers. Ada Lee knows she can be more than what society says she can be. Despite challenges and risks to come, Ada Lee leaves behind her life on the farm to pursue her dream of becoming a lawyer. Will her decision pay off?

Core ELA Connections

Texts	Theme	Genre
Narrative of the Life of Frederick Douglass, an American Slave	Ada Lee struggles to pursue a career in spite of legal and cultural unfairness to women. This text builds on the ideas of education, adversity, and ambition.	"Narrative of the Life of Ada Lee" is a work of historical fiction.

Differentiated Text Levels

ELL LEVEL	BEGINNING	INTERMEDIATE	ADVANCED	ADVANCED HIGH
WORD COUNT	257	416	456	567
LEXILE	390L	700L	830L	900L

Instructional Path

The print teacher's edition includes essential point-of-use instruction and planning tools
Complete lesson plans and program documents appear in your digital teacher account

Skill: Classroom Vocabulary

Objectives: Students will be able to learn and recognize routine classroom vocabulary in English.

Objectives: Students will be able to recognize routine classroom vocabulary when listening and reading, and produce classroom vocabulary when speaking and writing.

Skill: Making Connections

Objectives: Students will be able to learn and practice the skill of making connections when reading a text.

Objectives: Students will be able to make connections when reading.

First Read: Narrative of the Life of Ada Lee, an American Farm Girl

Objectives: Students will be able to perform an initial reading of a text using the strategy of using prereading supports.

Objectives: Students will be able to demonstrate comprehension of a text by responding to questions orally and in writing using textual evidence.

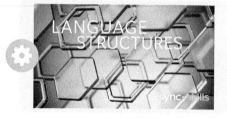

Skill: Language Structures

Objectives: Students will be able to grasp language structures.

Objectives: Students will be able to grasp language structures when reading.

Skill: Comparing and Contrasting

Objectives: Students will be able to compare and contrast.

Objectives: Students will be able to compare and contrast when reading.

Skill: Main and Helping Verbs

Objectives: Students will be able to identify main and helping verbs.

Objectives: Students will be able to identify main and helping verbs when reading.

Close Read: Narrative of the Life of Ada Lee, an American Farm Girl

Objectives: Students will be able to perform a close reading of a text in order to compare and contrast.

Objectives: Students will be able to demonstrate comparing and contrasting by participating in a collaborative conversation and writing a short constructed response.

Progress Monitoring

Opportunities to Learn	Opportunities to Demonstrate Learning	Opportunities to Reteach
Classroom Vocabulary		
⚙ Skill: Classroom Vocabulary	⚙ Skill: Classroom Vocabulary • Your Turn 💬 First Read • Classroom Vocabulary Focus	⚙ Spotlight Skill: Classroom Vocabulary
Making Connections		
⚙ Skill: Making Connections	⚙ Skill: Making Connections • Your Turn 💬 First Read • Practice Prereading Skill	⚙ Spotlight Skill: Making Connections
Language Structures		
⚙ Skill: Language Structures	⚙ Skill: Language Structures • Your Turn	⚙ Spotlight Skill: Language Structures
Comparing and Contrasting		
⚙ Skill: Comparing and Contrasting	⚙ Skill: Comparing and Contrasting • Your Turn 💬 Close Read • Skills Focus • Write	⚙ Spotlight Skill: Comparing and Contrasting
Main and Helping Verbs		
⚙ Skill: Main and Helping Verbs	⚙ Skill: Main and Helping Verbs • Your Turn 💬 Close Read • Write	⚙ Spotlight Skill: Main and Helping Verbs

First Read

StudySync

Narrative of the Life of Ada Lee, An American Farm Girl

Introduce the Text

As a class, watch the video preview ▶ and have students read the introduction in pairs to make connections to the video preview. Ask students various "wh" questions such as:

- What did you see in the video? How does it make you feel?
- What do you think the text will be about?
- Is there something in the video or introduction that surprised you?

ELL Beginning & Intermediate

SPEAKING FRAMES
- I see ____. I feel ____.
- I think the text will be about ____.
- I was surprised by ____.

Practice Prereading Skill

Remind students that Making Connections:

helps you better understand a text by connecting what you read to your own experiences, to other texts you have read, or to the world around you.

Have students work in small, homogeneous groups to make connections.

As students are working in small groups, circulate to listen for sample connections such as:

- *What happened to Ada reminds me of the time . . .*
- *This is really similar to the book . . .*

Activate Prior Knowledge and Experiences OPTIONAL

Have students make connections while practicing their oral language by discussing what they know about careers.

Generate a list (on the board or on paper) of any information or ideas your students have about careers.

Ask students to share where their background knowledge came from. For example, did their ideas come from a movie, friend, television show, book, or family member?

V VOCABULARY

secret
known by only a few people

earnest
sincere and serious

enroll
to register for or enter

grieving
to feel deep sadness

incomprehensible
unable to be understood

☰ READ

1   I sat down on the stool and dug my heels into the barn's dirt floor. "You know I love you, Bessie," I whispered dreamily to our dairy cow, "but I'm not going to be with you for much longer. I am going to college." A **secret** grin spread slowly across my face. It was the first time I had said my plan out loud. "I know what you're thinking, Bessie," I continued, patting her gently. Women could not go to college, but I had heard about a college on the east coast that would accept female students. The school was far away. The workload might be very hard, given my limited education. But I was determined to **enroll**. After all, I had taught myself to read. Learning from a teacher couldn't be harder than that. "It's going to be hard, but I will go to school and become a lawyer."

2   College was different than I had expected it to be. I missed my life on the farm, and the pile of books that rested on my desk practically reached the ceiling. They were filled with **incomprehensible** legal terminology that I hadn't much use for back home. I knew I needed to get some help if I were to

Reading & Writing Companion   **143**

◀)) AUDIO TEXT HIGHLIGHTING

Allow students to use the audio text highlight feature to follow along as they read. Alternately, you may wish to work directly with students or group them in twos or threes for partner reading or choral reading.

 Preteach Vocabulary

Model the first word and example for the class.

1.   The first word is *secret,* and its meaning is "known by only a few people."

2.   When I hear the word *secret,* I think of wishes or embarrassing stories I don't want anyone else to know.

3.   For example, I have a *secret* crush on my brother's best friend.

4.   This is an example of something that is *secret* because not many people know.

Continue this exercise with each word in the glossary, calling on individuals or groups of students to share out.

ELL Beginning

PRETEACH VOCABULARY
Use the gestures to clarify meanings.

- **secret** ("Zip" your lips and then hold an index finger in front of your lips to signal "shhhh.")

- **enroll** (Pantomime filling out a form at a desk.)

- **incomprehensible** (Shrug, raise your eyebrows, shake your head, and hold your hands out with your palms up.)

- **earnest** (Hold your hands to your heart and smile with your mouth closed.)

- **grieving** (Sit with your head in your hands looking downward so your face can't be seen.)

Classroom Language Focus

Remind students of the sight vocabulary and high-frequency words that they studied at the beginning of the unit. Point out that some of the words may be useful as they think about and discuss the text. For example:

- grow up (Ada **grew up** on a farm.)

- show up (When Ada **shows up** at college . . .)

- keep up (Ada struggles to **keep up** with her reading.)

- give up (Ada did not **give up** when . . .)

- grow up (When Ada **grows up**, she wants to . . .)

Narrative of the Life of Ada Lee, an American Farm Girl

NOTES

succeed. John Wilson was a young man in the law program who came from a long line of lawyers. One day, I flashed John a smile and told him I'd exchange home-cooked meals for some tutoring. He gladly accepted.

3   John and I worked together from then on. By the time we had earned our law degrees, we had grown quite close. We were married after graduation. It was my **earnest** wish that we would open a law office and continue working side by side. The state legislature had other plans. The state would not grant me a license to practice law because I was a woman.

4   My husband was not bothered by this turn of events. He had loved studying with me, but he was happy to provide for his family while I ran our home. I was devastated. I didn't have to go to college to be a homemaker. I spent my days **grieving** for the career I'd never have. I wished that I had never heard of the college, because then I'd be a happy wife. But then I wished something else. I wished that women could do anything we wanted to. I set out to find a way to change the law so we could.

TEXT TALK

1. What is the story about?
2. Who are the story's characters?
3. Where does the story take place?
4. How does the story make you feel?

ELL All Levels

SPEAKING FRAMES

Giving Information:

- This story is about ____.
- The story's characters are ____.
- This story takes place in ____.
- This story makes me feel ____.

Asking for Information:

- Can you explain ____?
- What do you think about ____?
- Why do you think ____?

First Read

Read the story. After you read, answer the Think Questions below.

THINK QUESTIONS

1. Where does Ada live in the beginning of the story? How do you know?

   Ada lives _____.

2. Write two or three sentences describing what happens when Ada goes to college.

   When Ada goes to college _____

   _____

3. What problem(s) does Ada face at the end of the story? Cite text evidence in your response.

   The problems Ada faces _____

   _____

4. Use context clues to confirm the meaning of the word *earnest* as it is used in "Narrative of the Life of Ada Lee, an American Farm Girl." Write your definition of *earnest* here.

   Earnest means _____.

   A context clue is _____.

5. What is another way to say that a text is *incomprehensible*?

   A text is _____.

Think Questions

Circulate as students answer Think Questions independently. Answers will vary.

QUESTION 1: Comprehension

Ada lives on a farm. She sits in a barn and talks to a cow.

QUESTION 2: Comprehension

Ada works hard. She meets a man named John. They get married.

QUESTION 3: Comprehension

Answers will vary, but may include the following examples:

- "The state would not grant me a license to practice law because I was a woman."
- "I spent my days grieving for the career I'd never have."

Student responses should provide an example from the text and an explanation that describes how the state did not allow Ada to become a lawyer.

QUESTION 4: Language

The author uses the word *earnest* when Ada tells about her deepest wish. This is a clue that *earnest* means "sincere."

QUESTION 5: Language

A text is impossible to understand.

Skill: Language Structures

Introduce the Skill

Watch the Concept Definition video ▶ and read the definition for Language Structures.

Narrative of the Life of Ada Lee, an American Farm Girl

Skill:
Language Structures

★ DEFINE

In every language, there are rules that tell how to **structure** sentences. These rules define the correct order of words. In the English language, for example, a **basic** structure for sentences is subject, verb, and object. Some sentences have more **complicated** structures.

You will encounter both basic and complicated **language structures** in the classroom materials you read. Being familiar with language structures will help you better understand the text.

••• CHECKLIST FOR LANGUAGE STRUCTURES

To improve your comprehension of language structures, do the following:

✓ Monitor your understanding.

- Ask yourself: Why do I not understand this sentence? Is it because I do not understand some of the words? Or is it because I do not understand the way the words are ordered in the sentence?

✓ Pay attention to **perfect tenses** as you read. There are three perfect tenses in the English language: the present perfect, past perfect, and future perfect. The word *perfect* means "completed." These tenses describe actions that are completed or finished.

- **Present perfect tense** expresses an action that occurred at some indefinite time in the past.
  > Combine *have* or *has* with the past participle of the main verb.
  > Example: I **have played** basketball for three years.

- **Past perfect tense** describes an action that happened before another action or event in the past.
  > Combine *had* with the past participle of the main verb.
  > Example: I **had learned** how to dribble a ball before I could walk!

TURN AND TALK

1. What does it mean to grasp language structures?

2. Why might it be difficult to understand language?

3. What can you do if you are struggling to grasp language structures?

ELL Beginning & Intermediate

SPEAKING FRAMES

- To grasp language structures means to understand ____.
- Language can be difficult because you may not understand ____.
- You could look at ____.
- You could think about ____.

ELL Advanced & Advanced High

SPEAKING FRAMES

- To grasp language structures means to ____.
- Language can be difficult because ____.
- You could look at ____, such as ____.
- You could think about ____. For example, ____.

ⓥ SKILL VOCABULARY

structure / la estructura *noun* the order of parts COGNATE

basic / básico *adjective* the most important parts without anything extra COGNATE

complicated / complicado *adjective* having many parts COGNATE

language structure / la estructura de lenguaje *noun* the order of words in a sentence COGNATE

- **Future perfect tense** expresses one future action that will begin and end before another future event begins.
  > Use *will have* or *shall have* with the past participle of a verb.

  Example: Before the end of the year, I **will have played** more than 100 games!

✓ Break down the sentence into its parts.

- Ask yourself: What actions are expressed in this sentence? Are they completed or are they ongoing? What words give me clues about when an action is taking place?

✓ Confirm your understanding with a peer or teacher.

Reading & Writing
Companion **147**

Discuss the Skill Model

1. What is the student trying to understand?

   The student is trying to understand the sentence "By the time we had earned our law degrees, we had grown quite close."

2. Why is the student struggling?

   The student is confused by the number of verbs in the sentence.

3. What strategies does the student use?

   Answers will vary, but should include: The student asks for help. The student thinks about verb tense. The student looks for clues.

ELL **Beginning & Intermediate**

Have students use the speaking frames and helpful terms to participate in the group discussion. If beginning students are hesitant to participate in a discussion, encourage them by prompting with *yes* or *no* questions.

Advanced & Advanced High

Have students use the speaking frames to participate in the group discussion.

SPEAKING FRAMES

- The student is trying to ___.
- The student is confused because ___.
- First, the student ___ in order to ___.
- The student also ___ to help her ___.

HELPFUL TERMS FOR DISCUSSION

- tense
- past
- asks
- subject
- perfect
- help

Narrative of the Life of Ada Lee, an American Farm Girl

⟳ YOUR TURN

Read the following excerpt from the text. Look at the bold-faced examples of past perfect tense. Remember that past perfect tense describes events that started and ended in the past. Then, sort the events into the order in which they happened. Place the correct letter in the chart below.

> **from "Narrative of the Life of Ada Lee, an American Farm Girl"**
>
> I sat down on the stool and dug my heels into the barn's dirt floor. "You know I love you, Bessie," I whispered dreamily to our dairy cow, "but I'm not going to be with you for much longer. I am going to college." A secret grin spread slowly across my face. It was the first time **I had said** my plan out loud. "I know what you're thinking, Bessie," I continued, patting her gently. Women could not go to college, but **I had heard** about a college on the east coast that would accept female students. The school was far away. The workload might be very hard, given my limited education. But I was determined to enroll. After all, **I had taught** myself to read. Learning from a teacher couldn't be harder than that. "It's going to be hard, but I will go to school and become a lawyer."

	Events
A	Ada teaches herself how to read.
B	Ada talks to Bessie about her plan to go to college.
C	Ada hears about a college that accepts female students.

First	Next	Last

 Your Turn   Ask students to complete the Your Turn activity.

First	Next	Last
Ada teaches herself how to read.	Ada hears about a college that accepts female students.	Ada talks to Bessie about her plan to go to college.

Narrative of the Life of Ada Lee, an American Farm Girl

Skill:
Comparing and Contrasting

★ DEFINE

To **compare** is to show how two or more pieces of information or literary elements in a text are similar. To **contrast** is to show how two or more pieces of information or literary elements in a text are different. By comparing and contrasting, you can better understand the **meaning** and the **purpose** of the text you are reading.

••• CHECKLIST FOR COMPARING AND CONTRASTING

In order to compare and contrast, do the following:

✓ Look for information or elements that you can compare and contrast.

- Ask yourself: How are these two things similar? How are they different?

✓ Look for signal words that indicate a compare-and-contrast relationship.

- Ask yourself: Are there any words that indicate the writer is trying to compare and contrast two or more things?

✓ Use a graphic organizer, such as a Venn diagram, to compare and contrast information.

SKILL VOCABULARY

compare / comparar *verb* to explain how two or more things are similar **COGNATE**

contrast / contrastar *verb* to explain how two or more things are different **COGNATE**

meaning / el significado *noun* the general message of a text

purpose / el propósito *noun* the reason the writer wrote a text

---

Skill: Comparing and Contrasting

Introduce the Skill

Watch the Concept Definition video and read the definition for Comparing and Contrasting.

TURN AND TALK

1. What does it mean to compare and contrast?

2. What type of information can be compared and contrasted in a text?

3. What can you do if you are struggling to determine what to compare and contrast in a text?

ELL Beginning & Intermediate

SPEAKING FRAMES

- To compare and contrast means to show how _____.
- You can compare and contrast information that is _____ or _____.
- You could look for _____.
- You could also use a _____

ELL Advanced & Advanced High

SPEAKING FRAMES

- To compare and contrast means _____.
- You can compare and contrast _____, such as _____.
- You could look for _____. For example, _____.
- You could also use a _____, like a _____.

⚙ Discuss the Skill Model

1. **What does the student notice when he starts reading the text?**

   He notices that there is a difference between what Ada expected college to be like and her actual experience.

2. **What does the student do first?**

   The student makes a note that shows what Ada's life was like before college.

3. **What does the student do second?**

   The student makes a note that shows what Ada's life was like during college.

4. **What does the student do with this information?**

   Answers will vary, but should include: The student makes a chart to compare and contrast the experiences. He shares his conclusion with a peer.

Ⓔ Beginning & Intermediate

Have students use the <u>speaking frames</u> and <u>helpful terms</u> to participate in the group discussion. If beginning students are hesitant to participate in a discussion, encourage them by prompting with *yes* or *no* questions.

Advanced & Advanced High

Have students use the <u>speaking frames</u> to participate in the group discussion.

SPEAKING FRAMES

- The student notices that there is a difference between what Ada ____ and her ____.
- He makes a note that shows ____. For example, ____.
- He makes a note that shows ____. For example, ____.
- He decides to ____. He also ____.

HELPFUL TERMS FOR DISCUSSION

- text
- during
- before
- expected
- chart
- conclusion

Narrative of the Life of Ada Lee, an American Farm Girl

🔄 YOUR TURN

Read the following excerpt from the text. Then, complete the Compare-and-Contrast chart by writing the letter of the correct example in the chart below.

---

from "Narrative of the Life of Ada Lee, an American Farm Girl"

John and I worked together from then on. By the time we had earned our law degrees, we had grown quite close. We were married after graduation. It was my earnest wish that we would open a law office and continue working side by side. The state legislature had other plans. The state would not grant me a license to practice law because I was a woman.

My husband was not bothered by this turn of events. He had loved studying with me, but he was happy to provide for his family while I ran our home. I was devastated. I didn't have to go to college to be a homemaker. I spent my days grieving for the career I'd never have. I wished that I had never heard of the college, because then I'd be a happy wife. But then I wished something else. I wished that women could do anything we wanted to. I set out to find a way to change the law so we could.

	Examples	
A	loved studying together in college	
B	wasn't allowed to get a license	
C	was allowed to get a license	
D	wasn't bothered by the laws against women working	
E	wanted to continue working together	
F	was unhappy about not being able to have a career	

Ada's Experience	Both	John's Experience

Reading & Writing Companion   Please note that excerpts and passages in the StudySync® library and this workbook are intended as touchstones to generate interest in an author's work. The excerpts and passages do not substitute for the reading of entire texts, and StudySync® strongly recommends that students seek out and purchase the whole literary or informational work in order to experience it as the author intended. Links to online resellers are available in our digital library. In addition, complete works may be ordered through an authorized reseller by filling out and returning to StudySync® the order form enclosed in this workbook.

⚙ Your Turn Ask students to complete the Your Turn activity.

Ada's Experience	Both	John's Experience
wasn't allowed to get a license	wanted to continue working together	was allowed to get a license
was unhappy about not being able to have a career	loved studying together in college	wasn't bothered by the laws against women working

Close Read

✏ WRITE

PERSONAL RESPONSE: Think of a goal that you are trying to achieve. Are there any challenges? Is there anything stopping you? Write a short paragraph comparing and contrasting your experience to Ada Lee's story. Pay attention to main and helping verbs as you write.

Use the checklist below to guide you as you write.

☐ What is a goal you have?

☐ What problems do you have to face?

☐ How does your experience compare to Ada Lee's experiences?

☐ How does your experience contrast with Ada Lee's experiences?

Use the sentence frames to organize and write your personal response.

A goal I have is _____.

This goal is important to me because _____.

A problem I have is _____.

To solve the problem, I _____.

My experience is like Ada Lee's because _____.

Unlike Ada Lee, _____.

Reading & Writing Companion **151**

Close Read

Model Skills Focus

Remind students of the Reading Skill Comparing and Contrasting. Tell students they can compare and contrast information within the text, across different texts, or even with their personal experiences. Direct students to the Skills Focus and remind them to track as you read aloud.

Compare and contrast Ada Lee's experience with a similar personal experience

Model Comparing and Contrasting for students:

- I am going to focus on Ada Lee's plan to go to college.

- When I was younger, I made a plan to go to a soccer camp during the summer.

- Just like Ada Lee, I was excited about my plan and I told my closest friends.

- However, my experience was easier. There were no rules or laws saying that I wasn't allowed to go. I didn't have to travel far to find a camp that I liked.

Complete Skills Focus

Use a Jigsaw strategy to have students complete the Skills Focus. Divide students into pairs. Have each pair focus on a single point of comparison, for example:

- Ada Lee teaches herself a skill
- Ada Lee struggles with a challenge
- Ada Lee asks for help
- Ada Lee achieves a goal
- Ada Lee decides to make a change

Circulate and monitor groups as they work.

Collaborative Conversation

Rearrange partners so that they are talking with someone who worked on a different point of comparison. Prompt partners to take turns sharing their personal comparisons with the events in text.

- How did your experience compare with Ada Lee's experience?
- How did your experience contrast with Ada Lee's experience?

- How did comparing and contrasting help your understanding of the story?

Collaborative Conversation

SCAFFOLDS

 BEGINNING, INTERMEDIATE Use the <u>word bank</u> to participate in the group discussion.

ADVANCED Use the <u>speaking frames</u> to participate in the group discussion.

BEGINNING, INTERMEDIATE	ADVANCED
Word Bank	**Speaking Frames**
• experience • different • like • connect • same • understand • unlike • realize	• I focused on ____. • It is similar because ____. • It is different because ____. • This helps me understand the text because ____

SCAFFOLDS

Write

Ask students to complete the writing assignment. Remind students to pay attention to verb tenses as they write.

ELL **BEGINNING** Write a response using the <u>paragraph frames</u> and <u>word bank</u>.

INTERMEDIATE Write a response using the <u>paragraph frames</u>.

INTERMEDIATE
BEGINNING

Paragraph Frames

- A goal I have is ____. This goal is important to me because ____.
- A problem I have is ____. To solve the problem, I ____.

- My experience is like Ada Lee's because ____. Unlike Ada Lee, I ____.

Word Bank

- difficult
- challenge
- motivated
- hard work
- succeed

No Risk, No Reward

In the Extended Oral Project, students plan, draft, practice, and deliver an oral presentation that ties into the theme of the unit and spans informative, argumentative, and narrative genres. Lessons provide explicit instruction to prepare students for the unique challenges of an oral presentation, and to help break down the genre characteristics of each prompt. At each step in the process, students focus in-depth on specific writing and speaking skills as they brainstorm, organize, and refine their presentation. Students also receive discussion prompts and frames to guide them in providing effective peer feedback as they practice and discuss in small groups before presenting to the class on the final day.

CONNECT TO ESSENTIAL QUESTION

Why do we take chances?

In this unit, students practiced effective collaborative communication skills, as well as making connections and comparing and contrasting, while reading and analyzing two texts about risks. Now students will apply those skills to work together in writing and delivering an informational presentation.

Developing Effective Presentations

The presentation revolves around the conflicts that arise when people can read each other's thoughts.

Form	Language and Conventions	Oral Language Production
Students may struggle with the demands of developing the presentation, such as breaking out advice into steps.	Students should be encouraged to experiment with new sentence patterns and types to make their presentation sound natural and logical.	Students may make mistakes when they transfer grammatical forms from their native languages into English. Remind students to monitor their use of pronouns.

SCAFFOLDS

ELL ENGLISH LANGUAGE LEARNERS

Vocabulary, discussion, and peer and teacher support in the Extended Oral Project is differentiated for Beginning, Intermediate, Advanced, and Advanced High English Language Learners. See individual lesson plans for additional scaffolding and support.

Instructional Path

 All Extended Oral Project lessons lesson plans appear in your digital teacher account.

Introduction

Objectives: Students will be able to identify the components of an informational presentation in order to brainstorm and plan their own presentation.

Objectives: Students will be able to record ideas for an informational presentation in writing.

Skill: Acquiring Vocabulary

Objectives: Students will be able to use a graphic organizer to make connections between words and acquire new vocabulary for their informational presentation.

Objectives: Students will be able to brainstorm new words to use in writing their informational presentation.

Plan

Objectives: Students will be able to plan and write a first draft of their informational presentation.

Objectives: Students will be able to organize their first draft using an outline.

Skill: Sentence Types

Objectives: Students will be able to apply knowledge of sentence types to revise the sentences in their informational presentations.

Objectives: Students will be able to vary sentence types orally and in writing.

Practice

Objectives: Students will be able to practice and revise their informational presentation based on peer feedback.

Objectives: Students will be able to practice an informational presentation orally and make revisions in writing.

Present

Objectives: Students will be able to observe and deliver an informational presentation in order to give and receive peer feedback.

Objectives: Students will be able to use varied sentence types in an informational presentation and give peer feedback orally and in writing.

Unit Overview

Integrated Reading and Writing

Extended Writing Project

English Language Learner Resources

Novel Study

End-of-Unit Assessment

Novel Study

Each Core ELAR Unit contains two texts designated for Novel Study. The Novel Study supports the close reading of the complete text through its associated Reading Guide and a series of comparative reading and writing lessons. Novel Studies are not a part of each grade-level's 180 days of instruction; however, teachers may choose to draw from them if they wish to incorporate materials from other disciplines or develop an alternative, novel-based approach to instruction.

Each novel comes with a **Reading Guide** that provides both teacher and student support. Each lesson provides key vocabulary words and close reading questions, as well as a key passage that will help teachers guide students through an exploration of the essential ideas, events, and character development in the novel. This passage will also serve as the point from which students will engage in their own StudySyncTV-style group discussion. Each novel study's **Comparative Reading and Writing** lessons contain resources to support comparative analyses. Students read passages of other texts drawn from across the disciplines and compare those passages to specific sections of the novel in written responses.

Suggested Novel Studies

Title	Genre	Summary	Themes and Topics
A Night to Remember (1955)	History	The biggest ocean liner ever built, the RMS *Titanic* was dubbed "unsinkable" because of its fifteen interior bulkheads. No one suspected an iceberg could rip them open.	• Disaster • Ocean • Eyewitness Account
Narrative of the Life of Frederick Douglass (1845)	Autobiography	The first widely published narrative by a formerly enslaved person was a sensation, helping to turn public sentiment against slavery in 19th-century America.	• Autobiography • Slavery • Freedom

A Night to Remember

Published 43 years after the legendary 1912 sinking of the *Titanic*, Walter Lord's *A Night to Remember* is the definitive account of the disaster. Chilling details from interviews with more than 60 survivors as well as from several other sources recount the collision with an iceberg, the filling of the lifeboats, and the rescue by the ship *Carpathia*. Through the experiences of passengers and crew, readers relive the last moments of the "village" aboard the world's largest ocean liner.

Walter Lord (1917–2002) wrote 11 books, but *A Night to Remember* is by far his most famous. On account of his expertise, he often lectured at meetings of the Titanic Historical Society, and when director James Cameron began filming the 1997 movie about the disaster, Lord was called in as a consultant.

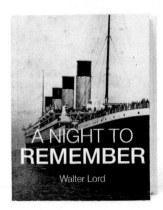

Narrative of the Life of Frederick Douglass

This autobiography by America's most famous formerly enslaved abolitionist chronicles his journey from the plantation—where he witnessed firsthand the brutality and injustices of slavery—through his years in Baltimore, where he learned to read. Marked by a series of epiphanies that continue even after Douglass's emancipation, the narrative is a meditation on the meaning of liberty and the shared responsibility of members of a society.

Frederick Douglass (1818–1895) was an activist, orator, and statesman who escaped slavery in Maryland to become one of the national leaders of the antislavery movement. In 1845, *Narrative of the Life of Frederick Douglass* was published; its vivid testimony leads readers along the road that led Douglass from chains to emancipation.

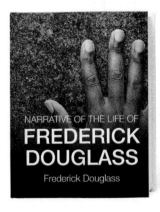

Unit Overview

Integrated Reading and Writing

Extended Writing Project

English Language Learner Resources

Novel Study

End-of-Unit Assessment

Spotlight Skills Review

A review day before the end-of-unit assessment gives you an opportunity to review difficult concepts with students using Spotlight Skills lessons. Spotlight Skills are targeted lessons that provide you with resources to reteach or remediate without assigning additional readings. Every Core ELA Skill lesson has a corresponding Spotlight Skill lesson. Spotlight Skills can be assigned at any point in the year, but the end of each unit provides a natural moment to pause, review data collected throughout the unit, and reteach skills students have not yet mastered.

Progress Monitoring

The Progress Monitoring charts that appear before every text in this unit identify standards and associated Spotlight Skills. On review day, you may want to give preference to reteaching skills that are not revisited in later units. You can see where skills are covered again in the Opportunities to Reteach column.

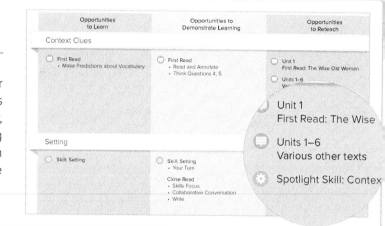

StudySync Gradebook

As students submit assignments on StudySync, their mastery of skills and standards is tracked via the gradebook. The gradebook can be sorted and viewed in a variety of ways. Sorting by assignment shows overall student performance, while sorting by standards or by Skill lessons displays student progress toward mastery goals.

Skills Library

Spotlight Skills are located in the Skills section of the StudySync Library. You can assign Spotlight Skills to individual students or groups of students. Search tools allow you to search by skill type or name.

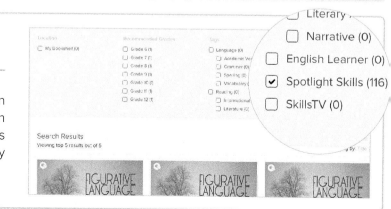

End-of-Unit Assessment

The end-of-unit assessment can be found in two places. The digital version of the assessment can be assigned from the Online Assessment tab inside your ConnectED account. The paper-based version of the assessment can be printed from the End-of-Unit Assessment tab inside this unit in your StudySync account.

Assessment Section	Content	Assessed Skills	
READING	The Scientific Revolution Genre: Nonfiction Word Count: 829 Lexile: 1060L	• Greek and Latin Affixes and Roots • Informational Text Structure	• Textual Evidence • Informational Text Elements • Summarizing • Figurative Language
	The *Friendship 7* Genre: Nonfiction Word Count: 463 Lexile: 1100L	• Informational Text Elements • Technical Language • Textual Evidence	• Summarizing • Informational Text Structure • Word Patterns and Relationships
	The Building of the Transcontinental Railroad Genre: Nonfiction Word Count: 495 Lexile: 1100L	• Informational Text Elements • Context Clues • Textual Evidence	• Summarizing • Informational Text Structure
	No Risk, No Reward Genre: Nonfiction Word Count: 872 Lexile: 1080L	• Greek and Latin Affixes and Roots • Informational Text Structure	• Context Clues • Informational Text Elements • Summarizing
REVISING and EDITING	Student Passage #1	• Infinitives • Gerunds • Participles	
	Student Passage #2	• Organizing Informational Writing • Introductions	• Supporting Details • Conclusions • Thesis
WRITING	Prompt: Informative Writing	• Informative Writing	

What's Next?

Assessment results can be viewed by item, standard, and skill to monitor mastery and make decisions for upcoming instruction.

RETEACH skills that students have not yet mastered, using Spotlight Skills or the Test Preparation and Practice book.

REVISE your teaching plan to provide more or less explicit instruction into a skill or text, using Beyond the Book activities for enrichment.

REGROUP students and levels of scaffolding based on standards progress.